The Australian Alternative Varieties Wine Show acknowledges the Traditional Owners of the country on which we grow vines, make wine and conduct our Show. We pay homage to their thousands of years of deep history and express gratitude for their ongoing culture, including looking after the land and water that we rely on, and gathering on country as we do now to celebrate life and share stories.

Contents

Foreword **Nothing comes from nothing**	Why we started the Australian Alternative Varieties Wine Show *by co-founder Stefano de Pieri*	*6*
Part One **Before the beginning – An alternative to what?**	Australia's wine grape landscape before the turn of the millennium: glimmerings of a wine revolution.	*10*
Profiles	*Dr Rod Bonfiglioli* *Mark Walpole* *Phil Reedman* *Kevin McCarthy and Kathleen Quealy*	*16* *22* *30* *36*
Part Two **2001 to 2004 – More than just a wine show**	The first ambitious years of the Australian Alternative Varieties Wine Show, a new spectrum of grapes emerges.	*42*
Profiles	*The Chalmers Family* *Steve Pannell* *Louisa Rose* *Helen Healy*	*48* *56* *64* *70*
Part Three **2005 to 2011 – Tipping points**	The AAVWS as it expands, the growth in new varieties such as tempranillo, fiano and pinot gris.	*76*
Profiles	*International Perspectives* *Ashley Ratcliff* *Corrina Wright* *Future Visions*	*82* *90* *98* *112*

Part Four **2012 to 2018** **– Natural evolution**	The AAVWS as it enters its second decade, a dynamic period of change for Australian wine culture.	*116*
Profiles	*Sue Bell* *Rollo Crittenden* *Fellowship of the vine* *Michael Trembath*	*122* *130* *136* *148*
Part Five **2019 to 2022** **– Wine in interesting times**	The AAVWS responds to local and global challenges, and continues to foster new alternatives.	*158*
Profiles	*Anita Goode* *Jonathan Creek* *Leanne Altmann*	*164* *172* *180*
Afterword **What next?**	Current and emerging wine trends in 2023: the revolution continues …	*188*
Glossary **An Alternative A-Z**	From aglianico to zweigelt: a guide to the grapes.	*200*
Best Wine of Show Artwork		*236*
Awards / sponsors		*238*
Acknowledgements		*257*

Foreword

Nothing comes from nothing

As philosopher and historian Claudio Magris once said, the problem with prefaces is they can pre-empt the story they're introducing – or, worse, spoil it. They can also be pyrotechnic exercises, there just to show how clever the preface writer is. But Max Allen is an excellent writer and storyteller, so I will leave all the storytelling – it's more *history*-telling, really – up to him.

Max does nothing flippantly. Everything is fastidiously researched and accurately reported. Unlike Max, I am abundantly flippant. That's how I got myself involved in this alternative varieties wine journey: I nearly always say yes to what appears like a good idea at the time, and deal with the consequences after. Build it and they will come. There's nothing particularly clever about that. It's more a case of mindless optimism.

In the late 1990s, the time was ripe for a big change in the Australian wine panorama, and initially the task seemed easy: help a local vine nursery to sell their new varieties of grapes. We decided to do this by organising a long lunch to draw attention to these varieties – fun, for sure – and then just see what happened afterwards.

What happened afterwards is in these pages.

At the time all of this started, Australia was full of the same four or five mostly French grapes – chardonnay, shiraz, cabernet, and so on. And they had taken food as their prisoner: because there were so few varieties on offer, different kinds of food had to squeeze in as best they could to conform. Except *French* food, of course, where butter, cream and chardonnay were in sync, and cabernet went well with entrecote and beef reduction.

Which authentic Italian dishes, by contrast – so dependent on vegetables, legumes, and tomatoes – could pair with an oaky chardonnay or a heavy shiraz? None! In fact, I contend that the standard Australian wine choices at the time were holding back the development of lighter, more creative cuisines.

Let's not forget, also, that many restaurants at the time were BYO. Diners brought to the table whatever they could afford, or their favourite wine, without necessarily thinking what food they were going to order. Sommeliers were rare – almost non-existent. It was more like a lottery than a rational approach to drinking with food.

It was logical, then, that this equation had to be adjusted. And I am convinced this imperative was in the minds of many players in the industry at the time. All it needed was a spark to set it alight. This became the role of the Australian Alternative Varieties Wine Show, which we started in 2001.

The show encouraged people to grow new varieties from scratch, making mistakes along the way, to be sure, but learning from experiments and failures, and eventually producing the first successes.

Above all, we imbued the project with love (or *passion*, if you think 'love' is too soppy). Over twenty-one years we have witnessed the development of a wonderful

Stefano de Pieri and Tim White at the Alternative Varieties Wine Show in 2004

camaraderie, driven by a sense of purpose and an old-fashioned desire to do good – good for the industry, for communities and individual growers and merchants, for gastronomy, and even for our international reputation. Many people helped along the way. We should be grateful to these pioneers.

We have been privileged to enlist the support of many wine judges and critics over the show's twenty-one years. But I must single out our first chief judge, Tim White. For as fastidious a pain in the neck as he can be, his very punctiliousness set the show on the right path from the start. All the others who have helped shaped the show are amply recognised in the chapters of this history.

'Nothing comes from nothing'. I once saw this profound statement written in big letters over two paintings in a dedicated room in the National Gallery in London. One was a mid-nineteenth century portrait of Madame Moitessier by Ingres. The other was Picasso's take on the Ingres canvas, *Woman with a book*, supposedly a portrait of Picasso's secret lover.

'Nothing comes from nothing'. That line has stuck with me and seemed appropriate when I was thinking about what to write in this preface. It occurred to me that the Alternative Varieties Wine Show may seem like a fluke; the serendipitous coming together of various individuals who were simply at the right place at the right time and had enough intuition to understand the opportunity.

But perhaps history itself had the biggest say. After all, historical processes have a certain inevitability given the right conditions.

Stefano de Pieri
co-founder of the Australian Alternative Varieties Wine Show

Mildura, 2023

Ready for the judges.

Part One

An alternative to what?

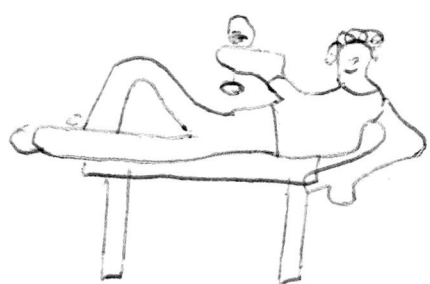

Saturday 6 November 1999. I'm sitting at a table in the dining room at the Grand Hotel in Mildura. On the plate in front of me – and the other 130 guests at lunch – is a *sformato* of porcini, one of the signature dishes of the hotel's celebrity Italian-Australian chef, Stefano de Pieri. There's a forest of wine glasses on the table, too. With this course, one of five that will see this long lunch stretch out almost to dinner time, we're drinking red wines from Italy made from refosco, schioppettino, primitivo; we've just tried some fiano, greco and vermentino with the antipasto; later in the meal we'll be tucking into some nero d'avola, negroamaro and aglianico.

Outside, as the sun beats down across the country, people are queuing up outside scout halls and churches across to vote in the Republic Referendum, participating in a process that, whatever the result, will set the course of Australia's future.

Inside, in the cool dining room at the Grand, there is also a serious side to this indulgent day. Throughout the afternoon, a group of speakers – viticulturists, winemakers, scientists – address the crowd and ask us to imagine a new future for Australian wine. A future in which grape varieties like the ones we're drinking could play a central role.

In 1999, most of these grapes are unfamiliar, little-known outside Italy; in some cases, they're newly rediscovered even in their homeland. We are being asked to take a leap of faith, to visualise a new reality where these grapes could become viable, exciting, accepted alternatives to the mainstream grapes – chardonnay, shiraz, cabernet – that dominate this country's vineyards.

We don't realise it at the time, but this Long Italian Lunch is a turning point in Australian wine history.

∾

In one sense, all wine grapes are alternative in Australia. Before the British stumbled ashore two and a half centuries ago with their claret and hock and their port and their brandy, there was no plant growing here quite like *Vitis vinifera*, the wine grapevine, and there is no record of Indigenous peoples using fruit to make wine here.

There are plenty of native Australian vines bearing berries that *resemble* wine grapes: one that grows in the bush along the south-eastern coast, for example, looks remarkably like ripe shiraz. There are quite a few examples, too, of fermented drinks made and enjoyed by Aboriginal and Torres Strait Islander peoples long before Europeans arrived, from the mead-like *way-a-linah* in Tasmania, produced from the sap of the cider gum tree, to the *mangaitch* of southwest Western Australia, made from the nectar of banksia flowers.

But the practice of planting a vine in straight rows, picking its fruit, and fermenting it into wine? That arrived in 1788 – literally, with the grapevines on the First Fleet.

Early settlers saw the planting of vineyards and the making of wine not just as a way of producing something to drink (and to get drunk), but also as an aspect of the broader colonial project: a way of imposing a 'civilising' influence on the landscape and people, making wild land productive and establishing ownership.

There was a commercial imperative to establish a wine industry here, too: when winemaking did eventually flourish in the nineteenth century, Australia was promoted as a 'vineyard of the Empire', with a duty to ship its produce back to the Mother Land.

Several entrepreneurs and pastoralists imported grapevines to the nascent industry in the early years of that century. The best known is James Busby, a young Scot who travelled through France and Spain in the 1830s, selecting dozens of cuttings to be shipped to the new colony. The ancestors of the shiraz and pinot noir vines from that original Busby collection still play a hugely important role in the modern Australian wine industry, but Busby was far from alone. Others – notably John and William Macarthur – were also busy importing vines in this era, notably pinot meunier from champagne in 1817, and riesling from Germany in 1838.

Although it's these well-known varieties from famous regions – and the less well-known Portuguese and Spanish grapes used for fortified wine production – that went on to establish themselves in Australian vineyards, Busby and his contemporaries also shipped many, many other varieties on a 'suck-it-and-see' basis. As Busby wrote in a letter to the British colonial office: 'It might at first seem superfluous to bestow attention on a collection which must include many [vines] of an inferior description … [but] it is perhaps the most remarkable fact connected with the culture of the vine that even a slight change of climate or soil produces a most material change in the qualities of its produce.'

As the nineteenth century wore on and growers became more familiar with local conditions, some adopted a more focused approach. Doctor Alexander Kelly, the founder of the Tintara vineyard and winery in South Australia's

Vine cuttings advertised in the Sydney Morning Herald, 1843

McLaren Vale, for example, published *The Vine in Australia*, a treatise on growing grapes and making wine, in 1862. In it he explained how Australia's climate was not like the 'classic' regions of Burgundy and Bordeaux and urged his readers to plant appropriately hardy *southern* French and Iberian varieties suited to warm areas – varieties such as marsanne, roussanne and mataro, and a grape he calls 'temprana', which was possibly tempranillo.

In the 1890s, another doctor, Thomas Fiaschi, brought Italian varieties sangiovese, canaiolo, mammolo, malvasia and aleatico from his homeland of Tuscany to Australia, and planted them in his Tizzana vineyard on the Hawkesbury River, north of Sydney. And as the nineteenth century ticked over into the twentieth, viticulturist Francois de Castella – son of the Swiss-born vigneron, Hubert de Castella, who helped establish the Yarra Valley as one of Australia's leading wine regions – imported several Mediterranean varieties such as tempranillo, durif and picpoul and trialled them at the Rutherglen Viticultural Station. He was particularly impressed with the 'remarkable character' of the tempranillo.

But despite this cornucopia of potentially exciting and grapes available to Australia's growers in the early 1900s, history would conspire to ultimately constrict what was planted to a handful of varieties.

A few kilometres from where we enjoyed the long Italian lunch in 1999, the old Chateau Mildura winery is a physical reminder of the bulk of wines produced in Australia for much of the twentieth century, particularly in hot inland regions like here in Sunraysia.

Built in the 1880s, not long after the Canadian Chaffey brothers had established this area as a fruit-growing colony by installing irrigation from the Murray River, the vineyard here at Chateau Mildura was initially planted with red and white grapes intended for table wines –

Dr Rod Bonfiglioli

— *scientist, grapevine specialist, co-founder of the Australian Alternative Varieties Wine Show.*

'Doctor Rod Bonfiglioli is a very busy man,' I wrote in mid-1999, in an article called 'The Fringe Dwellers', on emerging grape varieties. 'So busy, in fact, that the only time I can catch up with him is over coffee at Tullamarine airport after gets off a plane from Mildura and before he gets on a plane to New Zealand, then Argentina to look at new clones of malbec, then Italy, to the world's biggest vine nursery, Vivai Cooperativi Rauscedo.'

I remember that meeting. Rod was in a rush, every bit the globe-trotting 'mad scientist' character his friends and colleagues described: crumpled, wild haired, bemused as to why a journalist would be interested in talking with him. But he was also passionate about his work, which increasingly involved importing grapevines from Europe and other parts of the world into Australia.

'In his role as research scientist with the University of Adelaide,' I wrote,

'Bonfiglioli has been able to help the VCR nursery set up rigorous certification procedures for the 45 million vines they sell each year. But it's what VCR can help Bonfiglioli with that interests us here.'

Rod enthused about the new clones of VCR-sourced tempranillo due to come out of quarantine, as well as aglianico, sagrantino and vermentino. He was particularly driven by the concept of climate suitability.

'Italy has had a string of the hottest years ever experienced,' he told me. 'They're all convinced that climate change is very real. Now, a lot of shiraz in the Riverland and Sunraysia collapsed this year because it was too hot, so perhaps we should be doing the same thing – looking at more appropriate, more tolerant varieties from southern Italy, such as aglianico.'

Just a decade later, sadly, as the varieties he championed began to prove themselves in the Australian wine landscape, Rod Bonfiglioli died.

'Rod got liver cancer,' says writer Ruby Andrew, Rod's partner, who moved to Australia from her home in Canada in 2000 to live with him in his 'rather-the-worse-for-wear' cottage on the Murray River out by Chalmers' Nursery.

'He'd had hepatitis as a young man and was aware there might be complications at a later age. As it turned out it happened very quickly: he was diagnosed three months before he died.'

Rod was born in Glasgow in 1953 before moving to Oxford. His father, Kyril Bonfiglioli, was a notorious art dealer, *bon vivant* and author of the *Mordetcai* mysteries, a series of semi-autobiographical novels later turned into a disastrous flop of a movie with Johnny Depp.

'Rod grew up in an artistic academic milieu,' says Ruby. 'His family were highly cultured. When we first met in a friend's laboratory on Vancouver Island, I thought his accent was very posh – although in Mildura he sounded very different.'

Rod had hightailed it to Australia in his late teens, working as a psychiatric nurse in Darwin and in a tropical medicine lab in Brisbane, before finding his *metier* as an academic scientist relatively late in life, gaining a PhD on avocado viruses at the age of forty. This led to an interest in grapevine viruses in the mid-90s and work at Waite Diagnostics at the University of Adelaide, a job which took him around Australia and the world, keeping up with the latest techniques and technology, and advising vineyard owners.

Which is how he ended up at Chalmers, and how he met Stefano de Pieri and Mark Walpole and Phil Reedman and the other people who contributed to the conversation that led to the Long Italian Lunch and the Australian Alternative Varieties Wine Show.

'The thing was that they all liked and respected each other,' says Ruby. 'Rod and Phil remained best mates until he died. Alberto Antonini had a huge impact on him, as did Mark.'

These strong connections were maintained even after Rod and Ruby left for New Zealand in 2001. Rod had started consulting to Riversun nursery in Gisborne the year before, and owner Geoff Thorpe offered him a full-time position, setting up a plant diagnostics laboratory and vine certification system.

'He became known to everyone in the industry in New Zealand as "Doctor Rod",' says Ruby. 'Mainly because Kiwis often struggled with pronouncing "Bonfiglioli", but also out of affection for his plain-spoken expertise and willingness to help sort out problems in the vineyard.'

Ruby says that Rod did in some ways regret leaving Mildura and came to miss the camaraderie of the broader wine show community. But he went on to have a huge influence on viticulture in New Zealand, developing diagnostic tools for grapevine viruses, establishing best practice guidelines for disease management, and helping to import and promote new varieties.

'He even discovered a hitherto unknown grapevine virus and cheekily named it "The Alfie Virus" after our wee dog.'

Ruby says Rod was a natural scientist, gifted with intuitive insights about what might work. But crucially, science was just *one* of his passions. 'In the last few years of life, he became obsessed with oriental carpets!' she says. 'He told me he wanted to become a carpet merchant. We had trips to Singapore where we'd find ourselves sitting drinking tea talking carpets with these dealers. He was in his element.'

Ruby hesitates before continuing, aware that the word she is about to use carries so much weight.

'I thought he was a genius,' she says, finally. 'The way he blazed through things. He was only in Mildura for two years, but he touched so many lives. In this respect his legacy will outlast us all. I like to think of him as the Antipodes' viticultural equivalent to "Johnny Appleseed".'

Drinks in the rose garden at the Grand Hotel before the Long Italian Lunch in 1999

cabernet, malbec, red and white 'hermitage' (probably shiraz and trebbiano). By the 1920s, though, changing local tastes and an increasingly important export market of strong, fortified wines to the UK ('vineyard of the Empire', remember?), meant that most of the production had switched to sherry and port. Fermenting vats designed specifically for making flor-aged styles of dry sherry, with tent-like coverings to stop condensation dripping back into the wine, are still there today, long unused.

Because fortified wine and brandy production was so important during the first half of the twentieth century, Australia's vineyards were mostly planted to varieties suited to these kinds of drinks: grapes such as muscat gordo blanco, doradillo, pedro ximenez, grenache and mataro, all originally from the Iberian Peninsula. Crucially, another widely planted grape at this time was shiraz: it was mostly

Part One: Before the beginning   19

used in 'port', but its presence in so many vineyards would prove useful when, in the 1950s, the swing away from fortified to table wines started, slowly at first and then, during the 1960s and 70s, very rapidly.

The 1970s was when the modern Australian wine industry began. Winegrowers introduced drip irrigation and machine harvesting to the vineyards; cold-fermentation and stainless-steel technology created fresher, lighter styles of wine; packaging in bag-in-box casks saw wine become an affordable, accessible, everyday drink.

This prompted a renewed interest in grape vines and varieties.

South Australia, which had banned the importation of vines since the 1890s after the grape louse phylloxera arrived in Victoria, lifted the prohibition in 1964 which led to an influx of new potential. The book *Grape Varieties of South Australia,* published in 1967, paints a distinctly nineteenth-century picture of the varieties that had been grown in the state up until then: gouais, malbec, verdelho, sercial and so on. At the back of the book, though, is a list of recommended varieties that '… have been [recently] introduced or may be considered for introduction in the near future.' The list includes chardonnay, merlot, and pinot noir. At the time, in South Australia, these were the new alternatives.

In the 1960s, too, grapevine physiologist Allan Antcliff was busy sourcing new varieties and clones of existing varieties for the CSIRO's grapevine collection at Merbein, a few bends in the river away from Mildura. The CSIRO were embarking on a vine breeding program and needed as many different varieties as possible for their trials. As well as searching through Australia's old vineyards and European collections for promising material, Antcliff sourced varieties from the University of California at Davis and elsewhere into the 1980s. Around the same time, at Charles Sturt University in Wagga, viticulturist Libby Tassie was bringing in a few Italian varieties including arneis, nebbiolo and barbera.

The Long Italian Lunch at the Grand Hotel in 1999

This meant that by the 1990s, when Australia's wine boom was in full swing, the country's main vine collections were stuffed with all sorts of interesting grapes that could be propagated by growers – from arinto to fernao pires and bastardo to tempranillo, from bourboulenc to rolle and carignan, from three different Georgian grapes (mtsvane, rkatsiteli and saperavi) to a whole host of southern Italians including fiano, grillo, inzolia, montepulciano and negroamaro.

The sense of potential that this incredible varietal diversity offered was captured in 1980 in a paper published by leading viticultural experts Richard Smart and Peter Dry. The authors proposed a four-tier climate classification of Australia's wine regions, and allocated varieties accordingly – not only the 'classic' French varieties, but many Italian varieties, too, such as lagrein and pinot grigio in cool areas, sangiovese and garganega in warm areas, and negroamaro and malvasia in hot regions – all varieties that were available in Australia at the time.

Mark Walpole

— viticulturist and winemaker; AAVWS associate judge in 2006, judge in 2019, 2020 and 2021; speaker at the 1999 Long Italian Lunch, and at Talk and Taste in 2003, 2006, 2013 and 2019; committee member 2005-2022; inaugural winner of the Viticulturist Award, 2019.

Mark Walpole has always grown things. As a kid on his family's farm at Whorouly, in Victoria's northeast, he had his own vegie patch; as a young man he established a walnut orchard on the farm, planting the newer Californian varieties rather than the old French trees that everyone else had. Always thinking of alternatives. Plants ran in the family, too: his forebears in the late nineteenth century knew Baron Ferdinand von Mueller, best known as director of the Botanical Gardens, who gave them pear trees and took cuttings of native plants from their area for the herbarium in Melbourne.

After studying farm management in his early twenties, in 1987 Mark started working for Brown Brothers up the road at Milawa, preparing land for vineyards. At the time, the company was enjoying huge success in Australia with popular wines like sweet white spatlese lexia and light red tarrango, as well as being one of the first wave of wineries riding the export boom in the UK.

The Browns had always had an interest in new varieties, and not long after Mark started working for them, they established a viticultural research and development arm, both to keep up with the new plantings required to meet commercial demand and develop new wines that could become the next big thing.

Mark had arrived in exactly the right place at the right time. As well as taking on the role of grower liaison and getting to know the local tobacco famers turned vineyard owners – people like Fred and Arnie Pizzini, who had planted nebbiolo and barbera, encouraged by the Browns – Mark also planted his own vines on the family farm, including an experimental block of sixty-five varieties.

In 1995 Mark went on what would become the first of many vinous journeys to Europe to learn more about grapes and vines. His trip through France, Spain and particularly the north of Italy made him even more curious about less well-known varieties, and even more keen to share his enthusiasm with both his employers and anyone else who'd listen.

Mark was appointed chief viticulturist for Brown Brothers in 1997, the same year he met Tuscan wine consultant Alberto Antonini. Again, the timing was perfect: with Alberto's help, Mark brought in a whole heap of new varieties, including better clones of sangiovese than were then available in Australia, and a southern Italian red grape, aglianico, introduced to Mark by Alberto.

Many of the newer varieties – propagated at the Chalmers nursery at Euston – were trialled at Brown Brothers' new vineyard at Heathcote. These were also planted by Mark in the late 1990s at a property he'd bought on the edge of the Beechworth escarpment, a vineyard that he called Fighting Gully Road.

In 2003, Mark also planted the Greenstone vineyard on prime red soil in Heathcote, central Victoria, as a joint venture with Alberto Antonini and British Master of Wine and Italian specialist importer, David Gleave. From the first vintage a couple of years later, it was clear this was a vineyard to watch: the sangioveses made by top winemaker Sandro Mosele for Greenstone were stunning new expressions of both the variety and the region.

Importantly, too, as well as making wine for their own label, the Greenstone founders also sold grapes to other small winemakers, who would help spread the word about the quality, particularly of the new clones of sangiovese.

With Fighting Gully Road and Greenstone keeping him busy, Mark left

Brown Brothers in 2007. But by 2015, with Alberto expanding his own business internationally and David's company taking more of his attention, the trio sold the Greenstone vineyard to a group of investors headed by a Melbourne based media entrepreneur.

Then, sadly, in 2019, just as the sangiovese vines at Greenstone were beginning to mature and produce their best wines yet, they were burned in a grassfire. It's a terrible loss. What could have gone on to become one of the great, important vineyards of Australia were gone in an instant.

This loss was underlined – and the quality of the vineyard vindicated – in a bittersweet way a couple of years later, with a wine that had been made from Greenstone grapes in 2016.

That year, winemakers Matthew Di Sciascio and Andrew Santarossa had managed to purchase sangiovese fruit from the new owners of Greenstone. The wine they made from that fruit went on to win four trophies – for Best Museum Wine, Best Italian Red Variety, Best Red Wine, and Wine of Show – at the 2021 AAVWS.

Selling Greenstone didn't slow Mark Walpole down. As well as continuing to farm the family vineyards at Whorouly and build Fighting Gully Road into one of Beechworth's most renowned producers – particularly well-regarded for sangiovese and aglianico – Mark has also been the driving force behind a remarkable experiment in reviving an historic walled vineyard in Beechworth, planted the same way it was in the nineteenth century, with each close-planted vine trained on a single stake.

And he's still looking for new alternatives. At Fighting Gully Road he's grafted pinot noir over to grenache – he thinks it could be the coolest grenache site in Australia – and has recently added some new varieties he's imported himself, including petite arvine, a high quality white Swiss variety, also grown in the Valle d'Aosta in Italy, that he claims is the first high quality cool-climate white grape alternative since chardonnay or pinot grigio.

It's a big call. But given his track record it's one that other winegrowers would do well to heed.

Mark Walpole's numberplate

Sangiovese from Montrose, one of few producers of alternative varieties in the late 1990s

But for a long time, during the 1970s, 80s and 90s, very few in the wine industry were interested in taking advantage of this amazing viticultural resource. And those that did were often derided as odd-ball eccentrics.

∽

When I started getting into wine in the late 1980s and early 90s, I would occasionally come across bottles made by these 'odd-balls'. People like Italian winemaker Carlo Corino who had planted barbera, nebbiolo and sangiovese at Montrose vineyard in Mudgee in the 1970s; David Hohnen who had planted zinfandel around the same time at Cape Mentelle in Margaret River; or Bailey Carrodus and the Portuguese port varieties – and viognier – he'd planted at Yarra Yering. Wines like the unusual-tasting varieties emerging from Brown Brothers' 'kindergarten winery' in Victoria's northeast – some of which, like mondeuse and graciano, dated back to de Castella's day, and some of which were being trialled at the time by their

Part One: Before the beginning   25

adventurous young viticulturist, Mark Walpole. Wild-tasting chambourcin from Cassegrain in Port Macquarie; the first vintages of viognier from Yalumba in the Eden Valley; planted as recently as 1980 at the urging of the company's production director Peter Wall; and Coriole's first sangioveses, planted in McLaren Vale in 1985.

But these wines were rare exceptions in a marketplace saturated at that time by the 'classic' French varieties: chardonnay, cabernet, shiraz and, particularly in the 1990s, the fashionable sauvignon blanc and pinot noir. Indeed, that was the reason most of the obscure grapes had been planted – to give winemakers a point of difference in the market, rather than for any deeper (viti)cultural reasons. Looking back through the catalogue listing the hundreds of wines poured at the 1990 Exhibition of Victorian Winemakers in Melbourne, for example, I can find just one made by an Italian-Australian from an Italian variety: Bianchet's verduzzo from the Yarra.

The verduzzo was also in the line-up of the dozen or so Australian-made Italian varietal wines I helped assemble in 1993 for a tasting and article on the topic for *Divine Food and Wine*, a new magazine that had launched the year before. We stood at the end of the bar at Donlevy Fitzpatrick's recently opened George Hotel in St Kilda one afternoon (*Divine* had an office upstairs) and worked our way through the wines as sunlight and a steady stream of patrons flowed through the door. Despite only comprising a dozen wines, it was probably the most comprehensive tasting of Australian-Italian varieties ever undertaken to that point.

I was particularly impressed by Coriole's sangioveses, and a dolcetto from Mount Anakie in Geelong. And a brand-new wine from up-and-coming Mornington Peninsula winemaking couple, Kathleen Quealy and Kevin McCarthy: the 1993 T'Gallant pinot grigio: 'Everything about this wine shouts "Italian",' I raved.

I wrote that Yalumba were in the process of importing better clones of 'classic' Italian varieties, I enthused that more and more Italian-inspired wines were appearing in bottle shops and restaurants all over the country, wines that held great hope for the future.

I was jumping the gun a bit in my enthusiastic prediction of an Italian-inspired viticultural revolution in Australia's *vineyards*, though, because the bulk of the industry was heading in the opposite direction. Throughout the 1990s, driven by almost exponential export growth (particularly to the UK), most Australia's grape growers and winemakers were clamouring for more chardonnay, more cabernet and more shiraz.

Instead of becoming more diverse, Australia's viticultural landscape was becoming less so. Much less so.

As economists Kym Anderson and German Puga point out in their 2022 analysis of grape variety trends, in the 1960s more than 40 percent of the varieties grown for wine in Australia were Spanish in origin (the gordo and pedro and grenache I mentioned before), the share of French-origin grapes (cabernet, et cetera) was just under 20 percent, with Turkish grapes next at around 10 percent (thanks to sultana, a multipurpose variety grown both for eating and for winemaking).

'[But] by the early 1980s the shares of Spanish and French varieties had reversed,' they write, 'and by the turn of the century Spanish shares were less than four percent.'

In the 1990s, after a vine-origin war between the French and the rest of the world fought in the vineyards of Australia, the French have emphatically emerged victorious. But a resistance movement, a rebel alliance of like-minded souls determined to challenge this Gallic orthodoxy, is rallying its forces.

left: 'Italian Winegrape Varieties in Australia', published in 1999

right: winemaker Gary Crittenden speaking at the Long Italian Lunch in 1999

Flying into Mildura in November, in early summer, is the best way to get a feel for the stark contrast between what all this landscape once looked like – not that long ago – and what great swathes of it look like now.

This is ancient desert country, Mallee country, red sand and scrub. Just to the north is Lake Mungo, with its burial sites that pushed our knowledge of humans living here back 40,000 years.

From a plane, you can see the ancient patterns written in the earth. You follow the river, snaking its way through the red sand, leaving billabongs in its wake. Then you see the vineyards: huge geometric squares of green stripes stretching for kilometre after kilometre, all irrigated with water from the river. And, dotted between them, vast, refinery-like wineries, with their serried ranks of stainless-steel tanks.

In 1999, one of these wineries, Lindemans at Karadoc, just outside Mildura, is the home of a leading brand in the Australian wine export boom: Bin 65 Chardonnay. Thanks to the world's insatiable thirst for this sunshine-in-a-glass wine, many of those huge green vineyards you saw from the plane are now planted to just chardonnay, to be hoovered up into the bowels of Karadoc and spat out the other end as millions of bottles of Bin 65.

But the people flying and driving into Mildura for the Long Italian Lunch on this first weekend in November in 1999 have anything but chardonnay on their minds.

There's winemaker Gary Crittenden from Dromana Estate on the Mornington Peninsula. Garry makes chardonnay and pinot noir there but has also been producing wines from Italian varieties, from grapes grown in Great Western and the King Valley, since the early 90s. With viticulturist Peter Dry from the University of Adelaide, Jim Hardie from the Cooperative Research Centre for Viticulture and PhD student Alex McKay, he has also just published a book: *Italian Winegrape Varieties in Australia, Exploring the Potential of Barbera, Nebbiolo, Sangiovese, Vernaccia, Dolcetto and Arneis*.

There's Adelaide wine distributor and consultant, David Ridge, a passionate Italophile who established a group called Club Neb in 1998 to promote – and indulge in – his favourite nebbiolo wines from Piemonte. There's another distributor, Michael Trembath, one of Melbourne's leading importers of Italian wines with partner Virginia Taylor, and a convenor of Australia's first sangiovese seminar at The George Hotel in St Kilda in 1997.

There's sangiovese pioneer, Mark Lloyd of Coriole, and there's Mark Walpole, the Brown Brothers viticulturist who has not only planted over sixty different varieties in his own family vineyard in Victoria's northeast, but also helped several growers in the region such as Fred and Arnie Pizzini plant Italian varieties, to sell to Browns, to make under their own labels and to supply other makers like Garry Crittenden.

And there's Phil Reedman, the wine buyer from UK supermarket Tesco, sent to live in Adelaide in 1998 because the retailer is buying so much wine from Down Under. Phil caused a stir at an Australian Society of Viticulture and Oenology seminar on marketing earlier in 1999 by accusing his audience of winemakers and growers – in the nicest possible way – of being 'boring' because of their reliance on such a small number of 'classic' French varieties.

Phil Reedman

— wine consultant; AAVWS judge, 2002; speaker at the 1999 Long Italian Lunch, Talk and Taste 2002.

'I didn't tell them they were boring,' says Phil Reedman. 'Well, not exactly.'

He's talking about the Australian Society of Viticulture and Oenology seminar he spoke at in Mildura in 1999, where infamously, and influentially, he admonished his audience for their myopic focus on chardonnay, cabernet, and shiraz. At least, that's how we all remember it a quarter of a century on.

'What I actually said was, "If this wasn't such a public forum, I would call you boring." And that was excised from the published version of the seminar proceedings. I definitely did say that diversification of varieties should be done and would be a good thing.'

Either way, his deliberately provocative words made an impact, because they came out of the mouth of someone who wielded a lot of clout. Nottingham-born (he's retained his accent, even after living in Adelaide now for twenty-five years) Phil was buying huge amounts of Australian wine for leading UK supermarket Tesco at the time.

'The thirst was unquenchable back then,' he says. 'I would have regularly bought probably four or five million litres of wine. People were making good money.'

But he was frustrated by the fact he couldn't buy anything except the big three varieties.

'As hard as it is to believe looking back now, even merlot wasn't available in the quantity we needed to be able to have it sit on the shelves of all our stores fifty-two weeks of the year.'

By contrast, he says, the wine aisles at Tesco in those days had all sorts of different varieties from Chile, Argentina, the USA – and that's before you got into France or Italy or Spain and Portugal.

'Australia had just three grape varieties doing 90 percent of work,' he says. 'I didn't think that was representative or had the potential for sustainable growth.'

Phil worked for Tesco for another five years and then set himself up in Adelaide as a consultant; working with Australian wineries and retailers, sourcing wine for overseas buyers, teaching with the Wine and Spirit Education Trust, and helping the winegrowers association in South Australia's Riverland.

He has long been a big supporter of the Riverland. 'It's the best place in Australia to grow wines of a certain style at a certain price point,' he says. And he's excited that producers like Ashley Ratcliff, with his Ricca Terra and Terra do Rio labels, is doing such a good job of growing, making, and promoting alternative varieties. 'The other day, Ashley told me it was my comments at that Mildura presentation that spurred him to start doing things differently.'

A generation on from when he arrived in Australia and people started talking about alternatives, Phil says he's thrilled by how things have turned out.

'We're on the right track,' he says. 'McLaren Vale is awash with these varieties as are most areas. We're seeing the diversification paying off. And my successors at Tesco are certainly putting more interesting stuff on the shelves now.'

But, he says, the story is far from over. There needs to be continued evolution of the varietal mix.

'One thing I didn't talk about in 1999 was climate change,' he says. 'We need to keep pushing for more and more varieties appropriate to the climate we're moving into. We need to sustain the vision because the wine industry is a constantly moving target.'

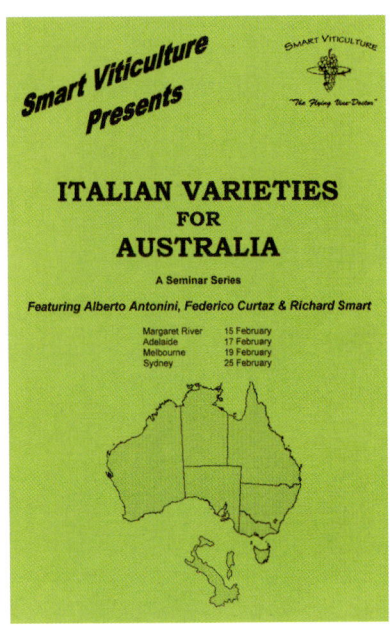

1999 Richard Smart seminar booklet

Many of the other hundred or so people descending on the Grand Hotel on this fine November day were at that ASVO seminar and have taken Phil Reedman's gentle admonishment to heart. They're curious to discover what the 'less boring' varieties taste like, and how they might be suited to Australian conditions. In fact, they're dead keen – the lunch sold out in two days after it was advertised.

Some of today's guests had also been at two other seminars, held by the ASVO in 1995 and 1997, exploring 'emerging' red Mediterranean varieties nebbiolo and sangiovese – as well as then-overlooked but long-established varieties grenache and mourvedre – and 'emerging' white varieties marsanne, roussanne, viognier and pinot gris. Ohers had met a group of visiting Italian growers and makers on a tour organised by the Cooperative Research Centre for Viticulture: Professor Franco Mannini of the University of Turin had talked about the resurgence of interest in Italy for non-classic varieties (i.e., negroamaro rather than nebbiolo); Jim Hardie of the CRCV had told attendees of a significant consumer interest in Italian wines that was predicated to grow in the early years of the next century. Italian varieties, he said, '… will certainly provide an alternative to pinot and cabernet and, to an extent, chardonnay.'

Another important precursor to this Long Italian Lunch was a series of yet more seminars organised by viticultural consultant Richard Smart across the country earlier in 1999, looking at the potential for Italian grapes in Australia. 'When wine moved out here 200 years ago,' Smart told attendees, 'French wine was at its height, so we took what we perceived to be the best. The French are good marketers, but I have to tell you that the best things in life are not necessarily French. We need more variety in our use of varieties.'

Erl Happ, one of Western Australia's pioneers of alternative grapes, also spoke at Richard Smart's seminar, and bemoaned the monocultural rush to sauvignon blanc then picking up pace. 'It is eminently possible that some grape variety hiding in the backyard of a cottage overlooking the Black Sea,' said Erl, echoing James Busby, 'will attain a remarkable expression in Australia that could create equal interest.'

∾

Another of the speakers at the Richard Smart seminar in 1999 was Italian winemaker and consultant Alberto Antonini. Smart had met Antonini when he sat next to him by chance on a flight to South America in 1996 and the two got talking. It was a random connection that would prove to be crucial to this story.

At the time, in 1996, Alberto was working for the large wine company Antinori, but was about to leave to set up his own consultancy, Gruppo Matura. He asked Richard who he should visit if we were to come to Australia. Richard suggested Garry Crittenden on the Mornington Peninsula, and Mark Walpole and the Pizzinis in the King Valley.

The timing was impeccable. Mark Walpole was looking for different grapes to trial in the new vineyards being developed by Brown Brothers at the time, and he quickly formed a good relationship with Alberto, who helped import new clones of sangiovese and nebbiolo from Italy and introduced him to the aglianico grape from the south of Italy.

Mark was also persuaded to import other, lesser-known Italian varieties by a well-travelled and passionate plant scientist, Dr Rod Bonfiglioli, then working on vine diseases at the University of Adelaide. Rod had come across grapes like sagrantino, vermentino and schioppettino during his time in Italy, and was convinced they had a future in Australia – despite being virtually unknown here at the time.

In the late 1990s, Brown Brothers were sourcing their grafted vine material from Chalmers Nursery near Euston, east of Mildura, and Mark asked Bruce Chalmers if he would look after these new clones and varieties once

Tim White speaking at the Long Italian Lunch in 1999

they'd come out of quarantine. In early 1999, Chalmers employed Rod Bonfiglioli to ensure the health of the vast quantities of vines the nursery was dealing with at the time. Encouraged by Rod's passion for alternative grapes, Chalmers had also signed a deal with Vivai Coopertivi Rauscedo (VCR), the world's largest vine nursery, based in northeast Italy, to bring in a large selection of their varieties.

Chef Stefano de Pieri was also swept up by Rod Bonfiglioli's passion for the potential of the varieties that Chalmers were planning to import. Stef, who was familiar to television viewers from his late-90s ABC series, *A Gondola on the Murray,* had been conducting his own one-man resistance movement for years in the restaurant at the Grand Hotel, opening Italian bottles for the steady stream of Australian winemakers and growers that passed through the dining room – where he was often met with apathy or even outright derision. Soon after Rod started at Chalmers in early 1999, he got into the habit of driving to Mildura after work in Euston and sitting with Stef late at night, the two of them opening bottles from Stef's cellar, dreaming up a vision of a different Australian viticultural landscape.

And planning, with Bruce Chalmers, a long Italian lunch for the first weekend of November. A showcase. A celebration. A symposium …

Finally, the last course arrives. An orange and almond cake served with three luscious golden sweet wines from the islands of Sardinia, Salina and Pantelleria. Despite being full of food and wine, I devour the dessert and the sticky nectar, my head swimming not (just) from the booze, but from the ideas bouncing around the room, the possibilities being conjured in the air.

Phil Reedman has encouraged everyone to broaden their viticultural horizons and look beyond the safe

Stefano de Pieri, Mark Lloyd and Bruce Chalmers at the Long Italian Lunch in 1999

and predictable triumvirate of chardonnay, shiraz and chardonnay. Stefano and Mark Walpole have told us how planting suitable Italian varieties could provide a sustainable future for overlooked and undervalued regions like Mildura. And Rod Bonfiglioli has insisted that this afternoon isn't just one more tasting of fine wines and fine food, that alternative varieties aren't just for niche players.

'This isn't pie-in-the-sky stuff,' he said. 'These are real opportunities. This is about sustainable regional development. All these varieties you've tasted today are here, or on their way, and have a real chance of being successful.'

It was a view echoed by Dr John Stocker, Chair of the Grape and Wine Research and Development Corporation – and patron of David Ridge's Club Neb. 'Regional Australia is entering its renaissance both politically and culturally,' he said, buoyed perhaps by the spirit of change potentially sweeping through the country that day. 'And it's vital we promote diversity in our regions: diversity in a cultural sense in the community and diversity on our palates.'

'What we're witnessing in this room is the embryo of how we need to think about wine in this country,' said Garry

Part One: Before the beginning   35

Kevin McCarthy and Kathleen Quealy

— *pioneers of pinot gris and skin-contact whites on the Mornington Peninsula; Kathleen: speaker at Talk and Taste 2003 and 2004, committee member/ ambassador from 2006.*

When Kevin McCarthy and Kathleen Quealy planted pinot gris vines on Victoria's Mornington Peninsula in the late 1980s, they were the first winemakers in Australia to give the grape variety a serious push.

It was a big punt at the time, to back a then virtually unknown new grape variety – especially when everyone wanted to drink chardonnay. But – thanks in no small part to the couple's irrepressible enthusiasm – it worked. Their first, small vintage was snapped up by legendary Melbourne restaurateur Hermann Schneider. And their second release, in 1993, was an immediate hit at the Dog's Bar in St Kilda, one of the era's most influential venues, founded by hospitality visionary Don Fitzpatrick and run by Neil Prentice, who now makes wine at Moondarra vineyard in Gippsland.

'I remember walking into the Dog's Bar,' says Kathleen, three decades later. 'Celia [her daughter] was on my hip. Neil was there and I gave him a bottle. He said, "Oh, this is *really* good", and he went and got Don and they all came out and made a big fuss.'

'Don went, "Fark, that's good",' says Kevin. 'And started pouring it for everyone in the bar. And put in an order for ten cases.'

Kevin was thirty-five, Kathleen was thirty-two. The pair had studied oenology in the 1980s, him at Roseworthy in South Australia, her at Charles Sturt Uni in Wagga. At that time, there was less of a cultural divide between grape growers and winemakers — or 'builders and architects', as she puts it — and more of a sense of holistic 'winegrowing'.

Kathleen was inspired by one of her lecturers, Max Loder, who had planted some pinot gris at Wagga. So, after she and Kevin met, got together, started having children and decided to establish their own winery, it was this grape that she was keen to plant — as well as other non-mainstream varieties.

'We also put in a nursery block of a whole lot of different grapes,' says Kathleen. 'And we went on a planting binge — we put in a whole lot of vineyards around the region, each with pinot noir, pinot gris, and an aromatic variety too: muscat or viognier.'

Thanks in part to the success of the early T'Gallant wines, other growers started planting and making pinot gris and/or pinot grigio. In 2003, corporate wine giant Southcorp (now Treasury Wine Estates) bought T'Gallant — not because they were interested in Kevin and Kathleen's thriving cellar door, but because they wanted a pinot grigio label they could grow into a big brand. Kevin kept working for the new owners, while Kathleen bought a vineyard on the Peninsula and set up her own, eponymous label.

By this time, Kevin had started travelling to Italy regularly. He and Kathleen had fallen in love with friulano and other lesser-known north-eastern Italian and Slovenian varieties, and Kathleen was keen to plant some or graft some over at her new vineyard. She couldn't find any cuttings available in the established nurseries. But at the AAVWS in Mildura, she met a grower, Denis Pasut, who had planted friulano back in the 1980s, using cuttings that had been imported by the CSIRO.

Around this time, in the early 2000s, Neil Prentice also introduced Kevin and Kathleen to the wines that Josko Gravner was producing on the Friulian border with Slovenia: so-called 'orange' wines made from white grapes fermented and matured on skins in big clay amphora-like vessels called *qvevri*.

'It sounded like something happening on the other side of the moon,' says Kevin. 'I was like, how good is this?'

After a trip to the region in 2006, Kevin came back keen to try the technique out for himself. So, when a marketing executive at Foster's (which had taken over Southcorp by then) asked him to come up with a new wine – 'something crazy' – he knew exactly what to do.

The result was the 2007 T'Gallant Claudius, an amber-coloured, cloudy blend of chardonnay, gewurztraminer and muscat grapes left for four months on skins. It was as revolutionary in its way as the first T'Gallant pinot gris and grigio wines had been fifteen years before. But it didn't receive quite the same reaction. It was influential in the industry – it paved the way for many other Australian winemakers to start exploring extended skin-contact whites – but wine drinkers weren't quite ready for this 'crazy wine from the moon'.

'It was unsaleable,' says Kevin, smiling.

Now, another fifteen years on, and the wine market in Australia is a very different place. Skin-contact whites are a more familiar sight in any bar, restaurant or bottle shop that has claims to being even vaguely on-trend. So, when Kevin decided at the beginning of 2020 to develop a new brand with daughter Celia (now a marketer) of well-priced Italian varietal wines showcasing grapes grown in Mildura, skin-contact whites – and Denis Pasut's vineyard – were a big part of the plan. The first release included a friulano, grown by Denis, which spent eleven days on skins, and won a trophy for Best Wine made from grapes grown in the Murray Darling region at the 2021 AAVWS.

And what about pinot gris? Well, the push that Kevin and Kathleen started in 1992 eventually led to the grape becoming the fourth most widely planted white variety in Australia less than two decades later. In fact, the grape jumped over into the mainstream to such a commercially successful extent that (spoilers) it was booted out of the AAVWS in 2009 – or, as the organisers prefer to say, the variety 'graduated'.

'I'm still pissed off,' says Kathleen, smiling. 'The reason why is because there is no wine show in Australia that takes pinot gris seriously to this day.'

Perhaps, I suggest, she should establish a breakout show, dedicated to the variety.

'A splinter show,' she says. 'I love it.'

'The Australian Pinot Gris Show,' says Kevin, pouring another glass, a twinkle in his eye. 'Yeah, sounds great.'

Max Allen speaking at the Long Italian Lunch in 1999

Crittenden. But he also sounded a note of caution, based on the lukewarm reaction he'd experienced in the wine trade and among consumers to his Italian varietal range, and the early polls suggesting a 'no' vote in the Republic Referendum.

'It might take a long time to convince the rest of the industry that Italian varieties have a future,' he said. 'Because people are reluctant to change – they don't often seek change. But that change must come.'

∾

I gave a presentation too. At some point. Apparently. (Look: there's a photo, so it must be true.) Three – maybe four – courses and half a dozen glasses of wine in. I'm one of two journalists who did: me, then writing for *The Weekend Australian*, and Tim White, wine columnist for the *Australian Financial Review*. We're both ex-Poms fascinated by this cultural shift taking place in front of our eyes.

Since the *Divine* magazine tasting of Australian Italian varieties in 1993, I'd been looking for and writing about – and spruiking – examples of the viticultural resistance movement. My studies ranged from conducting a tasting of pinot grigio and tempranillo and other 'new' grapes at the 1994 Exhibition of Victorian Winemakers, to writing about the wines of Garry Crittenden and other members of the rebel alliance in the mid-90s. These included people like the Pizzinis, and Peter Read, who was ahead of his time planting petit manseng and tempranillo and tannat in his Symphonia vineyard in the King Valley.

Thanks to Italian wine importers like Maurizio Ugge of Arquilla, I'd also been exposed not just to 'classic' Italian wines like Chianti and Barolo, but also to the wines and regions of the south: Campania, Puglia, Sicily had been going through their own revolution during the 80s and 90s, reviving the reputation of varieties like fiano and aglianico and nero d'avola.

Part One: Before the beginning

Tim White was on a similar journey of discovery during the 1990s after visiting vineyards in Spain, Austria and Greece, and wondering why the varieties grown there weren't being grown here. It was during one of those trips to Spain, that we were both on in 1997, that I fell deeply in love with tempranillo, returning to Australia a passionate advocate for the grape.

Like other wine writers, Tim and I were also being invited to judge at various wine shows around Australia at the time. A few days before the lunch in Mildura I was up to my eyeballs in riesling in the Clare Valley, judging their regional wine show. This is the other, crucial reason why we were both there on that first Saturday in November in 1999.

Before the long lunch, in one of the Grand Hotel's small conference rooms down the corridor from reception, Anna's Room, the two of us and a handful of others – including Rod, David Ridge and Michael Trembath – sat down in the morning and tasted, blind, all the Australian-grown examples of the sangiovese grape we could find. Flavours ranged from varietal pioneering vineyards like Montrose and Coriole to blends of sangiovese and cabernet from Primo Estate (then based in the Adelaide Plains) and Tintilla Estate in the Hunter Valley. Just thirteen wines in all, including a Poggerino Chianti Classico thrown in as a benchmark. The top wine of the tasting wasn't even 100 percent varietal: it was the 1995 Cherise Sangiovese Cabernet Sauvignon, made by Steven Hall from fruit grown at Coriole.

Dubbed, grandly, the Sangiovese Challenge, this small judging – a fleeting moment in time, an hour or so of sniffing, swirling, discussing, and scribbling – was arguably more important than the six-hour lunch and talkfest that followed. For the organisers of the day, Rod, Stef, and Bruce, applying this wine-show approach – a kind of scrutiny that the mainstream industry was familiar and comfortable with – was a very practical way of encouraging the adoption of new grapes in Australian

Jenni and Bruce Chalmers, Stefano de Pieri and Rod Bonfiglioli at the Long Italian Lunch in 1999

vineyards. A solid, easily understood framework around which a broader conversation about cultural change could be presented.

The results of the Sangiovese Challenge were announced during the long lunch. Mark Lloyd accepted the award for top wine, grinning proudly. The 130 people in the room, fuelled by fiano and fungi, clapped and cheered.

So, Stefano, Rod and Bruce decided to do it all again the following year. Except this time, it would be more ambitious.

Part Two

More than just a wine show

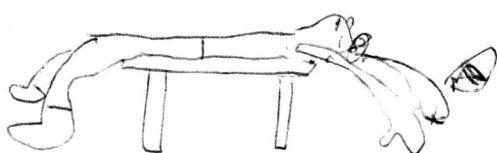

Saturday 4 November 2000. Rod Bonfiglioli is running around the Grand Hotel like a one-armed paperhanger. Judging is about to begin for the inaugural Australian Italian Wine Show, incorporating the Sangiovese Awards. The tasters are ready, the bottles organised, the glasses set up. But Rod's just realised he doesn't have a corkscrew. He's one of the organisers of this bloody event and there's not a single corkscrew to be found – in a hotel of all places!

Ruby Andrew, Rod's partner, remembers the moment vividly (the 'one-armed paperhanger' description is hers). 'As a naïve visitor from Canada,' she says, 'I was sent to ask Tim [White], Mark [Walpole], Stefano [de Pieri], and others whether they could contribute the necessary hardware. The comments about Rod's organisational skills were withering. It was classic Rod. He made wonderful things happen – usually in the midst of chaos.'

This was never going to be an ordinary wine show. Around fifty wines from twelve producers were sent to Mildura that November after the tasting had been announced earlier in the year: sixteen of them were sangioveses. Not a bad result at all, considering how few examples of Australian-grown Italian varietal wines existed at that point. But tiny compared to most wine shows,

above: Don Carrazza in 2004

preceding pages: judging underway for the 2003 Australian Alternative Varieties Wine Show

where hundreds or thousands of wines are entered and judged over many days.

And there was much more to this event than simply awarding medals and trophies to the top wines, which is the main outcome of most shows. The purpose was also to foster greater understanding and awareness of these non-mainstream grapes and to educate growers and makers and consumers about what was possible. And to do it all with the same sense of conviviality and the creation of networks that had marked the Long Italian Lunch the previous year.

So, the judging was held in conjunction with a special Sangiovese Dinner and tutored tasting, with food cooked by Stefano and featuring a full range of wines, selected with the help of Alberto Antonini, and imported from Italy. It was an expensive exercise that was generously paid for by Don Carrazza, the owner of the Grand Hotel, and Stef's father-in-law.

'That dinner was a whopping great big event,' remembers Tim White, who had been asked back to judge the show. 'Flight after flight of sangio. Maybe twenty or thirty wines. And a lot of local winemakers attending.'

None of the wines tasted by the show judges that day were awarded higher than silver medals, which is an indication of how Australian-made Italian varieties were still very much an emerging category. But in another break from 'proper' wine show tradition, this didn't stop the organisers from giving out awards (normally a wine needs to have been given a gold medal to qualify for a trophy).

The award for Best Sangiovese again went to Coriole in McLaren Vale, for their 1999 vintage. The award for Best White went to the 2000 Crittenden Arneis. And the Best Red – and Wine of Show – was the 1999 Cobaw Ridge Lagrein, made by Alan and Nelly Cooper from vines they'd planted only a few years before at their cool vineyard in the Macedon Ranges.

Alberto Antonini beaming in from Tuscany to the Talk and Taste seminar on sangiovese in 2003

Rod and Stef wrote a report on the wine show for *Australian Grapegrower & Winemaker* magazine, published in February 2001. The report finished with an announcement that was also in some ways a call to arms.

'For this coming November,' they wrote, 'we have decided to begin a new and exciting concept for Mildura. We will host a wine show … that will showcase all the new and emerging wine varieties being developed in Australia. These will include the Italian wines and any other new and interesting varieties from any other country. We know of many producers [who are] working with varieties that are new or relatively new to Australia and a common comment is that there is no show dedicated to new varietal wines or new wine styles. It is our intention to give these producers a platform on which they can show their wines to promote styles and varieties and also have them professionally judged by experienced winemakers and judges. We have already received a lot of interest and enthusiasm for this concept, and we expect the response will be tremendous. We look forward to seeing everybody at the Mildura Wine Show in November 2001.'

'Tremendous'. You can hear Stefano saying it.

Tasters at a structured wine masterclass at the 2003 AAVWS

Australia's wine shows emerged out of the nineteenth-century tradition of rural and capital city shows, organised by agricultural societies. Just as expert judges in white coats carrying clipboards have, for decades, assessed sheep and chickens and cakes and silage, so too have men (and for most of Australia's wine history it *was* all men) gathered in rooms at the same showgrounds and sniffed, sipped and spat their way through hundreds of glasses of wine. They would award medals and trophies for the best 'hermitage' or 'chablis' in an attempt to set benchmarks for each style and 'improve the breed'.

By the 1990s, it felt as though shows had moved away from these nineteenth-century agricultural roots and become more driven by marketing departments. Yes, many winemakers still used the shows as a way of assessing their wines against their peers (the exhibitors' tasting, where entrants get to taste all the wines after the judges have been through them, is always well-attended). But increasingly, medals – particularly gold medals and trophies – were primarily seen as another way of selling the latest chardonnay or shiraz in a marketplace stuffed full of other chardonnays and shirazes.

By the turn of the millennium, many in the wine industry were questioning the merits and relevance of shows. In 2001, the Australian Society of Viticulture and Oenology

The Chalmers Family

— *vine nursery operators, grape growers, winemakers, Bruce and Jenni Chalmers: co-founders and ongoing sponsors of the AAVWS, committee members/ambassadors 2001 - ; Bruce: speaker at the Long Italian Lunch, 1999, Talk and Taste, 2002, 2004, 2006; Kim Chalmers: associate judge 2014, speaker at Talk and Taste 2008, 2013, committee member 2005 - , brand and projects manager, 2015 - ; Tennille Chalmers: associate judge, 2014, judge 2020 and 2021, functions and partnership manager, 2015 - ; Bart van Olphen: associate judge, 2015.*

'Everything we've ever done has been leading up to crafting this wine,' says Tennille Chalmers, pouring me a glass of white. 'From bringing the cuttings in from Italy, to letting nature tell us what worked and what didn't, our lifelong career passion has been to make wine that expresses our connection to the Murray Darling region.'

It's the middle of harvest in Mildura, 2022. I'm sitting in the kitchen of Tennille's sister, Kim Chalmers, and Kim's Dutch-born husband, Bart van Olphen. The wine that Tennille has just poured is the inaugural, 2021 vintage of Mother Block, a blend of vermentino, ansonica, falanghina and pecorino. There's a Mother Block red, too: a mash-up of sagrantino, piedirosso, negroamaro, graciano, teroldego, nero d'avola and uva di troia.

These two wines are like a bottled manifesto of modern Australian winegrowing talking points – hardly any of which were part of the conversation before the AAVWS started. As well as being field blends of co-fermented climate-change-appropriate grape varieties, they're also vegan-friendly, packaged in lightweight glass, and have carbon neutral paper labels featuring an acknowledgement that the grapes were grown on Aboriginal land, on the country of the Njeri Njeri people.

'The thing is, this brand is not just good for Chalmers,' says Tennille. 'It could be good for changing the perception of the whole region.'

This year marks a quarter of a century since Tennille and Kim's parents, Bruce and Jenni Chalmers, started the process of importing a swag of varieties from Italy that were new to Australia. The couple had established a nursery on Bruce's family property east of Mildura in the late 1980s. A decade later, they were supplying the wine industry with four million baby grapevines a year – and, with the help of Rod Bonfiglioli, had signed an agreement with the Vivai Rauscedo Cooperativi and Gruppo Matura to exclusively bring over some of their collection of varieties and sell them to Australian growers.

Today Chalmers is a multi-faceted business. As well as continuing to operate the nursery – which in 2008 moved to Merbein, west of Mildura – the family have seventy varieties planted across vineyards in two locations, at Merbein and in Heathcote, central Victoria, and are selling grapes to dozens of other winemakers as well as producing wines under their own brands. Tennille covers sales and marketing, Kim is responsible for management and admin, and Bart is winemaker. Bruce and Jenni have been threatening to retire for years but are still very much involved with the business.

All of the family have also been heavily involved in some way with the Alternative Varieties Wine Show since its inception, including sponsoring awards, developing the database that underpins the show, organising – or speaking at – the Talk and Taste sessions, or judging. So heavily involved, in fact, that some in the industry have, at times, and (in a classic example of the Australian tall-poppy syndrome), grumbled that it's not the 'Australian Alternative Varieties Wine Show', it's the 'Chalmers Wine Show'. Just a big marketing exercise for a bunch of grapes that the family have exclusive rights to sell to the industry.

There's no doubting that self-interest is a factor in the Chalmers' continued backing of the show: it was partly Bruce's idea in the first place, after all. The family has invested a lot of money into new varieties: as Kim calculated for visiting wine journalist and AAVWS judge Walter Speller in 2015, at least

$350,000 went into putting the first seventy varieties and clones through the laborious quarantine and virus-checking and elimination process, and there has been another round of imports since then. And that doesn't include the millions of dollars of investment in infrastructure and propagation and marketing of these varieties. The family have been major players in the alternative varieties wine space, too, both as suppliers of grapes, but also making wine under their own labels – labels that have been launched at events during show week in Mildura.

So, yes, of course it's in the Chalmers' interests to see the show thrive. But there is a compelling argument that this vested interest is far outweighed by, and indeed has directly led to, the benefits that the show – and the promotion of alternative varieties in general – has brought to the wider wine industry and culture.

The time that Kim has spent 'hooning around' (her words) southern Italy in the early 2010s gathering information and experience – yes, that helps to sell more vines, but also expands everyone's knowledge of those varieties. The time Bart and Tennille and Kim hand-picked sixty different varieties off their Merbein vineyard to make tiny, bucket-sized batches of experimental wine, in a shed, using nothing but a sieve, some demijohns, and plenty of manual labour – yes, it was an attempt to attract sommeliers and independent retailers, always looking for rare bottlings of cool new wines. But it was also huge, instructive, energising fun.

As journalist Huon Hooke wrote in 2014 when the Chalmers were named Viticulturist of the Year by *Gourmet Traveller WINE* magazine: 'The family has contributed an enormous amount to warm-climate viticulture, to the cause of alternative grape varieties, to the diversity of Australian wine and to their fellow grape growers.'

It's hard not to be swept up by the Chalmers' enthusiasm for these new varieties, regardless of whether they will one day make someone lots of money or not. When I interviewed the family for an article in *The Weekend Australian* in 2015, the way Kim described bringing a new variety out of quarantine for the first time summed up that enthusiasm perfectly.

'Oh man, it's so exciting,' she said. 'When the vine gets its little toes into the ancient soil, into the sand and the limestone: it may have an Italian name but it's an Australian vine now. I just can't wait to see what happens when it grows up and starts producing wine.'

held a seminar, 'Who's Running the Show? – Future Directions for the Australian Wine Show System', which laid out a host of ways that things could be improved, modernised, and made more accountable.

In one sense, Rod and Stef's Mildura Wine Show – dubbed the Australian Alternative Varieties Wine Show in time for judging in November 2001 – was harking back to the early days of the agricultural shows – an attempt not so much to improve breeds as introduce them.

In most ways, though, the AAVWS would be nothing like traditional shows.

For a start, and most obviously, there were no wines entered made from chardonnay or shiraz or cabernet, or the other mainstream varieties that provided the bulk of entries at most shows. The AAVWS was only open to those varieties considered 'alternative': grapes that were relatively new in Australia, like pinot gris, as well as the more established varieties that were not as widely planted, like marsanne.

The judging panels, too, traditionally populated mostly by winemakers, in the AAVWS would be made up of people from a broader range of backgrounds – people who had experience and knowledge of the varieties being judged. In 2001, for example, the panel of judges assembled by chief judge Tim White, included importer and Italian specialist David Ridge, and Kate McIntyre, then working in retail but who would go on to become a Master of Wine, as well as winemakers Steve Pannell from McLaren Vale and Clare Halloran from the Yarra Valley.

Tim was not a typical wine show person, either – certainly not part of the 'establishment' of mostly older Australian wine industry stalwarts who'd been ensconced as chief judges in various shows around the country for decades.

Helen Healy and Tim White at the awards long lunch in 2004

Tim first started drinking wine in the UK in the 1980s, before he migrated to Sydney, and before his first wine-related article – entitled 'Terroirism' – was published in the *Australian Financial Review* in 1993. This meant that even before he arrived here, he already had more diverse tastes than many locals.

'At the time I was getting into Australian wines in London I also got to understand and much enjoy those from Italy,' wrote Tim in one of his *Fin Review* articles. '[I was] spellbound by Nicholas Belfrage's 1985 wonderful paean, *Life Beyond Lambrusco* (a book credited with helping to kickstart the modern appreciation for Italian wine). Then I ventured to the richer flavours of Spain which, weight and structure-wise, bridges those of Italy and Australia.'

In his columns, Tim quickly developed a reputation for idiosyncratic, evocative wine descriptions, a rigorous approach to tasting, forthright opinions and a way of scoring that combined both the theoretically objective hundred-point system made popular by US wine critic Robert Parker and, later in his writing career, a 'hedonic' score out of ten. His argument was that just because a critic thinks a wine is good – well-grown, well-made, all the elements in the right place – and gives it, say, ninety-five points, that doesn't necessarily mean the critic wants to sit down and *drink* a bottle. And vice versa.

'I also started writing about alternative varieties in the 90s,' says Tim. 'Not being deliberately contrarian, or to stir the pot, but out of a belief that there were other things to be growing, making and enjoying, other than the classic French varieties.'

This belief was reinforced during trips to Europe, to the vineyards and wine towns of Spain, Austria, and Greece. He remembers encountering gruner veltliner for the first time in Austria and sharing it with his readers back home; discovering the joys of great jamon and sherry in Jerez, tempranillo in Rioja, and writing about them in his column. 'This all got my brain clicking and thinking,' he says. 'I wrote about what I was experiencing.'

Tim travelled to Europe with people who were also helping change the gastronomic conversation. People like importer Paul de Burgh Day who was bringing in good wines from Spain, and writers like John Newton and Gay Bilson, who were exploring what a food and wine culture in Australia looks like.

'There was a lot of chatter about the interesting things happening in Europe,' says Tim. 'A lot of discussion about why and how we could be doing that here.'

In the late 1990s, Tim was also becoming a regular guest at the food and wine festivals and masterclasses that were springing up around the country. It was at one of these events, in Adelaide, that he found himself on a program of speakers with a bunch of celebrity chefs including Scotsman Nick Nairn and Mildura's Stefano de Pieri.

'I remember wandering up to Stef,' says Tim. 'He was quite famous at the time, because of *Gondola on the Murray* on the ABC. We got on immediately, and he, Nick and I ended up at a tasting of Langhe imports that David Ridge had organised at Bottega Rotolo. That's probably why I was invited up to judge in Mildura.'

Tim also brought an unconventional energy and an enthusiasm to the show that often lingered long after the last wine had been judged.

'One of my earliest memories of the show is playing pool in the back bar at the Grand late one night with a couple of the judges,' says Tim. 'We had Glen James' Billy Bragg CD playing. That was when my hair was still all gelled-up and Gary Glittery – as Gordon Ramsay once described it.'

ω

The last two years of the old millennium and the first two years of the new were dynamic times in many ways. The dot-com explosion and tech revolution in Silicon Valley inspired the establishment of two overly ambitious wine-related online Australian companies, WinePros (with the long-established wine writers Len Evans and James Halliday as figureheads) and WinePlanet (with me as editor), both of which would soon crash and burn in the dot-com bust.

The Australian export bubble expanded into the US in 2000 with the introduction of Casella's Yellow Tail brand (this will soon become particularly relevant to the future of one alternative variety). And the same year Brown Brothers released their first Moscato, a sweet, light, fizzy wine style that capitalised on the surging interest in all things Italian but was made using the same muscat of alexandria grapes they employed to make their once much-loved spatlese lexia, then in decline.

One of the most profound changes in wine around this time was the move away from corks towards screwcaps,

a move initiated in 2000 by a group of winemakers in the Clare Valley and rapidly taken up by other producers, in both Australia and New Zealand. The speed with which this change took hold is demonstrated by the fact that in 2002 the AAVWS introduced a trophy for 'Best Alternative Closure'. 'The show is alternative after all,' Tim White wrote at the time, 'and screwcaps are a more reliable alternative to cork, ensuring consistency and wine free of musty taint.' But they dropped the trophy just three years later because it was obvious that screwcaps were fast becoming the mainstream choice of seal across the industry.

And arguably the most seismic event of the early twenty-first century, the terrorist attack on the Twin Towers in New York, took place just a few weeks before the first AAVWS in 2001 – which was immediately followed by a federal election that saw the Howard government returned for a third term, swept up on a wave of fear and xenophobia. Not the first or last time the show is framed by momentous events.

I'm not going to go through all the facts and figures for all the shows that have happened in Mildura since 2001. That would be a bit dull for everyone concerned – and you can find all the major results at the back of this book. But it is worth looking at a few numbers from this first show, partly to see how things have changed in the ensuing twenty-one years, and to illustrate how *different* the AAVWS was – and is – compared to most mainstream large regional and capital city shows.

As a judge at, say, the Melbourne Show in 2001, your day consisted of donning a white coat, being handed your score sheet and pencil and clipboard, and sent off to work your way through sixty or eighty tasting samples in the one-year-old chardonnay class, tasting, spitting, writing notes, awarding scores out of twenty. Then you'd sit down with your two fellow panel judges and two associates (kind of like 'apprentice' judges) and collate the scores, agreeing on the wines you'll allocate medals to. Then you'd take a break, wolf down a bad coffee and do it all again, this time with fifty or more one-year-old shirazes. And after lunch another couple of brackets – a class of a dozen tannic, mouth-stripping cabernets if you were unlucky, followed by the muscat or tokay class if the gods were smiling on you.

All up, it wasn't unusual for a judge at these shows to taste 200 or more wines in a day. Exhausting, palate-numbing, mentally draining work. And if you did ever come across a viognier or sangiovese it'd be in the 'other whites' or 'other reds' class, judged almost as an afterthought. Hardly given the best chance to shine.

The basic principles of wine assessment at the AAVWS in 2001 were – and still are – the same. But there were no white coats (aprons, yes – wine-tasting can be a very messy business), judges tasted *much* fewer wines in a day, the class sizes were *much* smaller, and in most cases, like was grouped with like, even if that meant there might

Steve Pannell

— *winemaker; AAVWS judge, 2001 to 2004.*

In 2001, when Steve Pannell was asked to be one of the judges at the first Alternative Varieties Wine Show, he was group red winemaker at Hardys. It was one of the most senior production positions in the country. In 1996, aged just thirty-one, he'd won the then-prestigious Jimmy Watson at the Melbourne Wine Show for his first vintage of Eileen Hardy shiraz. By the early 2000s, as well as producing fine wines like Eileen, he was also responsible for churning out an ocean of cheap-and-cheerful chardonnay, cabernet, and shiraz for Hardys' all-important UK export market. He was, in many ways, part of this country's wine establishment.

By 2004, his fourth year of judging the AAVWS, Steve had left the security of corporate life and started his own wine brand, SC Pannell, with partner Fiona Lindquist.

'I'm tired,' he told me at the time. 'It's been a buzz to make millions of litres of Stamps and Nottage Hill. It really has. But I want to get back to hands-on winemaking. I like making wine – really *making* it. You know?'

Under his own label, Steve started producing non-mainstream grape varieties in non-mainstream styles: old, under-valued workhorse grapes such as grenache; new Mediterranean grapes like nebbiolo and tempranillo and touriga; blends of aromatic white grapes, and pale, dry rosés. Importantly, he began to win trophies for these groundbreaking wines, which helped encouraged other producers to also play with new grapes and styles.

For a while there, from 2009 to 2014, he had a particularly golden run, being awarded the Rod Bonfiglioli trophy at the AAVWS on four separate occasions for his own wines – including back-to-back for two vintages of his tempranillo touriga blend – and as the winemaker of the Protero nebbiolo which won the trophy in 2011.

These were not the wines Steve had grown up with. His parents, Bill and Sandra Pannell, had established Moss Wood in Margaret River in the early 1970s, a vineyard focused on the classic French varieties, cabernet, chardonnay, and pinot noir. By the early 2000s, though, after a number of vintages working in Italy, he felt it was time for a change. He was sick of turning up to judges' dinners at Australian wine shows with a bottle of great Barolo and having the wine dismissed as inferior to the French wines on the table.

'For years,' he told me in 2009, 'Australian winemakers have been seduced by the French and lulled into the false idea that we live in a country whose climate is like France. We were totally obsessed with so-called classic French varieties, we planted them in the most inappropriate places, and convinced ourselves that the wines were pretty good. And we struggled with the fact that other countries with climates much more like ours could grow and make wine as well. Well, the Francophile period is over.'

Steve has never been afraid to speak his mind. And sometimes it's drawn flak from others in the industry.

His passionate belief in making Australian wines that taste uniquely of Australia – and his frustration that sommeliers and wine show judges seemed to be obsessed with imported wines – led him in 2010 to set up an initiative called All for One Wine. At the time he described it as 'a national celebration of Australian wine along the lines of Movember or Earth Hour, a grassroots promotion', where people, winegrowers particularly, could pledge to drink only Australian wines from January 1 until January 26.

'This way, we could go into the [next] vintage with the idea fresh in our minds that if the wines that we like to drink aren't out there, we can make them,' he said. 'Let's take a risk, push the boundaries and most importantly make more wines that better suit the food we eat, the climate we live in – the way we live and the people we are.'

The reaction was generally positive among consumers, but there was push-back from the industry and the wine trade. New Zealand winemakers slammed the initiative as a 'myopic' boycott, while some local winemakers and bloggers called it naive protectionism – and worse. For a while there after the All for One Wine website was launched, a Twitstorm of arguments and accusations raged across the internet.

Steve was taken aback by the negative comments. 'I used to think we were a community,' he told me at the time. 'But when things get tough it looks like that community crumbles. That's the danger of new media, I suppose. It's a whole lot of people sitting in their rooms bah-humbugging. And that upsets me.'

But his possum-stirring was soon vindicated. At the AAVWS later in 2010, the theme of Talk and Taste, held in conjunction with the Australian Society of Viticulture and Oenology, was 'Think Global Plant Local'. Not only did this pick up on Steve's suggestion that we concentrate on what we can do best here rather than expecting to always find the best overseas, it also shone a light on alternative varieties as a way of achieving this goal.

'I remember when I first started dabbling around with grapes like tempranillo and grenache twenty years ago everybody was like, "What is this shit? You're a complete loop",' said Steve. 'And now look. Everybody wants to drink wine made from these varieties. Everybody wants to drink young unoaked red wines. How quickly it's all changed. I know it's been twenty years, but that's not very much time at all in the life of a vine.'

Judges and associates at the first show in 2001: Ben Canaider, Peter Godden, Rollo Crittenden, David Ridge, Tim White, Clare Halloran, Steve Pannell, Kate McIntyre and Donna Stephens. No, we're not sure what's going on here, either.

be only half a dozen wines or fewer in a bracket. Where there are only one or two examples of wine made from a particular variety, they were and still are put into mixed brackets. But these are often given the *most* attention and yield the most interesting results, rather than being considered as 'also-rans' – more on this later.

The 2001 AAVWS attracted 163 wines from sixty-nine producers. In some of the larger shows, you might easily have a *single* class of chardonnay with more than 160 wines in it. Here, those 163 wines were grouped into more than twenty classes: fifteen sangioveses in one: nine viogniers in another; five zinfandels; three gewurztraminers … and so on.

Interestingly, there was a class for grenache and/or mourvedre that year because grenache was then still considered non-mainstream, its reputation yet to be revived by Australian winemakers. And – remarkable from a 2023 perspective – there was no separate class for rosé because two decades ago rosé was nowhere near as fashionable or popular as it is today.

Part Two: 2001–2004 59

Only three tempranillos were entered in 2001 – but there were sixteen chambourcins. Chambourcin is a French hybrid grape – a crossing between a French *Vitis vinifera* variety and an American non-*Vitis* variety – that had been seized upon by a few producers in the 80s and 90s, particularly in humid, coastal regions, because of its resistance to fungal diseases. The wines produced from chambourcin can have good deep colour and plenty of flavour – but some people find the wild, slightly 'foxy' characters (typical in hybrid grapes) a little off-putting. Contrast this with 2022's AAVWS: just one chambourcin was entered – and it was a rosé at that – but we tasted eighty tempranillos and tempranillo blends.

Like other wine shows, the judges at the AAVWS awarded medals according to the usual twenty-point system: anything scoring 15.5 or more is a bronze medal wine, 17 is silver, and 18.5 and above is gold. Only one wine managed to get a gold medal that year, the 2001 Redbank Sunday Morning pinot gris, which went on to win the trophy for Best Italian Varietal, Best White Wine, and Best Wine of Show.

Now, I know what you're thinking. Surely if a winemaker (in this case Yalumba, who had bought the Redbank brand a few years before from founder Neil Robb) decides to label their wine 'pinot gris', and bottle it in a tall, Alsatian-style bottle, they are signalling to the consumer that the wine inside is likely to be French in style – i.e., quite rich, ripe and textural. Why – how – can such a wine win the trophy for Best Italian Varietal? Surely it should have been labelled 'pinot grigio' at the very least?

Well yes … and no. There was a lot of confusion in 2001 about the fact that the same grape had two different names, and some winemakers weren't as good as they are now at deciding which to use on their label. To try and sidestep this confusion, Tim White and the AAVWS committee decided, even though there were only thirteen entries, to split the pinot gris class into two so that those wines that were 'dry, crisp and crunchy' (more pinot grigio-like, regardless of what the label said) were judged

Best Wine of Show, 2001: the Redbank Sunday Morning Pinot Gris

together, and the wines that were 'rich and full-bodied' (pinot gris-ish) were also judged together. This is why the Redbank wine won the 'Italian' varietal trophy: it was judged in the 'dry, crisp and crunchy' – i.e., pinot grigio-style – class.

This was a groundbreaking move. No show had, to this point, gone to such trouble to give a new, emerging variety such an opportunity to be scrutinised so fairly by a panel of judges. But, again, it was also harking back to a time when wine shows judged primarily by style, rather than by variety. For most of the previous century in fact, before varietal labelling became widespread, wines were judged in classes according to accepted style guidelines: 'red burgundy', for example, was a wine that was 'full-bodied, with a soft finish', while 'claret' was 'medium-bodied, firm finish' – regardless of what grape varieties were used to make them.

In that sense, then, the fact that a 'pinot gris' won what was effectively the 'pinot grigio' trophy was *very* Australian.

The Alternative Varieties Wine Show wasn't the only party in town that week in November. In 2001 and for the most of the next ten years, it took place around the same time as the long-running Mildura Jazz Food and Wine Festival, and there were tie-in events held to promote the show to the visitors who'd flocked to this part of the world. Being held in the first week of November, it also coincided with the Melbourne Cup and the Spring Racing Carnival. This often led to memorable moments when the wine show people – teeth stained purple from a day judging tannic red wines, merry from the obligatory after-show cleansing ale – would cross paths in the pizza café or brewery next door with the racing people, sunburnt and boisterous in their crumpled suits and wilted fascinators.

Mildura is a cultural magnet for people from all over the country, a hub on the Murray in the middle of the outback, with a thriving cultural scene. As well as the jazz festival, there's a long-running writers' festival, arts festival, country music festival, and a major gallery connected to the Chaffey family's historic Rio Vista home.

The writers' festival began in 1994 in Stefano de Pieri's restaurant in the Grand Hotel; Stef has long been a supporter of the arts – and artists have long been fans of his food. Donata Carrazza, who was married to Stef and for many years was a partner in the restaurant, was instrumental in building Mildura as a cultural centre, as chair (now artistic director) of the writers' festival. Her father, Don Carrazza, owner of the Grand Hotel, has also been a big financial supporter of the artistic life of the city. And Helen Healy, who has managed the AAVWS since 2001, is also an event organiser and arts consultant who has worked on most of Mildura's other major public initiatives.

This cultural underpinning has always been a crucial part of the AAVWS, and a major attraction for visiting judges and others who have been involved in its development. Mildura is not just geographically well-placed to be the centre of the alternative variety scene – being in the heart of a major region and at the confluence of the three major wine-producing states – it's also a fabulously fun and inspiring town to hang out in. Every time you visit, you always come away buzzing with new ideas and new discoveries.

Tim White captured this sense of discovery and the embracing of the new in his column for the *Fin Review*, published the week after the third AAVWS in 2003.

"'Well, that's the best schonburger I've ever tasted,' said winemaker Natasha Mooney, voicing the thoughts of all the judges at this year's Australian Alternative Varieties Wine Show in Mildura. What on earth, or where on earth, is schonburger you might well ask. None of us judges had much of an idea about the grape variety's origins either. Was it Swiss, Austrian, German, or possibly

from the Alto-Adige region of northeast Italy? The answer turned out to be yes, yes, yes and, er, probably yes … The example entered in the AAVWS [came] from a small vineyard in northern Tasmania, just south of Devonport, called Barringwood Park. The 2003 vintage wine proved to be a fresh, gently floral white, not especially complex, but with good length and understated fruit flavours: we awarded it a silver.'

Tim described with glee the other 'exotica' in the show such as wines made from corvina and rondinella from the Veneto, saperavi from Russia and petit manseng from southwest France; unearthing these gems is one of the great joys of participating in the AAVWS. And he described how the judges broke with convention that year and discussed the gold medal wines at trophy time.

'Normally the trophy judging takes place in relative silence, with each judge listing their preferred wines for each trophy in the form of a secret, or reasonably secret, ballot. Instead, we tasted the wines in small groups, and openly discussed which examples provided the benchmarks for each style. All the judges agreed it was worthwhile.'

One of the difficulties in deciding trophies, said Tim, is that you're often comparing apples with oranges: 'How does one decide, for example, whether a brilliant example of a fresh young wine deserves to get up over an equally brilliant example of an older, mature one, or vice versa?' This was the dilemma in 2003, as the two wines in contention for Best White were vastly different but equally deserving wine styles: the 2002 Yalumba Viognier ('a stunning example of a variety which is only just starting to find a place in wine drinkers' hearts') and the '97 Tahbilk Marsanne ('a mature version of a venerable, but much underrated, wine style').

top: 2003 judge Natasha Mooney
bottom: 1997 Tahbilk Marsanne

Tim and the judges decided, bugger tradition, let's give the trophy to both. 'We then took this a step further and awarded both wines as the Best Wines of the Show,' he wrote. 'An alternative end to an alternative wine show.'

Louisa Rose

— *chief winemaker Yalumba; AAVWS judge, 2004 and 2005; speaker at Talk and Taste 2002, 2004, 2005, 2017; committee member from 2006, chair 2009 to 2016.*

As Louisa Rose gets up to accept yet another award, I think I detect more than a touch of emotion in her voice – and it's not just the pinot gris talking.

We're coming to the end of the Saturday long lunch in 2005 on Stefano's riverboat restaurant, the Avoca, moored on the Murray. Held the day after judging finishes each year, the lunch is fast becoming a Mildura institution during show week in November. One of the wines Louisa and her team at Yalumba have made, the 2004 Eden Valley Viognier, has won three trophies – again. For the first five years of the AAVWS, this viognier dominated the trophy tally, winning Best Wine of Show three times.

Louisa pays tribute to her boss, Robert Hill Smith, for having faith in a little-known variety years before it became the trend it is today. And she urges the growers and winemakers among the ninety or so people sitting down for lunch who might be starting out with viognier or any of the other varieties to get in touch if they need help.

'Please, ring me,' she says. 'We're there. We love to talk. Come and see us.'

Not all winemakers are supportive like this by any means – some can be cagey and self-centred and reclusive. But most understand that helping your neighbour make better wine benefits everyone. There is an undeniable spirit of competitive collaboration that runs through Australia's wine community.

Louisa Rose, who started working for Yalumba in 1992 and has been chief winemaker since 2006, has always been a strong supporter of the AAVWS. As well as judging the show twice (once stepping in at the last minute to cover for a judge who had to pull out) and speaking at Talk and Taste, she served on the committee – including spending a few years as chair – for a decade.

Louisa summed up this approach to competitive collaboration in Adelaide in 2007 at the Australian Wine Industry Technical Conference, a major triennial gathering of people from across the industry. The title of her talk was 'Creating our future – new varieties and styles'.

'The rest of the wine industry is there to help you,' she told attendees. 'And you're there to help them. Try and get your variety synonymous with your region. Look at the Mornington Peninsula and its association with pinot gris, for example. Become the expert. There's not much knowledge out there about some of these varieties, so you need to create knowledge.'

Some winemakers obviously listened to her advice. McLaren Vale has become a hotbed for nero d'avola, the King Valley the home of prosecco, the Adelaide Hills synonymous with gruner veltliner.

'There needs to be a critical mass,' she said. 'There needs to be enough people out there drinking your chosen variety. And not necessarily your wine: as long as they're drinking your variety, it's going to help you.'

2003 AAVWS flyer

Tim also commented on how disappointed the judges were with the sangioveses, the largest class in the show with forty-eight entries (fifty-four including sangiovese blends). The disappointment is understandable: the whole show began four years previously as the sangiovese awards. It also highlights an important addition to show week that had been introduced in 2002: a seminar program called Talk and Taste scheduled for the Friday afternoon, after the judging was complete.

This concept of holding seminars was inspired by the presentations given during the long Italian lunch in 1999 and it has proved to be a crucially important part of the AAVWS. The events draw people to Mildura, to hear the latest developments in the alternative wine space, to meet old friends, make new ones, and build new networks. They've even encouraged some winemakers to dip their own toes in the alternative water.

In 2002 Talk and Taste included Bruce Chalmers presenting 'A grower's and nurseryman's perspective on alternatives varieties', and Italian agronomist and winemaker Federico Curtaz, who spoke on 'Modern and traditional viticulture objectives in Italy and their application to Australian conditions'.

'I remember Federico,' says Tim White. 'He was that little geezer who'd come all the way from Sicily and lost his luggage en route to Mildura. I remember wandering down from my room at the Grand and in the spirit of bonhomie giving him my Mambo shirt.'

Yalumba's Louisa Rose – also a judge that year – gave a talk on viognier in Australia. And I gave an overview of tempranillo, sharing my surprise that the variety had exploded from half a dozen producers in 1998 to sixty growers with 150 hectares in twenty-five regions in 2002. I noted that the Yendah Vale tempranillo had won a trophy at the Perth show in 2000 (for 'early drinking red') and that the variety was the third most popular red at the Brown Brothers cellar door.

The mood wasn't quite so optimistic at the following year's Talk and Taste, entitled 'Sangiovese – Let's Get it Right'. A sangiovese – the 2001 Scaffidi Talunga from the Adelaide Hills – had won the trophy for Best Red at the show in 2002, but there was a sense that the variety wasn't living up to its potential more broadly.

'The principal reason for this,' wrote Tim White, '[is] that the main clone of sangiovese planted in Australia, H6V9, simply doesn't appear to be much chop.' (This is the clone that the CSIRO had imported back in the 1960s.) 'It does OK on some sites, if a lot of work is put into the vineyard, but generally it produces pretty washed-out wines. There is an argument that once the plantings have gained some maturity they'll improve, but I'm not convinced. Fortunately, there are now some really schmick new clones available and the first wines from these show a lot of promise.'

That promise took a while to be fulfilled. The topic of the 2006 Talk and Taste was 'Sangiovese: *still* the challenge' (my emphasis). It wasn't until almost a decade later that sangiovese-based wines started winning trophies again, culminating in the 2021 Best Wine of Show, the 2016 Valentino Sangiovese – a wine made from those 'really schmick new clones'.

In 2003, wine drinks giant Southcorp, known today as Treasury Wine Estates, owner of such brands as Penfolds, Wolf Blass and Rosemount, bought Kevin McCarthy and Kathleen Quealy's T'Gallant business. This was a turning point in the fortune of pinot gris. From being an emerging variety a decade previously, the grape – in its grigio form – now had the backing of one of the world's biggest wine companies. Casella's Yellow Tail brand, which was enjoying stratospheric sales in the US in the early to mid-2000s, was also about to start soaking up as much pinot gris fruit as the company could get its hands on, encouraging Bruce Chalmers and others to plant hundreds of hectares of the variety. It was well on its way to becoming mainstream.

This sense of commercial optimism was set against a world, and a country, dealing with huge threats and instability. Back then, our TV screens and newspapers were full of news of the Iraq War, SARS, and the bushfires that ripped through Canberra early in the year – challenges that, in retrospect, look like a grim rehearsal for the first three years of the 2020s.

Meanwhile, in the wine industry, an oversupply of grapes was building, and the Millennium Drought was beginning to bite. By 2004 it was becoming increasingly obvious that the export boom could not be sustained, and that too many of the wrong varieties had been planted in the wrong places. Not only that, but quite a few of those vineyards had been planted for the wrong reasons, as part of managed investment schemes, or to secure precious

The 2004 awards long lunch was on the Avoca paddleboat

Chair of the AAVWS committee Robin Day (left) and Kathleen Quealy at the 2004 awards

water rights along the inland river systems, rather than because they had a secure commercial contract.

At the same time, the smart growers and winemakers were beginning to get together and organise their own groups and develop networks, sharing information and experience, tasting each other's wines, offering advice and help.

In 2004 the winemakers of the Barossa Valley hosted the first Shiraz Alliance, a series of tastings and seminars and lunches and dinners that brought winemakers from around Australia and around the world together to celebrate the grape. After the event, Louisa Rose and Yalumba hosted a get-together for growers and winemakers of tempranillo: an in-house affair – not, like the Shiraz Alliance had been, also open to the public – where producers could taste and speak freely, offering constructive criticism, helping 'improve the breed' in the spirit of the AAVWS' Talk and Taste program. It was an event that was repeated over subsequent years, with me – an interested but not commercially invested third party – acting as moderator.

Also in 2004, the first Biodynamic Wine Forum was held in Beechworth. This was a hugely influential event that encouraged several producers to convert to this form of organic farming in their vineyards. It's no coincidence, I think, that some of the highest-profile producers to head down this path – such as Paxton and Gemtree vineyards in McLaren Vale – were also actively engaged with planting and promoting alternative varieties, particularly tempranillo. Thinking about different ways to grow grapes wasn't confined to the choice of variety.

In November 2004 the AAVWS judging moved to the Mildura Function Centre. Well, that's it's *official* name. It's actually the club house of the Mildura Demons footy team. A room big enough to hold all the wine samples

Helen Healy

— arts and events consultant, Mildura city councillor; manager of the AAVWS from 2001.

Helen Healy had been running the Alternative Varieties Wine Show in the early 2000s for a couple of years when she picked up the phone.

'"Hey sis",' said a man's voice at the other end. '"Can we enter your show? We're an Aboriginal winery – that's pretty alternative."'

Helen wasn't surprised. She knew this job was going to be different even before she started working on it.

'In 2001 I'd only been in town for a couple of years,' she says. 'But I'd heard about the events Stef and Rod had put on in 1999 and 2000. A friend had gone along to one. Had a wild time. Ended up in the pool at the Grand with some of the other people at the dinner …'

Helen grew up in the Mallee and moved to Mildura in the late 90s as a partner in a graphic design firm. When this closed, she was asked to organise a local event and discovered not only that was she good at it, but she also loved it. So, she set up a business that would go on to win awards for event management.

'There was a cultural surge in Mildura in the late 90s, early 2000s,' she says. 'Stef's *Gondola on the Murray* TV series changed everything. New restaurants opened; new people came to town. There was a real buzz.'

All this activity in the arts and food and scene resonated with Helen. She is a musician, songwriter, and performer, has taught dramatic arts, and infused the AAVWS with this background. But the wine aspect of the show was new to her.

'I didn't really drink wine before I started working on the show,' she says. 'To train me up, [chief judge] Tim White took me to a tasting. He didn't instruct me at all, so I had to just learn by observing. I was wearing a white shirt – which was a mistake. And no-one told me not to swallow all the wines.'

In a food, wine, and arts community as tight as Mildura's, it hasn't always been easy running the show over the last twenty-one years. There have been falling outs, cross words, and challenges. With 700 entries, a dozen judges, dinners, awards ceremonies, and countless stewards lugging boxes, opening bottles and pouring – and always, endlessly cleaning glasses – juggling the many demands of the show year after year has required an efficient and determined manager. But Helen has persisted and her persistence has paid off.

'In the early days it was hard to get the local wineries involved, particularly the larger ones,' she says. 'Now the bulk of our stewards and associate judges come from the big local companies. There's really good buy-in from the big companies, and they're involved as supporters.'

A couple of years ago, Helen was elected to Mildura Rural City Council and today she is the deputy mayor. But she's still heavily involved in managing the show. And she's glad that these days, everything – from exhibitors filling in entry forms to the judging itself and the distribution of the certificates to each medal winner after the show – is done online. She remembers, for example, how the show's first judging manager, Bruce Hall, compiled and entered all the early judging notes manually.

'Those years we spent hours sitting in my backyard stuffing hundreds of envelopes with exhibitor labels and certificates seem like a *long* time ago now.'

on one side of a screen (entries were nudging 400 at that point, from over 130 different producers), and large tables on the other side to hold the judges' glasses. A big kitchen, too, for all the glass-washing that the ever-growing team of stewards was lumbered with.

It's a room full of character. The names of teams and medal winners and past glories, painted in gold on dark wooden panels on the wall. A balcony where the judges can relax, or check up on emails, or just stare out at the footy oval in between tasting – and, memorably one year, watch the Crusty Demons freestyle motorcyclists rehearsing for a show that night. Much more conducive (Crusty Demons notwithstanding) to concentration – and conviviality – than the cooler, less soulful, modern Alfred Deakin Centre where the judging took place in prior years. The footy club has (apart from one year) been the 'home' of the AAVWS judging and exhibitors' tasting ever since and has become part of the fabric of the show.

The previous year, in 2003, and for the next five years, the Awards Long Lunch on the Saturday took place not at the Grand Hotel but on the Avoca Paddleboat, moored on the banks of the Murray River, which Stefano and Donata were running at the time. It was a glorious, unusual, and unique setting that really grounded – or, rather, immersed – guests in the culture and spirit of Mildura. Again, it helped build a sense of conviviality – hugely important for a wine show with an agenda, like the AAVWS. Having a hell of a lot of fun is a great way of spreading a message.

The trophies in 2004 went, fittingly, to two of the key drivers of alternative varieties in the 1990s: the Pizzini family in the King Valley for their 1998 nebbiolo, and T'Gallant (albeit now under corporate ownership) for the Tribute pinot gris. That same year also saw the first wines produced by the Chalmers family from the vines they'd imported and planted at Euston in the late 90s.

Disheartened by the lack of interest from Australia's larger wine companies in some of their new varieties, the Chalmers developed their range of wines, called The

2002 Pizzini Nebbiolo, Wine of Show in 2007

AAVWS

AUSTRALIAN ALTERNATIVE VARIETIES WINE SHOW

MILDURA

THURSDAY 4
Structured Wine Tasting with Tim White
Nebbiolo and Sangiovese AAVWS medal winners and comparable international wines.
6pm. Mildura Grand Hotel. Cost $66

FRIDAY 5
Viticulturalist's Tour of Chalmers Nursery
Tour of one of Australia's largest producers of grafted vines, with over 30 alternative varieties.
Morning tea and lunch provided.
7am - 12.30pm. Depart by bus from the Mildura Grand Hotel at 7am. Cost $66

Intensive Winemaker's Workshop
A hardcore workshop covering flavours, brettanmyces and tastings with Mark Sefton, Stephen Henschke and Adrian Coulter.
9am - 12noon. Mildura Grand Hotel. Cost $77

Seminar 'Wood you like a Pinot Gri/s/gio'
Featuring some of Australia's foremost winemakers, marketeers, researchers and writers including Robin Day, Prue Henschke, Alan Kennett, Stephen Henschke, Mark Sefton, Kathleen Quealy, Louisa Rose and Huon Hook. Followed by a panel session and tasting with new and old world Pinot Gri/s/gios.
1pm – 5pm. Mildura Grand Hotel. Cost $110

SATURDAY 6
Public & Entrant Tasting of Show wines.
Cost $10 includes tasting glass.
Mildura Function Centre. Twelfth St. Mildura. 10am – 11am

AAVWS Awards Long Lunch
Legendary awards presented by Stefano de Pieri on the Murray, with wine tutoring by Show judges throughout the lunch.
Seating is limited.
12 noon Avoca Riverfront Café. Cost $110

INFORMATION (03) 5021 5100
www.aavws.com
BOOKINGS
Mildura Arts Centre on (03) 5018 8322
or the Mildura Visitors Information Centre on (03) 5018 8376
* All tickets sold by our ticketing agent incur a $2.20 booking fee.

2004 AAVWS poster

Details from the 2004 show judging

Murray Darling Collection, as a way of showing that the viticultural proof is in the vinous pudding. They collaborated with wine importer Jamie Broadway. Jamie was soon to also become co-owner of the Gertrude Street Enoteca in Gertrude Street in Melbourne, established with his partner, cookery writer and chef Brigitte Hafner, who not long before had cooked with Stef in Mildura (I hope you're keeping up with this web of connections). The winemaker was Sandro Mosele, then developing a reputation for high quality pinot and chardonnay at Kooyong on Victoria's Mornington Peninsula.

I'll never forget tasting the 2004 barrel and tank samples of the vermentino ('delicious, crisp, fennel and almond-flavoured') aglianico ('gutsy, imperious and robust – like a cross between zinfandel and durif, but with more finesse') and schioppettino ('glaring pinky-purple and bursting with flavours of raspberries and spice') – the first Australian-made examples of these grapes I'd tried. It felt like a breakthrough moment, a vindication of Rod Bonfiglioli's crazy dreams.

The Talk and Taste program that year included a viticulturists' tour of the Chalmers vineyard, an intensive winemakers' workshop with a panel including Mark Sefton and Adrian Coulter from the Australian Wine Research Institute, and a discussion and tasting entitled 'Wood you like a Pinot Gri/s/gio' (not the first or last time bad puns would be employed at the AAVWS),

2004 judge Huon Hooke

featuring such industry luminaries as Robin Day, former chief winemaker for Orlando Wyndham, influential viticulturist Prue Henschke, and Sydney wine writer Huon Hooke.

Huon and Sydney wine merchant Jon Osbeiston were also judges that year, again a deliberate attempt on Tim White's part to broaden the experience base of the show's participants – except this was a case of bringing in a couple of 'old farts' (Tim's affectionate phrase) to lend gravitas to what had been predominantly next-gen-dominated judging panels.

Huon had been writing about the alternative variety movement for a while. In a remarkably prescient article in the *Sydney Morning Herald* back in 2000, he'd imagined visiting an inner-city bar ten years in the future, where the front of the wine list is full of vermentino, greco and aglianico, and the chardonnay and shiraz and cabernet are lumped up the back under the heading 'Boring Varieties'.

'The use of non-winemaker judges was strategic,' says Tim. 'We were thinking how we could maximise exposure for the show. It was perceived by some as being this little regional show, but it was a national show, and it was important to get that message out. Also, we needed people to know it wasn't just about promoting Italian varieties. Jon was and is a very influential figure in the Sydney wine trade – although I don't think he'd judged a wine show before – and I was good friends with Huon. Getting them involved really helped with exposure.'

Part Three

Tipping points

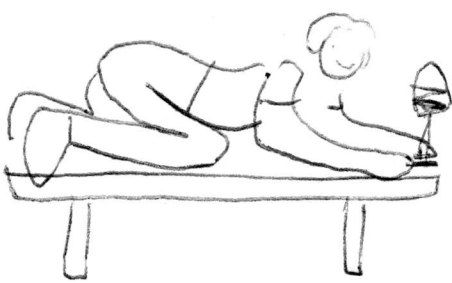

Saturday 7 February 2009. It's only nine o'clock in the morning but it must be at least 50°C in this shed. Sweat's trickling into my eyes and onto my glasses as I stand precariously on a table, holding a camera, trying to stay still enough to take a photo of thirty-two different bunches of grapes laid out on the floor below me (you can see the photo on page 200). I've spent the last couple of hours finding and picking these bunches from various sections of the vineyard here at Chalmers in Euston, an hour's drive east of Mildura, and it's already one of the hottest days I've ever experienced.

I've come here for two reasons: to take photos of the different varieties for a book I'm working on, and to participate in a 'flavour tasting day'. As I finish up in the shed, 150 winemakers and growers, prospective buyers of these varieties, are converging on the Chalmers vineyard to see the grapes on the vine and then taste the wines each variety produces. The wine-tasting is accompanied, of course, by a relaxed lunch cooked by Stefano de Pieri and his team.

Except, in 2009, this isn't the Chalmers' vineyard anymore. They sold it in 2008 to Macquarie Agriculture, who were primarily interested in the property's hundreds

preceding pages: Spit painting by Max Allen and the 2008 AAVWS judges

right: Kim Chalmers and ABC TV crew at Chalmers vineyard on Black Saturday, 2009

of hectares of valuable pinot gris, thought to be the largest planting in the southern hemisphere. Bruce is still involved with managing the place, though, and the original plantings of all the varieties the family imported are still here (for now – Macquarie will eventually get rid of them, but not before the Chalmers can take cuttings and re-establish new mother blocks at their Merbein vineyard).

And the lunch isn't very relaxed.

I got here as early as I could this morning because the forecast was for a particularly hot and windy day. Well over 40°C, they'd said, with brutal northerlies blaring down from the desert. Another blistering day on top of a string of blistering days the week before. Bruce Chalmers lent me an ATV, told me where to find the varieties I wanted to shoot and sent me on my way.

It's not too bad at first, when the sun is still low in the sky and the vines provide some cool shade. But by the time everyone returns from the vineyard tour and sits down for lunch, it's clear this is no ordinary day. Sprinklers and fans act as an impromptu evaporative cooling system, but the ferocity of the sun and fierceness of the wind soon nudge the mercury up to 46°C.

AAVWS
AUSTRALIAN ALTERNATIVE VARIETIES WINE SHOW
MILDURA

Welcome to the
2006 Australian Alternative Varieties Wine Show
Awards Long Lunch
11 November 2006

Food by Seasons at dining room one
accompanied by
2005 AAVWS gold medal wines

Starters
Eggplant fritters w/spicy tomato salsa
Mildura Brewery Beer
2005 Redbank Sunday Morning Pinot Gris
2005 Yalumba Y Series Viognier 2005
2004 Yalumba Eden Valley Viognier 2004

First course
Basil & lime cured ocean trout w/ rocket fennel citrus salad
2005 T Gallant Pinot Grigio
2004 T Gallant Imogen Pinot Gris
2005 Murray Darling Collection 'Murray Cod' Vermentino

Second Course
Roasted tart of potato, roasted capsicum, leek & capers w/ prosciutto & basil pesto
2004 Casella Wines Yellowtail Reserve Pinot Grigio
2005 Brown Brothers Pinot Grigio
2004 Yarra Burn Pinot Gris

Third Course
Gnocchetti w/ veal & porcini ragout
2006 Murray Darling Collection Negro Amaro
2004 Dunns Creek Estate Barbera

Fourth Course
Braised local beef cheeks w/ soft polenta & gremolata
2004 Yalumba Tempranillo95% & Grenache5% & Viognier5%
2004 Stuart Wines Co. Tempranillo Buddha's Wine

Fifth Course
Extra mature Ironstone Cheddar w/pecorino romano & local muscatels & crackers
2003 Westend 3 Bridges Reserve Durif
2003 Ferngrove King Malbec

Dessert
Summer berry pudding w/ crème anglaise
2005 Trentham Estate La Famiglia Moscato

www.aavws.com

2006 Long Lunch menu

A TV crew from ABC's *Landline* program are there and they capture lots of positive comments from attendees.

'It's great on a day like today to see how well some of these varieties are actually standing up to quite hot conditions,' says Yalumba chief winemaker Louisa Rose.

'They sound like [they have] funny names,' says Barossa winemaking legend Stephen Henschke, 'but they're really interesting varieties.'

'The great thing about today,' I say when they point the camera at me, 'is the opportunity to taste all these grape varieties traditionally from southern Europe and northern Europe and other parts of the world, all on the vine at the same time.'

But when the cameras aren't rolling, everyone's nervously checking their phone for messages, worried about the extreme fire danger that has been predicted for today.

I'm due to fly back to Melbourne from Mildura later that afternoon. Not being a good flyer at the best of times, I decide that I'd rather not be up there in that horribly volatile sky, so I accept an offer of a lift from Alan Cooper, who's driving back to his Cobaw Ridge vineyard in the Macedon Ranges and can drop me off close to the city.

As we head down the highway, the car thermometer clicks up to 49°C and the ferocious sunlight outside paints the landscape a sickly shade of bruised yellow. We listen to news reports on the radio of one fire after another breaking out here and jumping containment lines there. It sounds like half the state is burning.

The fires that raged that day killed 173 people and injured more than 400. Over 450,000 hectares burned and more than 2000 houses were destroyed. Up to a million animals perished.

In early 2009, it seemed, everything was falling apart.

Appearing on the telly as a kind of spokesperson for the alternative variety movement was a sign of far how I'd crossed the line from observer to participant – a line that should arguably never be crossed if you claim to be a journalist.

I had been chief judge at the AAVWS since 2005. When Tim White stepped down the year before and told me he wanted to put my name forward to the committee as a replacement, he'd assured me it wouldn't be too onerous. 'It's pretty easy,' he said. 'Not much work at all.' And when I started, it certainly seemed we were more concerned with making the show more fun to judge, and the results more meaningful, than facing up to the existential threat of climate change and global instability bearing down on us.

In 2006, for example, we ditched the small, International Standard tasting glasses in favour of large, roomy Riedel glasses. This made the stewards' job more difficult (all that polishing!) but made a huge difference to the quality of judging. The larger bowl size of the Riedel glasses emphasised both the flaws and imbalances as well as the subtle aromas in each wine, meaning poor entries were more easily discarded and more elegant, restrained styles were given a chance to shine.

The AAVWS wasn't the only show in Australia to be moving in this direction. In the mid-2000s many other wine shows in Australia – notably the big capital city shows in Adelaide and Sydney – were also instigating changes: using Riedels or other, large-bowled glasses, and questioning the dominance of old-school winemakers among the ranks of the judges, making sure new blood was entering the system, inviting people from the retail and restaurant worlds to participate.

And making sure that the judging panels were balanced in other ways. Starting in 2005 and continuing in most years since, the gender balance of the judges invited to

International Perspectives: guests from around the world

2003	*Paul White, wine writer, New Zealand*
2003	*Alberto Antonini, consultant, Tuscany (via livestream)*
2006	*Joelle Thomson, wine writer, New Zealand*
2008	*Rebecca Gibb, wine writer, New Zealand*
2010	*Jo Burzynska, wine writer and sound artist, New Zealand*
2010	*Stefano Dini, viticultural consultant, Italy*
2013	*Pietro Scafidi, researcher, Sicily*
2013	*Alessio Planeta, winery owner, Sicily*
2014	*Walter Speller, wine writer, Italy*
2014	*Lado Uzunashvili, winemaker, Georgia*
2015	*Jo Burzynska, wine writer and sound artist, New Zealand*
2015	*Nick Hoskins, viticultural consultant, New Zealand*
2016	*Sarah Ahmed, wine writer, UK*
2017	*Eddie McDougall, winemaker, entrepreneur, Hong Kong*
2018	*Madeleine Stenwreth, Master of Wine, Sweden*
2019	*Michaela Morris, wine writer, educator, Canada*
2020	*Cha McCoy, sommelier, educator, United States*

International judge Jo Burzynska at AAVWS 2015

Australian wine history is full of the influential ideas and hard work of people from outside Australia. This country's first, early nineteenth-century vignerons all came from somewhere else, of course. But even after Australian-born growers and winemakers began to establish an industry, notable outsiders – from a string of German-born winemakers such as Wolf Blass to the UK-born writer, spruiker and show judge Len Evans – have continued to shape the way we think about and drink wine.

The Australian Alternative Varieties Wine Show is no different. Only one of the three co-founders of the show – Bruce Chalmers – was born here. The other two, Stef and Rod, were Italian and English. And outlined in Part One, it was a chance meeting between Australian viticultural consultant Richard Smart and Italian viticultural consultant Alberto Antonini on a plane in 1996 that set in motion the course of events that ultimately led to the first show being held in 2001.

Ever since then, the show has invited people from all around the world to join the judging panel as an international guest and/or contribute to a Talk and Taste session, both to contribute their experience and expertise, and to tell others what's happening here when they return home.

Initially, most of the international judges came from not that far away – just across the Tasman Sea in fact, from New Zealand / Aotearoa. Partly this was a financial decision: in its early years, when entry numbers were much lower than they are today, it was cheaper to fly someone in from Wellington than Washington. But also, the committee invited a lot of Kiwi judges because, until 2018, New Zealand wineries were eligible to enter the show. The number of Kiwi entries was never that huge, but it was important to maintain that connection and keep that perspective.

New Zealand sound artist and wine writer, **Jo Burzynska**, felt right at home at the AAVWS when she judged in 2010, collaborating with Kim Chalmers on an aural experience for the attendees.

'I still recall the thrill of entering the awards lunch drinks,' said Jo in a video address at the 2022 Talk and Taste. 'Hearing one of my compositions

Profiles 83

that I'd created from recordings of the winemaking process, joined by one of Kim's compositions, and the sounds of a grape harvester. I remember there being a little consternation amongst some of those present, but then I witnessed winegrowers suddenly recognising what the unusual aperitif soundtrack was made from. So, it was initially a bit strange but became intriguing and more enjoyable with recognition. A bit like the alternative varieties themselves.'

In the second decade of the show, the international judges' net was cast further afield. **Sarah Ahmed**, UK-based writer, and expert in Australian and Portuguese wines, was keen to taste as many examples of touriga and arinto and fernao pires as she could when she judged in 2018.

'It was really exciting to see how those Portuguese grape varieties are performing in Australia,' said Sarah. 'In Portugal, producers are very much thinking about climate change and digging deeper into native varieties that have been overlooked. So, I think it's completely the right direction to go [in Australia].'

Flying winemaker **Eddie McDougall** said his judging experience helped give him a broader understanding of alternative varieties, which are increasingly popular in east Asia.

'In bars across the region, we're seeing varietals other than shiraz or cabernet or chardonnay,' he said. 'Australian fiano, sangiovese, pinot grigio, prosecco. All these are starting to ruffle feathers over here. And it's the new generation of wine drinkers that are starting to really appreciate and create this drive. People are thirsty, people are becoming more intrigued by what else Australia has to offer.'

Given the show's historic connections with Italy, it was particularly instructive to have people like **Walter Speller** – Italian specialist at *JancisRobinson.com* – and **Stefano Dini**, Italian viticultural consultant, as judges. Both went on to become even more involved, with Walter hosting a seminar with the Chalmers and Jane Faulkner in London in 2015 called '21st Century Vino', looking at Italian varieties in Australia, and Stefano helping

International judge Eddie McDougall, right, judge Fiona Donald, left, at Talk and Taste 2017

the Chalmers import the coveted nerello mascalese variety into the country.

'I would love to do something like 21st Century Vino again,' said Walter. 'To show how strong these varieties are and the marketability of them. The crown of this would be of course to organise a tasting of Australian Italian varieties in Italy. In the lion's den!'

'I'm happy to help to introduce a variety new in Australia like nerello,' said Stefano. 'Some Italian producers criticise me because they think that this variety is born for a place and shouldn't move. Probably they are afraid that other producers will be competition for them. But I think that this variety should be well known in the world, and one way to do that is to show what other producers in other countries can do with it.'

The last word should go to **Alberto Antonini** who, although never a judge, has been a part of Talk and Taste and a champion of alternative varieties here.

'I always believed Australia has an amazing diversity of biodiversity and terroir,' he said. 'And many of these grapes have found another home here, to contribute to the making of premium wines. Also, it's interesting to see how the consumer is evolving: wine consumption is becoming more and more a kind of experience. People don't want to just drink the same wine every day. They want to learn more, and Australia has plenty of options to offer with the diversity of terroir, but also with more grapes that can be successfully grown in your country.'

Profiles 85

2007 AAVWS dinner menu

TRENTHAM ESTATE

Australian Alternative Varieties Wine Show Dinner

Wednesday 7th November 2007
$70 per person
7:30pm

Canapés:

2007 Moscato

- Smoked salmon mousse on crispy bread
- Seared scallop in Asian spoon with marinated vegetables
- Vegetable quiche bites
- Asparagus and prosciutto spears

Appetizer:

2007 Vermentino

Seared garfish with fennel mayonnaise and salad

Entrée:

2006 Viognier

Rosemary and garlic marinated Quail on ratatouille with crushed kipfler potatoes and jus

Main:

2004 Petit Verdot Tannat / Mystery wine

Rabbit and wild mushroom pie with baby vegetables and rabbit glaze with herbs

Dessert:

2003 Taminga

Quark and vanilla bean soufflé with blood orange and mint salad

the show has been evenly split. This seems unsurprising now. But even as recently as the mid-2000s the wine show world was still overwhelmingly male-dominated – if not a fully-blown boy's club. At the time we didn't make a big deal out of the fact that the AAVWS was adopting a more equitable approach – and was probably one of the first shows to do so – because, well, it was just the right thing to do.

Another innovation introduced in this period was to give the pink wines a proper chance. I'd long felt that rosé shouldn't be judged in wine shows: it is, after all, the epitome of 'just shut up and drink it' wine. So, during the show in 2006 we chilled down the twenty-five wines in the rosé class to *drinking* temperature (i.e., nice and cold), before we tasted them blind, in a line-up – as you

left: cover of the Beer and Bowls songbook

right: 2010 singalong at Beer and Bowls

would any other class. Afterwards, we sat down to discuss, take notes, and give medals over lunch. The next year Sergio de Pieri – Stefano's older brother, who spends half the year in Mildura, half back in Italy – cooked a big pot of pasta for us in the footy club kitchen, and we ate that while we judged the rosés.

It was a lovely experience, and helped us get some good results, but ultimately it was of course impractical, especially as the entry numbers were creeping up by this point (close to 600 wines from over 200 producers were entered in 2007). It wasn't the only impractical innovation, either: in 2010, in an attempt to provide truly meaningful results to the exhibitors, we decided to record the judges' impressions of the wines and transcribe them from the audio recordings. I'd argued that the heart of a wine show is the judges' discussions – frank and fearless conversation about style, about faults, about quality – and that if there was some way we could capture this discussion it would help the whole process of refinement and improvement back in the vineyard and winery. As it turned out the workload, with Jenni Chalmers valiantly transcribing and editing the audio, was nightmarish in its scope, and it was ditched the following year.

2008 chief judge Max Allen: spit painting in progress

The wine show's extra-curricular program also expanded during this period in the mid-2000s. As well as the dinners that were already part of the carnival of side-events that took place each year, 2007 saw the introduction of a new, informal event that would go on to become an AAVWS tradition: beer and bowls.

∾

The Mildura Bowls Club, a short walk from the Grand Hotel, is a classic example of the 1950s red-brick sports facilities you find all across Australia, complete with a portrait of the Queen inside and a sweeping view from the rooftop terrace across Rio Vista Park to the slow-flowing Murray River. The perfect location to unwind after the awards long lunch on the Saturday, with a couple of ends of barefoot bowls, beer in hand. And, inevitably, a singalong, with Kim Chalmers and Helen Healy on guitar, and me on mandolin.

Bruce and Jenni's daughters, Kim and Tennille, had come back to Mildura and started working in the business in the mid-2000s, and their energy and enthusiasm added another layer to the AAVWS experience. Kim was a composer and musician, who had spent some time living in Italy with Sergio de Pieri, a renowned organist; Tennille had worked in the hospitality scene in Melbourne. I'd mentioned I played mandolin in the car on the way to a dinner featuring the Murray Darling Collection (MDC) wines in the Mildura Station Woolshed during show week in 2005. Somehow, towards the end of dinner, Helen and Kim had managed to find a mandolin and we worked our way through a few songs. The next year I brought my own and joined Kim and Helen and band – including local winemaker Melissa Tucker on violin – in some raucous covers. By the time beer and bowls had become entrenched a few years later, Kim and Helen had compiled and printed out a songbook, so everyone could sing along.

As well as music, the AAVWS committee indulged my artistic urges in 2008.

I'm a big fan of the British artist Andy Goldsworthy, best known for his ephemeral sculptures made from leaves and ice and stones in the landscape. In the 1990s, Goldsworthy created a series of 'paintings' by laying a large blank canvas in a sheep paddock and placing a round salt lick in the middle. The resulting images – a flurry of muddy hoofprints surrounding a white circle – were extraordinary. So, I convinced Helen Healy to buy a big piece of plain, un-primed canvas that I laid out at one end of the footy club, placed a bowl in the middle, and invited the judges to spit wine into it. We displayed the 'spit painting' during the exhibitors' tasting on the Saturday; it's the image that opens this section of the book, on page 76.

This sense of creative exploration also influenced the content of the Talk and Taste program. As we argued at the time, 'While serious issues such as climate change, water use, uncertain economic times and sustainability are all incredibly important, there is also room for an entertaining, thought-provoking afternoon of tasting and talking that might help to push the limits of wine style, wine perception and wine enjoyment.'

In 2008 the theme was 'The Weird and Wonderful World of Wine'. The first session, hosted by consultant David Le Mire and international judge Rebecca Gibb, looked at 'The Wackiest Wines in the World'. The line-up looks tame now – it included a blend of malagousia and assyrtiko from Domaine Gerovassilliou near Thessaloniki and a rosé from brand-new Adelaide Hills winemaker Anton van Klopper, made with no additions – but back then was quite challenging: I had to bring bottles of Josko Gravner's amphora-fermented ribolla back from Europe in my hand-luggage for the session because no-one in Australia was importing it at the time. (Jamie Broadway had brought some in a few years before but found hardly anyone was interested.)

The second session saw winemaker Matt Gant and sommelier James Erskine, who was beginning to work with Anton in the Hills and would go on to become a

Ashley Ratcliff

— viticulturist, wine producer; AAVWS committee member 2010 - , chair 2017–2020; speaker at Talk & Taste, 2011.

There's a fair chance that you've drunk wine made from Ashley Ratcliff's grapes and not even realised it. As well as growing and making wine under his own labels – Ricca Terra, Terra do Rio, 22 Degree Halo, among others – Ashley also sells lots of different grapes, including many alternatives, to lots of other producers, from Coonawarra to Margaret River, from McLaren Vale to Melbourne, from major producers to tiny garage winemakers.

Ashley and his wife Holly are based in the Barossa, where Ash worked for Yalumba for many years as viticulture and production manager. They bought their first eight-hectare vineyard in Barmera, in South Australia's Riverland in 2003. It was a much more affordable investment than the Barossa, and the chardonnay grapes growing on the site were then in demand. Grape prices soon fell, though, and water prices rose. The Ratcliffs were faced with a choice: get out or get smart. So, they started buying more vineyards, and planting –

and grafting, and encouraging others to plant – a whole host of climate-adapted, interesting, emerging alternative varieties, under the Ricca Terra Farms umbrella.

Now, Ricca Terra covers 80 hectares of vineyards in the Riverland, and for the last decade has been at the forefront of alternative grapes. Along the way, Ashley has also encouraged many others in the region to think differently about their vineyards, their businesses, and their community.

In 2009 Ashley became the founding chair of the Riverland Alternative Wine Group. I remember attending the first meeting of the group in 2009, with one hundred growers and winemakers – many from the larger companies – crowded into the Renmark Club thirsty to learn about vermentino and nero d'avola, fiano and montepulciano, with another 250 people having to be turned away.

I've talked to Ashley a lot over the years about his visions for the Riverland. And I've watched as his impressive leadership skills and extraordinary energy have helped instil a sense of optimism and pride in the region's growers and producers.

His advocacy and vision for a sustainable inland wine industry were recognised in 2013 when he picked up several gongs: he was named Horticultural Grower of the Year by ABC Rural, picked up the Wine Industry Award at the Riverland Wine Show – an award normally given out to winemakers – and was named Viticulturist of the Year by the Australian Society of Viticulture and Oenology.

When broader industry enthusiasm for alternatives dwindled a few years later because of the rising demand for mainstream grapes – fuelled by booming exports to China, most of which was shiraz – Ashley launched wines under his own labels, first Ricca Terra, mostly blends of Italian varieties, then Terra do Rio, mostly Portuguese varieties, to help spread a confident message about the viability of alternatives.

'Growers were saying, "Well, I can make $800, $900 a tonne selling shiraz, why bother with alternative varieties?"' he says. 'Then, of course [after the collapse of the Chinese market], it swung back to a pretty dismal place. But those people who had alternative varieties stayed at a high point [selling grapes] as the tide dropped out. Alternative varieties created a point of difference – and there's probably no more important time in the history of the wine industry where a point of a difference is going to have some commercial benefits.'

Jane Faulkner and Stefano Dini at the AAVWS in 2010

winemaker himself. They wanted to push the boundaries of food and wine matching from the tried-and-tested (oysters and Muscadet) to the hyper-regional (Fairbank rosé with Holy Goat La Luna cheese, both from Sutton Grange in central Victoria) to the decidedly unusual (Matt's Minchia montepulciano with coffee ice-cream). Again, at the time, it was the first taste for many in the room of *vin jaune* – the sherry-like flor-aged savagnin from Jura – with comté cheese.

And the day finished with a session hosted by me and Kim Chalmers, exploring the idea put forward by provocative Californian wine consultant Clark Smith and others that the music you listen to can affect the way you taste what's in your glass. This was a fascinating exercise – but a step too far for some of the participants.

∾

It wasn't all fun and games during this period of the show's history. There was also a sense that alternative varieties – some of them at least – were on the cusp of becoming accepted in Australia and overseas, and telling the story was the crucial next step to pushing them over the line. As a result, we made sure the judging panels included journalists such as Jane Faulkner from *The Age*, and New Zealand wine writers Joelle Thompson and Jo Burzynska. In addition, we invited sommeliers such as Sophie Otton, then at the City Wine Shop in Melbourne, and Matt Skinner, then at Jamie Oliver's Fifteen; and importers such as Sally McGill from Red and White and Rob Walters from Bibendum. It was also why the theme of the 2005 Talk and Taste was 'Marketing Alternative Varieties', hosted by experienced industry elders such as James Irvine – the only person then making sparkling wine from the petit meslier grape – and Robin Day, former head of winemaking at Orlando, now making garganega and lagrein under his own small label.

That same year, 2005, Yellow Tail, the hugely successful brand launched in the US by Riverina wine company Casella, introduced a pinot grigio to the range. In 2007,

Pouring more viognier for the man in the tinny at the 2007 awards long lunch

Barossa winery Peter Lehmann reported selling their entire vintage of tempranillo to UK supermarket chain, Sainsburys. And as we were all enjoying the AAVWS awards long lunch that year on the Avoca paddleboat on the Murray, a bloke drifted past in a tinny with a fishing rod and a bottle of white wine. Somebody spotted him, told the others on the Avoca and we all raised their glass.

Someone shouted out, 'What are you drinking, mate?'

'Viognier!' came the reply.

As the show expanded in the second half of the 2000s, more trophies were introduced. In 2005, to underline the founders' original intention to build awareness of the inland irrigated regions, one of those new trophies was for the top-scoring wine made from Murray Darling fruit. The inaugural gong was won jointly by Trentham Estate for a moscato – a style then becoming hugely popular

– and the second vintage of the MDC vermentino, an emphatic early endorsement of this variety's suitability to hot, dry growing conditions.

Other trophies introduced in that period include the Chief Judge's Wine to Watch (for an entry that may not have scored highly in the judging but the chief judge feels is worthy of attention or tells a compelling story), the Stewards Choice (like the 'packing room prize' at the Archibald portrait awards) the Best Spanish Varietal (changed to Best Iberian in 2015 to capture the growing number of Portuguese varieties entered into the show) and Best Blend. After all, in their homelands, many of these varieties are seldom traditionally found as varietal wines; often they're grown together and blended together because of their complementary characteristics.

In mid-2008 the AAVWS took the show on the road. They hosted a lunch and tasting for wine trade, sommeliers and public at the Royal Sydney Yacht Squadron, featuring previous winners from the show and some Talk and Taste-like presentations. Stefano de Pieri spoke about the need for alternatives in Australia; Bruce and Kim Chalmers spoke about growing and selling new varieties; Clare Valley winemaker Kerri Thompson spoke about being a judge at the show and what makes it different from other shows; and Helen Healy spoke about Mildura, putting the show into cultural context.

In October the same year, I hosted a tasting of alternative varieties for wine media at Australia House in London, comparing wines that had done well in the show – and were then available in the UK – with European versions of the same grape. Coriole's fiano alongside a fiano from Campania; Yalumba's viognier alongside one from the Rhone; the SC Pannell nebbiolo alongside a Barolo, et cetera. In most cases, tasters preferred the Australian example; writing in the *Guardian*, Victoria Moore particularly looked forward to trying more Australian tempranillo, mourvedre and petit verdot.

All of which paints a picture of a local wine community, and an international market, brimming with enthusiasm for diversity and reinvention – exactly the kind of scenario Tesco's Phil Reedman had called for a decade before. The reality was, in many ways, quite different.

∾

In the late 2000s, Australia's wine industry was suffering from a huge oversupply. There were too many vineyards planted to the same few familiar grapes, too many wineries, too much of the same kind of wine, and not enough people either at home or abroad who wanted to drink it. The world's love affair with our wine had cooled off: in 2008 exports fell 11 percent by volume and 18 percent by value, and that trend looked set to continue. A brand of Australian chardonnay called Down Under was selling in the US for just $3 a bottle – which horrified growers back home, many of whom had their contracts cancelled by the big wineries and had no way of selling their fruit. And this was before the shockwaves of the Global Financial Crisis began to reverberate around the world.

Even Australian drinkers were bored with their own country's product.

Sales of domestic wine dropped by 4 percent in 2008, and although sales of imported table wine jumped by a massive 67 percent, it was almost exclusively New Zealand sauvignon blanc that accounted for the surge. We couldn't, it seemed, get enough of yet another 'classic' French variety, this time transplanted to the Land of the Long White Cloud.

By the late 2000s the Millennium Drought was really hurting farmers and grapes growers. Frosts in late 2006 followed by terrible bushfires leading into the 2007 vintage resulted in ravaged crops. Climate change was on everyone's mind, thanks in part to the release that year of Tim Flannery's book, *The Weathermakers*, and of Al Gore's consciousness-raising film, *An Inconvenient Truth*. Furthermore, there was the publication of a report on wine and climate change by the CSIRO's Leanne Webb and Penny Whetton (also an author of the 2007 'Intergovernmental Panel on Climate Change' report), and the University of Melbourne's Professor Snow Barlow.

As I wrote in my 2010 book, *The Future Makers* (a title inspired by Flannery), when the triennial Australian Wine Industry Technical Conference took place in Adelaide in July 2007, global warming and water security were front and centre issues.

'More than 1,600 delegates to the conference, all battle-scarred from the vintage they'd just endured, listened as Richard Smart told them that "climate change is the biggest challenge the Australian wine industry has faced in its history." Smart outlined the potential problems; Leanne Webb showed how temperatures are predicted to rise in wine regions across Australia; Penny Whetton told the conference that climate observations are running at the high end of the various modelled predictions; and Snow Barlow urged those assembled to make sure they ended up on the side of the angels. I was sitting in the middle of the audience. All around me winemakers were shaking their heads as the reality of the situation was driven home to them.'

Faced with such clear signs that climate change was all-too-frighteningly real, already among us, and already wreaking havoc, many winemakers realised that they might have little choice but to change the varietal mix in their vineyards.

'In 2006, we didn't have much demand for vines,' Bruce Chalmers told me at the time. 'Not surprising, really, given the glut of the last few years. But since the 2007 season began, we have been getting more and more interest in our alternative varieties. People wanting to plant white grapes like vermentino and fiano, and Italian

2009 AAVWS Judges: Leigh Krake, Jane Faulkner, Sue Bell, Tim White, Max Allen, Peter Leske, Simon Hanley, Kim Bickley, Kerri Thompson, Tony Harper

red grapes like lagrein and nero d'avola, which have adapted amazingly well to the growing conditions up here.'

One of the varieties that seemed to be a no-brainer for a hotter, drier Australia was the Spanish white grape albarino (known as alvarinho over the border in Portugal). Wines made from albarino in Spain's Rias Baixas region had become popular internationally in late 1990s, and it seemed like a good white companion to the increasingly trendy red tempranillo.

Barossa winemaker Damien Tscharke outlined his pioneering experience with the variety in an article for the *Wine Industry Journal* entitled 'Albarino: a good choice for a changing climate', published in November 2008. 'After a few great experiences tasting [Spanish examples of the] varietal wine I was determined to produce an Australian albarino,' he wrote. 'It was clear the plant and fruit would adapt well to our Mediterranean climate.'

Corrina Wright

— *winemaker; AAVWS judge, 2007, 2011, 2014, 2022; speaker at Talk and Taste 2007 & 2014; president AAVWS committee 2021-*

Corrina Wright became an alternative variety pioneer in McLaren Vale twenty years ago, after a good-natured argument with her uncle, Don Oliver – fifth generation grape grower and viticulturist.

The Oliver family have been farming and growing grapes in the region since the 1840s but have mostly sold fruit over that time – including to Penfolds for inclusion in Grange. The Olivers only started producing wine under their own label after Corrina suggested they should, while she was still working as a corporate winemaker in the 1990s.

'In 2002 uncle Don wanted me to make a white wine,' Corrina told me a few years ago. 'I was being annoying and refusing to make one from our existing plantings of chardonnay, semillon or sauvignon blanc. I didn't think they performed all that well in McLaren Vale.'

Encouraged by Mark Lloyd, who was also trialling new Italian varieties at Coriole, Corrina had other ideas for the family vineyard.

'So, I convinced him to let me try fiano, which I thought would be much better for our region. After we planted it, we had the drought, and the fiano sailed through. So that convinced him it was worthwhile – and he knew I was happy with it in the winery.'

More alternatives followed: vermentino, tempranillo, sagrantino. Then, in 2011, Oliver's Taranga became the first South Australian producer to plant the red Spanish grape, mencia. Corrina had tasted a lot of red made from the variety in Bierzo, in northwest Spain, and thought it might be a grape that could do well in the Vale. She started asking around the vine nurseries and discovered Yalumba in the Barossa had imported mencia and had just released some mother vine material from quarantine. So, she put her order in for the first few propagated cuttings, planted them out in spring that year and made her first wine in 2014.

'The grapes are quite different to anything else I've seen – definitely nothing like shiraz or anything else we've got in the vineyard already. Which is lucky – or why else would you bother planting a new grape in the first place?'

As well as taking the lead on alternative varieties in the region and being an active supporter of the AAVWS since her first stint as judge in 2007, Corrina has played a leadership role in other areas of the industry. She has chaired wine shows, has sat on numerous boards (including, presently, the Australian Wine Research Institute), was instrumental in developing the Australian Grape and Wine Diversity and Equality Charter and is an advisor to the Australian Women in Wine Awards – all of which contributed to her being named the 2019 Australian Society of Viticulture and Oenology's Winemaker of the Year.

She also embodies the spirit of good-natured fun that lies at the heart of the AAVWS. Speaking at a dinner in Mildura in November in 2022, celebrating the twenty-first birthday of the show, she had the audience in stitches, describing her fangirl crush on celebrity chef Frank Camorra and how she embarrassed herself sitting next to him at the judges dinner one year: 'I used all my words,' she said. 'He was overwhelmed and exhausted by entrée.'

It's less like an address from the president of a committee and more like a stand-up routine.

He discovered that the CSIRO had sourced albarino from the Spanish national vine collection in 1989, so he tracked down some mother vines at the South Australian Vine Improvement nursery in Nuriootpa and propagated enough to plant his first hectare in 2001, releasing his first vintage in 2004.

By 2008, another thirty or so Australian growers had jumped on the albarino bandwagon, many describing its performance in the vineyard as 'a winemaker's dream'. The variety was also developing a strong following among curious wine consumers.

And then, disaster.

In late 2008, Jean-Michel Boursiquot, the French ampelographer who had helped identify Chile's merlot as carmenere in the 1990s, visited the Barossa and raised doubts about the albarino vines he saw there. Samples were sent for DNA testing and in February the following year, Wine Australia announced the results.

'It's not often that an obscure grape variety, new to Australian vineyards, makes the six o'clock TV news,' I wrote in *The Future Makers*. 'But that's what happened in early 2009 when DNA testing revealed to Australia's small-but-burgeoning band of albarino growers that the vines they had planted were in fact savagnin, the white grape used in France's Jura region to make the sherry-like *vin jaune*. Turns out there was a mix-up 20 years ago when the CSIRO imported some vine cuttings from Spain – and those vines were the source block for almost all Australian plantings.'

Not surprisingly, Australia's 'albarino' growers were furious – especially as many of them had adopted a Spanish brand and/or Spanish imagery on their labels to match the Spanish varietal name. First Drop's albarino was called 'Matador'; Rollo and Zoe Crittenden's was 'Los Hermanos'. One grower described the whole episode as, 'Like being handed a newborn baby in a maternity ward, only to be told a few years later that it wasn't your baby

2009 AAVWS invitation postcard

after all' – and he was only half joking. Some adapted – 'pivoted' we might say these days – and embraced the cock-up, using it for their marketing advantage. Most went into denial, deciding to wait a few more years for *real* albarino vines to be imported and made available.

It's not the first or last time such misidentification has occurred. Another French ampelographer, Paul Truel, revealed during his visit in the 1970s that the grape many in Victoria had known as malbec since the nineteenth century was in fact dolcetto. And a few years after the albarino 'episode' other varieties – carignan, grillo, petit manseng – would turn out not to be what we thought, thanks to DNA testing. (For more on this, see the Alternative A-Z at the back of the book.)

But there was something about the scale and the timing of the albarino fiasco, during such a difficult period for the wine industry, that arguably took some of the shine off the alternative variety movement for a while. It made growers a little more cautious of backing new grapes, and almost certainly contributed to the early closure of the CSIRO's Merbein collection later that year.

By time the AAVWS came along in November 2009, everyone was in a very reflective mood. And sombre: a couple of months before the show, sad news came through from across the Tasman that Dr Rod Bonfiglioli, one of the co-founders of the show, had died, at just fifty-six years old. As a tribute, the trophy for Best Wine of Show would from now on be named in his honour.

∽

The show reached a milestone in 2009: ten years since Rod, Stef and Bruce had conceived the Long Italian Lunch that sowed the seeds of its inception. So, to mark the occasion, the theme of Talk and Taste for this year was 'Back to the Future'.

The first part of the seminar consisted of Tim White and I presenting a tasting of gold and trophy winners from the previous decade, from well-established wines like the Tahbilk marsanne and Yalumba viognier to new, game-changing wines like the Arrivo nebbiolo, made using recently imported clones of the Piemontese grape, and Quealy Senza Nome, made using the recently planted white variety, friulano.

The seminar finished with a wide-ranging discussion about the future, based on a survey I'd sent out to lots of people who'd been associated with the show over the years, from those who were there at the beginning like Stefano and Phil Reedman to those who'd judged for the first time that year like winemakers Peter Leske and Sue Bell. I asked them to imagine what Australian wine landscape might look like in 2025.

Why this date? In 1996, the wine industry had launched the now-infamous *Strategy 2025* document, with its bold mission to make Australia the most influential and profitable wine country in the world. The sheer audacity of the plan galvanised winemakers (and investors) and inspired an explosive – and as it turned out, unsustainable – boom. The 2025 target was not only met but surpassed in just nine years, and many think it contributed in a major way to the massive oversupply of wine in the mid- to-late 2000s.

Max Allen at the 'graduation' ceremony for pinot gris in 2009

Reading the responses to my questions now, with 2025 just around the corner, is fascinating, and I've reproduced some of them on page 112. Almost all the trends that define wine in Australia in the mid-2020s – greater diversity of wine styles, lighter wines, concerns about health and wellness, sustainability, et cetera – were predicted by the members of the AAVWS family back then, including, remarkably, punitive tariffs imposed by an Asian country, crippling wine exports overnight.

As part of the seminar, I showed a slide of the Gartner Hype Cycle. This well-known graph was developed in the 1990s to help people understand what happens after a new *technology* is introduced – the rapid rise to the 'peak of inflated expectations', the steep fall into the 'trough of disillusionment' then back up the gentler 'slope of enlightenment' to the 'plateau of productivity'. But I showed it as a fun way of discussing new varieties in Australia. One variety in particular.

∽

By 2009 it was clear that pinot gris was no longer an emerging alternative variety but was well on its way to the 'plateau of productivity'. So, the AAVWS committee voted to boot the grape out of the show – or, to give it a more positive spin, hold a 'graduation' ceremony for it at the awards long lunch, held the day after Talk and Taste.

Not everybody was happy with the decision. Kathleen Quealy, one of the pioneers of the grape, thinks it still deserves a forum today like the one it was given at the AAVWS. But it was clear to most of us that it had become thoroughly mainstream, enjoying the kind of growth over the previous decade that other varieties can only dream of.

Not only that, but pinot gris had also become the subject of a fascinating initiative to help consumers choose their preferred style. Dreamed up by Kevin McCarthy of T'Gallant and developed by the Australian Wine Research Institute, the 'Pinot G (PG) Spectrum' was a bit like the

Alla Griglia

November 3rd 2011

2011 Chalmers Nero d'Avola Rosato, Heathcote

2011 Chalmers Vermentino, Heathcote

King George whiting, herb & lemon pangrattato

2010 Chalmers Fiano, Murray Darling

Grilled polenta, baccalá mantecato, baby capers

2011 'St Marty's' Vino Nuovo & 2011 Chalmers Nero d'Avola, Heathcote

Grilled eggplant, tomato ragu, Mozzarella di bufala

2009 Chalmers Aglianico, Murray Darling

Grilled quail, local asparagus spears

2009 Chalmers Sagrantino, Murray Darling

Grigliata mista, hand-cut potato chips, mixed leaves

2009 Chalmers 'Aurora' Malvasia Istriana/Picolit Passito, Murray Darling

Almond Biscotti & Polenta Biscotti

2011 AAVWS Chalmers dinner

sweetness scale you might find displayed on the back label of a bottle of riesling, which runs from 'bone dry' to 'very sweet'. But, instead, it had 'crisp' (i.e., pinot grigio) at one end and 'luscious' (i.e., pinot gris) at the other.

This echoed the way the AAVWS had been splitting pinot gris into different styles since 2001 but the PG Spectrum was backed up both by human tasting and by spectral analysis. In other words, the AWRI had discovered they were able to gauge what kind of pinot gris was inside a bottle – whether it was crisp and crunchy or rich and round – just by shining a light through it.

It wasn't the only example of technology being employed to better understand and promote alternative varieties. Behind the scenes at the AAVWS, 2009 also saw the development of a database that aimed to capture in unprecedented detail as much information as possible about the wines that were being entered in the show. And, by extension, how alternative varieties were being grown and made across the country. Now, when each winemaker filled in their entry form, they were asked questions about where the grapes for each wine were grown, what clones and rootstock they were, crop yield, soil type, growing method, fermentation, and maturation details – the list goes on.

This was a huge undertaking that took significant resources, both in a financial sense, but also in time: as well as capturing the information from 2009 onwards online, information about each wine entered from 2001 to 2008 was also transferred manually. And this all coincided with concern over the financial viability of the show.

In early 2009 manager Helen Healy predicted there would be a drop in entries at that year's AAVWS due to concerns over the global financial crisis. Entries were then expected to drop further after pinot gris 'graduated'. And as the fee that winemakers pay for each entry provides essential income for the show, losing pinot gris – at the time 13 percent of the show's total – would be a significant drop.

Everyone was relieved, then, when entry numbers for the 2009 show were *higher* than the previous year (clearly in an economic crisis winemakers need publicity more than ever). And everyone was surprised when entries *didn't* crash in 2010, instead only dipping slightly to 570, thanks to the fact that quite a few new producers entered the show.

This year, 2010, was when the inland regions started to fulfil the promise flagged at the Long Italian Lunch in 1999.

The trophies for Best White, Best Italian Varietal and Best Wine of Show in 2010 all went to a deliciously lively dry white bianco d'alessano from Salena Estate in South Australia's hot Riverland. Bianco d'what? No, I'd not heard of it either. Luckily, one of the judges that year was Stefano Dini, an Italian viticulturist, and he informed us that bianco d'alessano is a white grape originally from Puglia. According to Salena winemaker Melanie Kargas, it handles the heat very well in the Riverland, ripening late in the season with bountiful flavour and natural fresh acidity, meaning that she doesn't have to manipulate it with aromatic yeasts or added acid.

The trophy for Best Red went to an aglianico from Calabria in the Riverina, another southern Italian varietal from another inland, Italian family-owned winery. And the Stefano de Pieri Tre Viti Bianco – a mash-up of Murray Darling-grown moscato giallo, greco and malvasia made by Cellarmasters – won the trophy for Best Blend.

Yellow Tail malbec – from another inland producer, Riverina-based Casella – also won the trophy for Best Commercial Wine in 2010. This trophy had been introduced in 2008 to encourage larger players in the industry to enter the show and to reiterate the founders' insistence that alternative varieties aren't just for boutique wineries but are viable on a large scale.

2010 AAVWS event flyer

The next year, 2011, was yet another vintage from hell for many growers in south-eastern Australia, but for different reasons. The Millennium Drought had broken the year before, and La Niña was squelching around all over the eastern seaboard. The summer was cool and humid, the rain leading up to harvest was drenching. Rivers flooded, dams burst, and vines were slammed with disease. Old-timers said they had to go back to the mid-1970s to find a season that compared to this one.

But while the broader wine industry continued to mope and lick its wounds after yet another challenging vintage, a growing number of groups at a grassroots level were busy dreaming up new ways to respond to the challenges, to bring about the change they wanted to see. And alternative varieties were often very much a part of that.

In 2008 twenty wineries in the Granite Belt region of southeast Queensland banded together and formed the evocatively named 'Strange Bird' touring trail, encouraging visitors to seek out the sixteen different grapes, from barbera to viognier, then being grown across the region.

In 2010 six tempranillo growers and makers from across Australia – Yalumba, Gemtree, La Linea, Tar & Roses, Mount Majura, Mayford – many of whom had made connections through the AAVWS, established 'TempraNeo', a series of seminars and tastings held around the country introducing trade and media and consumers to the Spanish variety.

The November the same year, to coincide with the AAVWS, I wrote an article in the *Weekend Australian* about my love of chargrilled sardines – one of Australia's most under-fished and therefore sustainable fish species – washed down with a col glass of vermentino – one of Australia's most drought-tolerant and therefore sustainable new varieties.

'In fact,' I wrote, 'I have a vision: an Aussie sardine and Aussie vermentino-led recovery. Worried about reduced water allocations in the Murray Darling basin? Worried about food security? Never fear: sardines and vermentino are here. We need a new national marketing campaign. Forget cans of piss-weak lager and chucking another prawn on the barbie. I'm thinking flash-mob sardine grill-ups in suburban shopping strips; the sudden waft of charcoal smoke and Eskies full of crisp, dry vermentino. Delicious, cheap, good for you, and totally sustainable. Resistance would be useless. Who's with me?'

Turns out, quite a few people. Winemakers started getting in touch asking how they could get involved. Amanda Pritchard, a PR person specialising in food and wine who had done some work for the AAVWS, also read the article and helped turn my silly rant into reality. The following January, a dozen vermentino producers turned up at the Adelaide Central Market – followed by other venues in Melbourne and Sydney – with Eskies full of wine and barbecues loaded with sizzling sardines.

2011 Vermentino and Sardines poster

There's nothing new, of course, about winemakers banding together to promote their product. The Wine and Brandy Producers Association (as it was called back then) was handing out free wine in South Australian shopping centres back in the 1960s, and winemakers have been travelling to London for the annual Wine Australia tastings for decades.

The crucial difference is that this latest wave of collaboration wasn't organised by the industry's statutory marketing body, but by the winemakers themselves. Indeed, much of this grassroots activity was fuelled by frustration with that marketing body's perceived lack of action. Collectively, these producer-led initiatives injected an exciting energy into the Australian wine scene – an enthusiasm and optimism that had been lacking for much of the previous decade.

∞

At the turn of the next decade of the new millennium, more and more Australian growers were also talking about sustainability, about soil, and about organic and biodynamic farming.

The first Australian and New Zealand Organic Wine Show was held in Sydney in 2006. One of the top wines at that event – a 2002 kerner from certified biodynamic Robinvale Wines on the Murray – went on to win two trophies at the 2007 AAVWS, for Best Murray Darling Wine, and Stewards Choice. Then the 2008 vintage of the same wine won the inaugural trophy for Best Certified Organic Wine at the AAVWS the following year – and the same trophy again in 2009.

The 2002 kerner in particular was (is!) the most extraordinary demonstration of the benefits of biodynamics – a cool-climate grape, grown in a hot-climate vineyard, that went on to mature magnificently in the bottle for well over a decade. It was one of the wines included in a presentation on biodynamics at the 2007 Talk and Taste, hosted by winemaker Kerri Thompson, then experimenting with the techniques in her vineyards, and Brisbane wine bar owner, Tony Harper, both of whom judged at the AAVWS that year.

In November 2008, a couple of days after the show in Mildura, I drove across to the Riverland and presented a tasting of organic and biodynamic wines at the regional association's annual 'Some like it Hot' symposium, explaining to a room full of hardened local growers at the Renmark Club how adopting more sustainable viticultural practices could help them adapt to the changing climate. I took some of the musical spirit of the AAVWS with me and played Gloria Gaynor's classic 'I Will Survive' as my introduction. I'm not sure it was all that well received – but the wines were.

In July 2009 organics and biodynamics were front and centre at the Australian Society of Viticulture and Oenology's annual conference in Mildura, looking at vineyard soil health. And I chaired a session on organics and biodynamics at the Australian Wine Industry Technical Conference in Adelaide in 2010. That people would one day be talking about biodynamics at such mainstream wine industry events was inconceivable a decade before.

Then, in March 2011, as part of the Melbourne Food and Wine Festival, more than sixty members of Return to Terroir, an international group of winegrowers all following biodynamic principles of organic farming in their vineyards, brought 340 of their wines to Australia and spent two days exhibiting them to the public and the trade. The group included some of the very top names in wine – Leflaive in France, Foradori in Italy, Nikolaihof in Austria; Cullen and Castagna in Australia, Millton in New Zealand – and the event made a huge impression on the new generation of sommeliers, retailers, writers, and makers who attended.

It was the inspiration and precursor in many ways of a new wine and food festival called Rootstock that would be held a couple of years later in Sydney and would nudge the wine conversation in Australia in yet another direction.

But we're getting ahead of ourselves. First, we need to go back briefly to that unforgettable first week in February 2009.

༄

It's the Wednesday after Black Saturday. I'm in the upstairs kitchen and dining room at Gertrude Street Enoteca in Melbourne, tasting a bunch of new releases that two winemakers, Anton van Klopper from the Adelaide Hills, and Tom Shobbrook from the Barossa, have brought with them from South Australia. As Anton and Tom open bottle after bottle, they offer up various delicious plates of things shot, caught, grown, and gathered by the two of them on the way over.

The wines have been made with as little as possible added or taken away. It's one of my first experiences of the natural wine *ethos* – not just regarding the wines themselves, but the whole philosophy and approach to living that comes with it. Soon, Anton and Tom will be joined by two other collaborators: ex-sommelier and 2008 AAVWS judge, now Adelaide Hills winemaker James Erskine, and the late, much-missed Sydney artist-provocateur Sam Hughes, who blurs the boundaries between winemaking and art by fermenting whole semillon grapes in ceramic egg-shaped vessels and then 'bottling' them in small ceramic egg-shaped vessels.

The group soon acquires a name: Natural Selection Theory (it's the headline of a slightly dismissive newspaper article about them that they gleefully appropriate). They aren't the first to make wines without preservatives: some of Australia's oldest organic vineyards such as Botobolar in Mudgee have been doing this for decades. Nor are they the first to ferment white grapes on skins, inspired by the likes of Josko Gravner: Kevin McCarthy made his first Claudius, a skins-fermented blend of chardonnay, gewurztraminer and moscato giallo, in 2007.

But the intentionally disruptive nature of the group *is* new. And it will go on to shape the next decade in many ways. As Sam Hughes wrote at the time, his egg project – and, by extension, the Natural Selection Theory movement – 'represents a fault line in the history of Oz wine culture: after this nothing shall be the same again.'

Future Visions

Thinking about 2025 in 2009

Rebecca Gibb, associate judge at the AAVWS in 2008

Shane Kerr at the AAVWS 2019

James Erskine judging the AAVWS in 2008

Matt Gant judging in 2006

Head steward Bob Shields in 2008

Sam Connew at AAVWS 2008

Peter Leske (and Kathleen Quealy) in 2009

David Ridge, judge at the first AAVWS in 2001

Huon Hooke at the AAVWS in 2004

As part of the Talk and Taste session at the AAVWS in 2009, I asked the judges, committee members and supporters of the show to gaze into their crystal balls and think about what Australia's wine landscape might look like in 2025.

Not all the predictions have come true of course – and some were completely missed. A lot of people thought back then, for example, that by 2025 the northwest Italian red grape barbera would become one of the most popular new alternative grapes. Instead, it's the southern Italians, nero and montepulciano that have particularly resonated with Australian drinkers. And no-one picked prosecco as a possible monster wine trend of the very near future.

Because the predictions were made at the tail end of the Millennium Drought, there were a lot of gloomy scenarios depicting the desertification of Australia's inland wine regions, the collapse of the Murray Darling river system, and a major vine-pull scheme leading to a reduction in the size of the national wine industry – none of which has happened (yet).

But some predictions were uncannily accurate.

'Doesn't history repeat itself?' asked **Rebecca Gibb**, UK-based wine writer and soon-to-be Master of Wine. 'Plague, famine, drought, war. The rich getting richer, the poor getting poorer. Why is the next fifteen years going to be any different?'

'Gruner will pop its head up somewhere in the next fifteen years,' said **Shane Kerr**, Trentham Estate winemaker (this was before the first Australian gruner had been released). 'And chardonnay will make a comeback, but the styles will have a bit more finesse rather than the big, fat and oaky wines of yesteryear.'

'If I were a marketer,' said **Stefano de Pieri**, 'I would invest in a campaign to promote all manners of rosé and light reds – light both in structure and alcohol – with a tinge of fruitiness, in balance with the savoury characters so needed for food, and not particularly related to varieties.'

This – lighter wines – was the most common theme among all the crystal ball-gazers.

'We'll see more red wines released fresher, *a la nouveau* style,' said sommelier-turned winemaker **James Erskine**. 'Grenache will rise in the restaurant scene and be followed by the public. There are so many awesome under-utilised old grenache vineyards that could make fine, savoury, spicy delights.'

Winemaker **Matt Gant** also predicted the grenache renaissance. 'In 2025 drought tolerant varieties like grenache will be playing a significant role in our warm climate regions,' he said. 'And there will be substantial plantings of southern Italian, Portuguese and Greek varieties to be made into single varietal wines and blends.'

Bob Shields, winemaker, and head of stewards at the show from 2004 to 2008, missed the mark in predicting a push for the genetic manipulation of yeast and vines by 2025 – but he got a whole heap of other things spot-on, from officially allowing the addition of water to grape must (this became legal in 2017) to the growth of 'light, chillable, reds and rosés, alfresco whites; wines with low alcohol levels in response to heightened health concerns; and a "wine cooler" revival' (they're not quite wine coolers, but the hard seltzer craze of the late 2010s is pretty close).

Winemaker **Sam Connew** had a lot of fun dreaming up future scenarios. Some were just plain silly: '[by 2025] James Halliday's eyebrows will become a winemaking relic, similar to the Shroud of Turin.' Some were wishful thinking but are still good ideas: 'All new vineyards [will be] legislatively required to be planted on salt-, drought-, and phylloxera-resistant rootstock, and can only be irrigated with recycled water; all wines to be exported will be bottled in PET or equivalent to reduce carbon footprint; all new wineries must be established using solar energy for all of their electricity requirements.'

But many came true.

Julia Gillard becoming Australia's first female PM; somebody turning savagnin into 'an Aussie version of *vin jaune*'; the merging of the country's various wine industry bodies; China becoming the biggest export market; supermarkets Coles and Woolworths buying wine brands and wineries … Sam Connew predicted it all.

Winemaker **Peter Leske**'s tongue-in-cheek future export scenario, looking back from 2025, also turned out to be spookily accurate, even if he got the country and the date wrong: 'Our burgeoning exports fell by 90 percent in two months in 2017 after the Indian government applied a 200 punitive punitive tariff to members of what they named the Foreign Imperialist Cluster.' Just substitute 'China' for India and '2020' for 2017 and this is pretty much exactly what happened.

Wine importer and distributor, **David Ridge**, talked about a future 'increased fragmentation in all areas of beverages,' (foreshadowing the rise of craft spirits, local breweries, garage winemakers, et cetera), and that wine drinkers will in 2025 be bombarded with information about wine from 'a more bewildering [even more so than now!] number of directions.'

Stefano de Pieri wondered how this fragmentation will change the way we think and talk about wine.

'Wine is a cultural manifestation,' he said, 'and culture moves fast now. It forms in unpredictable clusters of interests. It is not monolithic anymore. So, my question is, how do we structure a discourse on terroir, say – which is a slightly metaphysical concept even for the reasonably experienced drinker – for people who do not think or communicate inside the boundaries of tradition? And would they care anyway?'

Similar thinking informed the most challenging – in the context of a seminar at a wine show – and arguably prescient comments, from Sydney wine journalist **Huon Hooke**.

'Wine competitions will have ceased having any credibility by 2025,' said Huon. 'The range and diversity of wine styles will be too challenging for blind judging to cope with. There will be wild wines – much wilder than the most eccentric wines available now. Assessing them without some knowledge of the aim and philosophy of the maker will be meaningless – [but] these factors will become ever more important to drinkers.

'As with the art world, where long ago the ability to draw the human body went out the window, so too will "anything go" in wine. In this sense there will be a reversion to the past, where faults were tolerated. In the past this was because faults were not understood. In the future it will be because people won't care – they will care most about what they enjoy, and their own idea of what is good will be supreme.'

Huon predicted that, 'What drinkers know and feel about the idea of a wine will be as important as its taste. That is, the philosophy of the maker and how the wine is produced; what kind of person he/she is, their ideals and ethics, the way they relate to their land and care for the environment.'

Part Four

Natural evolution

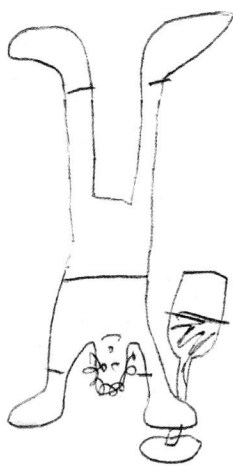

Friday 7 November 2014. More than one hundred winemakers, growers, wine judges, and show stewards are crowded into a conference room at the Mildura Working Man's Club listening to Lado Uzunashvili talking about the wines he makes in Georgia.

It's a different setting for Talk and Taste this year – fitting, because the topics under discussion have also shifted away from the Italian and French and Iberian varieties that have dominated in previous years. The theme of the afternoon-long seminar is 'The Ancient in Modernity'. As well as Lado's presentation (called, in the grand AAVWS tradition of lame jokes and puns, 'Georgia on my Mind'), there's a panel discussion and tasting of unconventional vinification methods titled 'Winemaking 101 – Not!' looking in part at the practice of fermentation in clay vessels, such as the big amphora-shaped *qvevri* of Georgia.

Lado Uzunashvili migrated to Australia from Georgia in the 1990s, but now spends most of his time back in his homeland making wine at that country's high-profile new estates. He has plenty of experience with the red Georgian grape, saperavi, famous for its deep, dense colour and bold, tannic quality: he helped McLaren Vale vigneron

preceding pages: behind the scenes at the 2018 show

left: 2013 AAVWS judges Dave Brookes and Sue Bell

right: chief judge Jane Faulkner in 2015

Hugh Hamilton plant and make some of this country's first examples of the variety.

'Lado is such as an inclusive, fabulous guy,' says Jane Faulkner, who, in 2014, was in her third year as chief judge at the AAVWS and chaired the Talk and Taste that day. 'Everyone just fell in love with him. He was talking about *qvevri* and of course a lot of people in the audience didn't know what *qvevri* were. But because of Lado's personality there was a sense of open-mindedness in the room.'

There's a similar willingness to engage with the second session of the day. Winemaker Glenn James presents his Pandora, a blend of white fiano and vermentino grapes co-fermented in amphora. Bart van Olphen presents some of the #bucketwine micro-ferments he and Kim and Tennille Chalmers produced the year before. And international judge, writer Walter Speller, presents what he describes as 'several wines of a distinctly left-field character', including skin-fermented whites and naturally sparkling reds.

'I had expected that the audience, consisting of a large number of winemakers, would dismiss these wines,' says Walter. 'Great was my surprise when only one winemaker

2014 long lunch chefs Frank Camorra and Stefano de Pieri

complained that the wines were faulty, volatile and undrinkable … and even greater when other Australian winemakers defended the styles saying they were exciting, refreshing and original.'

By 2014, Jane Faulkner was a 'veteran' of the AAVWS. She'd judged at the show almost every year since 2005 and attended – or presented – many of the Talk and Taste sessions. But she says this one, on 'The Ancient in Modernity', was her favourite.

'My mind was opened up that day,' she says. 'I hadn't been to Georgia at that point, but going subsequently made me really understand it, culturally and politically. It's fascinating how a people can continue to make wine, with all the challenges of history they've had to face; how they can preserve a culture when they're constantly being bombarded on every level.'

In 2014, the show had come a long way from its beginnings in 1999, when discussion revolved mostly around a few grape varieties from a handful of European regions. Now we were looking in more depth at how culture is created, at philosophical challenges, and at crumbling paradigms.

∽

'I've always loved wine,' says Jane Faulkner. 'We always had wine at the table, growing up. We're all obsessed with taste in our household. My brothers too. We love eating and drinking. And my parents were rather open minded. So, we drank lots of different wines. Things that didn't grow here.'

I'm talking with Jane over a glass of wine, reminiscing about the show, about her time as judge and then chief of judges. I'm curious about her journey into wine; about how and why she started to think about wine differently.

Jane says that her parents, like many wine drinkers in Melbourne, drank the usual Australian staples – Wynns, Penfolds – but also had Italian friends, so drank Italian wines as well: 'Dad thought Italian food was the best thing he'd ever encountered,' she says. Her parents also spent some time in Malaysia, where they were exposed to amazing food and wine: 'Mum and Dad used to drink Chateau d'Yquem that they could buy for five bucks. Best times of their lives, they said.'

After Jane started working as a journalist at *The Age* in the early 90s, she also started doing wine courses, and when a new lifestyle section of the paper was launched in the late 1990s, she became food and wine editor.

'That's when I heard about what the Chalmers were doing, and about the show,' she says. 'And then finding other people who were involved, like Mark Walpole and the Pizzinis. It was all these little entry points, leading me to Mildura. I thought, hold on a minute, what's going on? And then I sort of got hooked.'

Jane brought an irrepressible energy to her role as chief judge. She reminds me of the 2011 awards long lunch, when I passed the chief's baton to her.

Sue Bell

— *winemaker; AAVWS judge in 2009, 2011, 2012, 2013, 2014, 2019 and 2022; speaker at Talk and Taste in 2013 and 2018; committee member 2022.*

Sue Bell thinks that winemakers have both a responsibility and a great opportunity to help create a better Australia.

'I firmly believe that an industry that respects regional expression has a huge ethical role to play in the future,' she said. 'If we make wine as a commodity, we are pushing a drug and should be taxed accordingly and suffer public wrath. But when we grow, make and sell wine ethically and sustainably with respect for culture we are getting back to what it's all about: a substance that enhances life and society, that doesn't damage and strangle it.'

This is one of many thought-provoking opinions put forward by Sue Bell in 2009, when I asked the AAVWS family for their visions of the future for that year's Talk and Taste. I shouldn't have been surprised that Sue's answers to my questions would be among the most considered and provocative: Sue has long been a champion of collaborative thinking, an advocate for change and a leader of diversity and inclusion in Australian wine.

Before establishing her own small winery and cellar door, Bellwether, in Coonawarra in 2008, Sue worked for several large wineries, including a stint in Mildura in the mid-90s – where, she says, she developed an addiction for Stefano's food – and at Stonehaven in Padthaway, on South Australia's Limestone Coast. Bellwether is in an old, renovated shearing shed; it features a kitchen garden and glamping facilities (in bell tents, of course), and regularly hosts gigs, get-togethers and workshops.

'Clearly, wine isn't just a business for Sue,' I wrote a few years after she opened her cellar door. 'She's also, importantly, deeply involved in her community. She is chair of the Limestone Coast Grape and Wine Council and has been heavily involved on two recent projects identifying and recording what makes the region tick – from a detailed review of the ancient geological past to an audio-visual record of the region's human history. "I have chosen to live in a country community and can see a lot of good that having a successful wine industry does for a region," says Sue. "It's about building pride – not just when the wines win medals in shows, but from providing jobs and bringing in tourism. This leads to community pride, people being able to show off the uniqueness of their place."'

This sense of community was on full display a year or so later at Sips in the Sticks, an Adelaide Food and Wine Festival event showcasing a bunch of Sue's female winemaking friends, held at Bellwether. It was a wonderfully multicultural affair: the shearing shed was built by Chinese labourers in the 1860s; lunch was cooked by women from the recently arrived local Afghan community. And it was a celebration of women: guest of honour, Senator Penny Wong, contrasted the event with recollections of growing up with a feminist mum who drank Chapel Hill wines because they were made by Pam Dunsford – the only female winemaker she could find at the time.

Sue has taken a similarly collaborative approach to her winemaking, sourcing region-appropriate varieties from friends' vineyards across Australia to make small batches of wine: cabernet, malbec, and shiraz from Coonawarra and Wrattonbully, riesling and chardonnay from Tasmania, vermentino from Heathcote, nero d'avola and montepulciano from the Riverland.

Sue is also a regular judge and chair of judges at wine shows around Australia – including the AAVWS – and a Dux of the prestigious Len Evans Tutorial. Which all sounds like serious wine industry business – except Sue always approaches everything she does with a twinkle in her eye.

Returning as a tutor to the 2022 Evans Tutorial, for example, she encouraged the scholars to work song lyrics into their tasting notes, to see if any of the old fellers who run the event would notice. She's also often the first to start singing when the guitars come out at the end of the AAVWS long lunch.

At the Talk and Taste in Mildura in 2022, I quoted some of what Sue had written thirteen years earlier. In particular, her observation of how serious challenges to the wine industry – such as the oversupply of grapes that had come about at the time because of the deflating export bubble – had the potential to change the culture for the better.

'The benefit of the current glut and global financial crisis,' Sue said in 2009, 'is that people are getting back to focussing on the domestic market. Australian wine drinkers are increasingly more savvy and daring, and are helping to build an even bigger foundation for the future. We were kidding ourselves trying to flog so much cheap wine overseas yet not focus on improving the knowledge and culture of Australian drinking.'

I asked her: does she think that we're in a better place now, bearing in mind the existential challenges of the pandemic and the trade war and the extreme weather events?

'I think we're definitely in a better place in some ways,' she said. 'And in others we're in a much worse place. We've been looking down a dark barrel for a few years. It's interesting coming out of the pandemic, seeing people drinking at home, how some of them started to drink more broadly. They couldn't travel overseas, so they travelled through wine. And they've come out hungry for new things, more adventurous in wine. And the beauty is, the varieties that we were tasting in 2009, that were gangly and adolescent back then, are now in the ground in the prime of their life. And that's really exciting.'

After she judged at the AAVWS for the first time in 2009, Sue wrote me a letter – not an email, a letter – thanking me for encouraging discussion and debate as chief judge and saying what an inspiration the show is.

A lot of us feel the same way about her.

2012 AAVWS judges and associates: Clare Dry, Gabrielle Poy, Stuart Kilmister, Sue Bell, Krystina Menegazzo, Jane Faulkner, Tony Harper, Mike Hayes and Matt Gant

'I did my kookaburra impression,' she says. 'Remember that? You said, "And we'd like to announce that Jane is taking over" and I did a kookaburra call. I just do stupid things like that sometimes, to make people laugh. And then I reflect, and I think, *Oh my god, why did I do that?*'

∾

In the early 2010s, when Jane took over at the AAVWS, a new generation of adventurous Australian producers were starting to release wines that were *so* different and *so* challenging, they were a wake-up call to both the industry and the consumer. Wines like the Natural Selection Theory's egg-fermented semillons; the first *pet nats* (sparkling wines that finish ferment in the bottle and are not disgorged, meaning they're often cloudy and quite funky-tasting) from Gilles Lapalus at Fairbank in central Victoria and James Erskine in the Adelaide Hills; and the first amphora-fermented wines from producers like Brad Hickey in McLaren Vale.

Some other wine shows were beginning to embrace new ways of thing, too. James Erskine, who'd judged at the

AAVWS in 2008, instigated changes when he took over the running of the *Adelaide Review*'s annual Hot 100 tasting in 2010. He started assessing wines by style rather than variety, judging wines with food, encouraging debate and discussion and emotional responses – not just looking at how well the wines are made, but also how they made you *feel*.

At the same time, some very high-profile restaurants – and their increasingly influential sommeliers – were embracing the wild, the funky and the new. When influential American chef David Chang opened Momofuku Seibo in Sydney in 2011, sommelier Richard Hargreave packed the list with impossible-to-find wines from the gods of natural winemaking in France. When Rene Redzepi opened a much-hyped Noma pop-up in Sydney a few years later, his head sommelier Mads Kleppe created a wine list that just featured white wines, skins-fermented 'orange' wines, and pet nats, all produced according to Kleppe's strict criteria.

'I'm very picky about the wines I list,' Mads told me at the time. 'As far as possible, they must be grown in a sound way, without synthetic chemicals. For me this is most important. They must be from nice people; people I have met and enjoy drinking wine with. And they must be made in a non-intervention way, not fined [clarified] or filtered, preferably with no sulphur [dioxide, added as a preservative]. Wines made this way have a different tension, a different texture, a different energy [to conventional wines].'

This ethos also informed the selection criteria for Rootstock Sydney, the enormously successful and influential wine and food festival that ran from 2013 to 2017. Founded by writer Mike Bennie, sommeliers Giorgio Di Maria and James Hird, and sake importers Linda Wiss and Matt Young, the festival saw winegrowers and makers from Australia and around the world converge. They were united by a desire to think differently about wine, and linked, unofficially but umbilically, to a growing number of similar, joyous, disruptive events happening around the world, such as the Real and RAW natural wine fairs in London.

Rootstock inspired a bunch of other events locally. Throughout the 2010s, natural wine gatherings (and natural-ish wine gatherings) popped up all over the place. It was a huge encouragement to up-and-coming producers and retailers and wine bar owners, who could see how much the thousands of people who attended Rootstock and the other events were enjoying these wines.

But the disruptive nature of the Rootstock movement wasn't universally well received. Some in Australia's wine establishment – the veteran journos, senior sommeliers, chief wine show judges – became quite cranky about the threat it posed to their influence. Some started defiantly wearing 'I love SO2' t-shirts; some wrote articles denouncing natural wine as a fad or – worse – a con being foisted upon the public by a bunch of hippy zealots. And some went into denial: at a Melbourne Food and Wine Masterclass I co-hosted during these early years of the decade, a couple of my fellow presenters refused to even *taste* the wild and funky pinot noir I'd selected to tell the story of the nascent natural wine movement.

The tension was, perhaps, unavoidable. It was, perhaps, the whole point.

After all, deeply entrenched wine hierarchies and long-accepted ways of doing things were being questioned. The old order was being overthrown.

∾

In 2012, eminent UK wine writer Jancis Robinson with co-authors Julia Harding MW and vine specialist Dr José Vouillamoz, published *Wine Grapes*, an encyclopaedic guide to 1368 varieties used for commercial wine production around the world.

top: 2015 AAVWS wines lined up for judging

bottom: 2013 S.C. Pannell Tempranillo Touriga

Jancis had written a similar, if much less comprehensive guide back in 1986. Called *Vines, Grapes & Wines*, it grouped varieties into a clear hierarchy: 'classic' grapes such as cabernet, 'major' grapes such as grenache, and 'minor' grapes such as marsanne. *Wine Grapes* by contrast listed the varieties alphabetically.

'The alphabetical approach was primarily a question of making the readers' lives easier,' Jancis told me at the time. 'Flipping between sections in a 1200-page book would not be easy. [But] I think with everyone being much better informed about less well-known grapes nowadays, we'd have had a riot on our hands if we had tried to categorise them by quality or status.'

A pragmatic decision, then, but also one that demonstrated a new way of thinking about grape varieties. An acknowledgment that newly-trendy, ancient regions such as Etna in Sicily and Jura in France were producing wines as desirable in today's market as all but the loftiest 'icons' perched on top of the old classifications of wine, from grape varieties no-one had paid any attention to just a decade or so before.

The AAVWS was slowly beginning to expand away from the longer-established northern European Italian and French varieties, too, spreading the love among varieties traditionally from warmer, more southerly homelands, and younger, fresher styles of wine.

In 2012, for example, Steve Pannell walked away with the Rod Bonfiglioli award for wine of show with a savoury, four-year-old nebbiolo. But the following year – and, remarkably, the year after that – he won the same award for a much brighter juicier style of one-year-old red made from the Iberian grape varieties tempranillo and touriga. A wine that captured the trend, still with us today, for lighter, crunchier reds.

The mid-2010s also saw more and more southern Italian grape varieties take out the top awards at the show. There was an incredible run from 2015 to 2018 when Coriole and Hither & Yon, both from McLaren Vale, shared the Best Red trophy with wines made from nero d'avola. The southern Italian whites had a similarly strong run through this period: from 2009 to 2018, the Best White award went either to a fiano or a vermentino – apart from just one year, 2013, when it went to a cortese.

The theme of 2013's Talk and Taste was 'Spotlight on Sicily', with special guests Alessio Planeta, representing his family's winery, one of the island's most progressive, and Dr Pietro Scafidi of the University of Palermo, who, the year before, had co-authored a paper outlining what lessons warm-climate growers in Australia could learn from the Sicilians.

The southern Italian varieties, particularly fiano and nero, were clearly finding their feet out in the wider world of Australian wine. So, the focus of the Talk and Taste sessions then began to shift to other locations. First Georgia in 2014, and then less obvious – but no less exciting – parts of Europe.

2015 Hither & Yon Nero D'Avola

Rollo Crittenden

— *winemaker; AAVWS associate judge in 2001, judge in 2007, 2016 and 2022; presenter at Talk and Taste in 2007.*

When he was in his late teens and early twenties, Rollo Crittenden enjoyed wine at the family dinner table, like the children of most other winemaking families. But unlike most, the bottles on the Crittenden table often weren't cabernet or shiraz – or, as their Dromana Estate vineyard was on the Mornington Peninsula, pinot noir and chardonnay. Instead, they were nebbiolo.

'It was a great night whenever Dad dragged a bottle of particularly good Barolo out of the cellar,' says Rollo.

Rollo's parents, Garry and Margaret Crittenden, were among the first to plant a commercial vineyard on the Peninsula in the early 1980s. Rollo and his sister Zoe – who now run the business – grew up among the vines. And while Garry initially planted the fashionable French varieties; cabernet, chardonnay, pinot; he became increasingly fascinated by Italian wines and flavours.

So, in the early 1990s, he started buying barbera and nebbiolo grapes from the Pizzini family in the King Valley, and dolcetto from Best's in Great Western, to make wine for release first under his Schinus label, then under the Crittenden 'i' brand. Garry was convinced that these grapes had a great future in Australia and became quite evangelical about it. As I wrote in an article on his new wines for *The Age* in 1995, he was farming 'a loose alliance of like-minded people with the aim of promoting Italian grape varieties to the wine drinker.'

One product of this 'loose alliance' was the publication of a book, *Italian Winegrape Varieties in Australia*, a guide for prospective vignerons co-authored with viticulturist Peter Dry from the University of Adelaide, Jim Hardie from the Cooperative Research Centre for Viticulture and PhD student Alex McKay. The book was published a few months before the Long Italian Lunch in Mildura in 1999.

Garry spoke at the lunch and told guests – more members of the loose alliance – that, despite all the positive press the Italian and alternative varieties were receiving at the time from supportive journos like me, the reality was that the market was not quite ready for them.

'It's not a simple matter of just selling these wines,' he said. 'At cellar door, the shutters go up in people's minds when you offer them strange-sounding Italian varieties. They're just not comfortable with what they don't know. And once they try the wine they're still challenged.'

We've come a long way since then, says Rollo, and that change is due to the hard work people like his father did back then, to change people's minds.

'Garry really had to push to have these varieties accepted,' he says. 'It's a lot easier to sell things like sangiovese and pinot grigio now, and all these other varieties because of what has been done by the previous generation.'

Rollo started working alongside his father in 1998, a role he continued after the Dromana Estate business was sold, and the family went back to operating from their original property; re-named Crittenden Estate; in the early 2000s. The interest in Italian varieties and styles continued under the Pinocchio and Geppetto labels. And Rollo and Zoe also branched out into Spanish varieties and styles, launching a brand called Los Hermanos.

As well as buying grapes for this new range, the Crittendens also decided to plant the Spanish white grape, albarino, in their Mornington Peninsula vineyard. Except, as mentioned elsewhere in the book, it wasn't albarino – it was the French grape, savagnin, from the Jura region.

At the time, the wines of Jura were little-known in Australia. Sommeliers and wine geeks were yet to embrace the sherry-like *vin jaune* or seek out Jura's cool natural winemakers. But Crittenden Estate assistant winemaker Matt Campbell had tasted *vin jaune* and visited Jura, so, in 2011, he left a barrel of the Crittenden savagnin un-sulphured, which encouraged a 'veil' of flor yeast to grow on the surface of the wine inside the cask. When Rollo tasted the layers of complex flavours in the wine, both winemakers realised they were onto something, and decided to repeat the exercise in subsequent years.

Not surprisingly, given its unusual character, the wine – called Sous Voile, 'under the veil' –took time to build a following. But finally, consumers and wine show judges *got* it: it won the award at the AAVWS for Best White in 2017, and it now sells out every year, with demand outstripping supply.

'It's been amazing,' says Rollo. 'Absolutely amazing. As a wine that started out as a mistake, it's one of the greatest mistakes that has ever happened to us.'

Rollo was an associate judge at the first AAVWS in 2001 and has returned three times since.

'It helps you refine your own styles both in terms of viticulture and winemaking,' he says. 'You come away thinking, Gee, why are people using so much oak in this beautifully elegant variety of wine? Okay, well, I'll make sure that I don't go down that avenue as well.'

He points out that the show is not just about the judging; it's very much a collective learning platform for winemakers and growers who want to do something different.

'And having it in Mildura is the key to its success,' he says. 'It's that central point that pulls in South Australia and New South Wales and Victoria. It's the meeting point. I don't think it would have been nearly as impactful or successful had it been in a capital city.'

wines lined up for judging at the AAVWS in 2015

'In 2015 we decided to hold a Talk and Taste session called "Cool Runnings",' says Jane Faulkner. 'Yes, the southern Mediterranean varieties were really important to sustainability in a changing climate in the warmer regions. But we can't always *just* talk about that. I thought it would be good to visit some other varieties that were also beginning to take off as viable alternatives in cooler climates. Varieties like gruner.'

The Austrian white grape, gruner veltliner, had been in Australia for many years, in the CSIRO's collection. But it wasn't until the mid-2000s that anyone thought to grow it commercially.

The Carpenter family at Lark Hill in the Canberra District were inspired to plant after a visit from Jancis Robinson. 'She was walking around the vineyard, and she just suddenly demanded: "Why aren't you growing gruner veltliner?"' remembers David Carpenter. 'It was a bit of a WTF moment. We knew that gruner came from Austria and that it made a dry white wine but that was about it.'

The Carpenters managed to track down some gruner vines in Tasmania – remnants of the CSIRO imports – and started planting in 2006, at the same time as Joe Holyman at Stoney Rise vineyard in the Tamar Valley, using the same source material. Larry Jacobs and Marc Dobson at Hahndorf Hill vineyard also started importing their own gruner clones from Austria around this time, and by 2009, Australian gruners began to enter the show, picking up their first award – Chief Judge's Wine to Watch, given to the 2012 K1 by Geoff Hardy from the Adelaide Hills – in 2012. The grape would go on to achieve great things, snagging Best Wine of Show in 2018 (from Artwine's Adelaide Hills vineyard) and 2020 (Hahndorf Hill), and Best White in 2022 (Linear Wines, made from Tumbarumba fruit).

Other non-Italian white grapes stood also out at the show during this time.

The first commercial vintage of the Jim Barry assyrtiko from the Clare Valley, the 2016, was named Chief Judge's Wine to Watch in that year. Winemaker Peter Barry had fallen in love with the grape on a trip to its homeland in Santorini a decade before and had decided to import cuttings. It was, and still is, a truly inspirational wine, and it would be great to see more Australian growers planting it (at the time of writing, the Barrys are yet to release the variety for commercial propagation).

Jane had also given her 'wine to watch' nod the previous year to two other whites of interest. One – an albarino (the real thing) from Maori-owned wine label, Aronui – was brand new, the other – an ugni blanc made from centenarian vines by Simon Killeen in Rutherglen – was a nod to old Australian grape-growing traditions.

And at the 2017 show, Crittenden Estate from the Mornington Peninsula won the trophy for Best White Wine with the 2013 Cri de Coeur Sous Voile Savagnin. This was a significant achievement for many reasons. For a start it showed that it's possible to turn a disaster (the

top: Gruner Veltliner t-shirt seen at 2022 Talk and Taste

bottom: Crittenden Estate Cri de Coeur Savagnin Sous Voile

Jane Faulkner and Frank Camorra at the awards long lunch in 2014

misidentification of 'albarino', as outlined in the last part of the book) into an opportunity. It was also entirely in keeping with the show's ethos that the first winner of the new trophy for Best French Varietal wasn't a well-known grape like viognier or gamay, but a grape that until recently hardly anyone in Australia had heard of – a truly *alternative* alternative.

But the most important thing about this win was the fact that the wine was a style that undoubtedly would have been rejected by most show judges in Australia – or at least misunderstood – less than a decade before.

Inspired by *vin jaune* from the Jura, in eastern France, the Cri de Coeur savagnin was matured in barrel under a layer – *sous voile* – of flor yeast, which gave the wine a yeasty, sherry-like, nutty, oxidative complexity. If you're not expecting these characters, or if you've never tried wines like this before, they can be difficult to wrap your head around, and challenging to taste. But once you understand them, you grow to appreciate their deliciousness.

Part Four: 2012–2018

Fellowship of the vine: welcome to the family

2014	*Sarah Limacher, sommelier, Sydney*
2015	*Adam Walls, wine buyer, educator, Newcastle*
2016	*James Scarcebrook, communicator and winemaker, Melbourne*
2017	*Katie Spain, writer, Adelaide*
2018	*Simone Madden-Grey, writer, Melbourne*
2019	*Grant Scicluna, retailer, Melbourne*
2020	*none – and we all know why …*
2021	*none – (see above)*
2022	*Alexandra Pritchard, educator, Adelaide.*

Katie Spain

James Scarcebrook

Grant Scicluna

'Look, I don't want to be too over-the-top about it,' says **Katie Spain**. 'But doing the AAVWS fellowship was pretty life-changing for me. If I hadn't had that week in Mildura in 2017, I might not be talking to you now.'

These days, Katie is a widely published wine writer, columnist, editor, book author and presenter. In 2021 she was named Wine Communicator of the Year by the Wine Communicators of Australia, and in 2022 she was named Best Rural Print Journalist at the Rural Media Communicator Awards. But in 2017, she says, she was just beginning to dip her toe in the water of wine storytelling – and it was spending the first week in November, immersed in the culture of the AAVWS, that made her decide to plunge in.

'Sue Bell [winemaker, AAVWS judge and committee member] really pushed me hard to apply for the fellowship,' says Katie. 'And I'm forever in her debt for doing that.'

Katie wrote about her experience for Australia's *Wine Business Monthly* magazine. She described standing in the Chalmers vineyard, surrounded by varieties that were alien to her – nosiola, malvasia, arneis, refosco – chatting with a bunch of wine industry legends. These included Mike Hayes (2017 Australian Winemaker of the Year), Mark Walpole, Nick Dry (then nursery manager and viticulturist at Yalumba), and Bruce Chalmers.

'I feel like Kate Hudson in *Almost Famous*,' she wrote. 'Only these blokes are wine gods, not rock gods, and I'm trying to get into their heads, not their beds.'

'There was a such a sense of excitement in Mildura that week,' Katie tells me. 'And that really grabbed me and made me want to give this writing thing a real crack, to tell these stories.'

The fellowship has become one of the show's most important initiatives when it comes to building networks of like-minded people. As Katie describes it, 'The team behind the AAVWS is all-inclusive and focused on spreading awareness about alternative varieties. In 2014 they instigated a fellowship for wine enthusiasts to experience the show and become ambassadors for varietal misfits.'

Another of those ambassadors is **Adam Walls**, who works for Wine Selectors in Newcastle.

'The weekend opened my eyes to the momentum that alternative varieties are currently experiencing in Australia,' Adam wrote after his fellowship in 2015. 'The AAVWS is the driving juggernaut behind this and the weekend in Mildura is a dynamic and unique experience. I loved how the show brings together wine professionals and the public in an atmosphere that celebrates fun and knowledge just as much as scores and medals. More a festival than a show.'

James Scarcebrook, the 2016 fellow, has gone on to establish his own wine label, Vino Intrepido (specialising in Italian varietals), and has both returned to judge at the show and joined the committee.

'It was a fantastic opportunity in 2016, to see more and more alternative varieties being planted for people to explore and experiment and try new things – even some varieties that I didn't know existed in Australia,' says James. 'It was fantastic, too, six years after doing the fellowship, to come back and see how much further things have come.'

And **Grant Scicluna**, who works at the Wine House store in Melbourne and was the 2019 fellow, is determined to spread the alternative varieties gospel among more cautious, premium-end consumers.

'The curious drinker wants a new experience as well as pleasure,' Grant explains. '[But] this yearning has yet to fully infuse in the premium wine market's high end, to whom an independent retailer like Wine House primarily caters. Each conversation I have with wine buyers in the high end of the premium market is an opportunity to grow the desire for alternative varieties.'

For Kate Spain, this aspect of the fellowship – telling the stories of alternative grapes to anyone who'll listen – is the most important.

'I've encouraged so many other people to apply since 2017,' says Katie. 'I tell them to go for that opportunity because I know how profound an experience it can be. It's like having a big crystal ball glimpse into the future.'

Back in the early 2000s, a couple of adventurous Australian wine importers had shipped some *vins jaunes* and other wines from the then obscure Jura region and struggled to sell a bottle because the styles were alien to retailers and sommeliers here. By the late 2010s, thanks in part to what I call The Rootstock Effect, our wine culture had matured enough to embrace the style in a wine show and award it a trophy.

∾

During her time as chief judge, Jane and the committee introduced a few other new trophies to the show. In 2012, wines were eligible for fourteen awards. By 2018, Jane's last year, there were nineteen trophies up for grabs. And one of the reasons for the introduction of these new trophies was the sheer number of new varieties and styles being entered throughout the decade.

The exception was 2012, Jane's first year as chief, when entry numbers dropped to 476 – the lowest since 2006. Not only that, but these 476 wines came from just 147 producers, the smallest number of entrants since 2003. This was a result of the very challenging and low-yielding 2011 vintage. And it turned out to be an anomaly, because in 2013 entry numbers soared back up to 593 – a record for the show at that point, and a serious challenge for the organisers.

'The show in 2013 nearly killed the judges,' says Jane. 'After 2012 we didn't expect the numbers to go up that much. And we couldn't get the footy club as a judging venue, so we used a smaller space, a gallery up the road from the Grand Hotel. Gorgeous space, but too many wines for the two panels of judges.'

Jane says the judging had to continue until eight o'clock in the evening to get through the sheer number of wines. Suddenly, the AAVWS, which prided itself on being different from other, mainstream shows, was struggling with the issues that plagued those bigger shows: too many wines, too large brackets, too much potential judging fatigue.

Head steward Paun Danenberg at the 2014 AAVWS

'It was way too much,' says Jane. 'I was singing and dancing my heart out for those judges because they were tired. For me, being chief is always about looking after the judges. With the amazing hard work of Paul (Danenberg, head of stewards) and his team, we made it work. But after that, I said to the committee, "You've got to have more judging panels." Simple as that.'

It was a turning point in the show's evolution. And a risky decision for the committee to make. Going from two panels of three judges to three panels of three judges – and from two associate judges to three – is a big bump in costs (travel, food, accommodation). And there was no certainty that the entry numbers would increase by enough to offset those costs.

It was the right decision. In 2014, entries leapt to 685. In 2015, that number nudged up to 716 wines from 234 entrants, still the highest ever number of producers entering the show. And in 2016, entry numbers increased again to 743.

By this point it was clear that, barring another disastrous vintage or unforeseen global events, the growth in entry numbers would continue. So, the committee decided to add another panel of judges. This turned out to be very good timing, because in 2017 entries hit 780 wines, and have stayed at around that number every year since (with some obvious exceptions, caused by 'unforeseen global events', that we'll come to in the next part of the book).

2014 AAVWS judges and associates: Stuart Kilmister, Walter Speller, Brad Wehr, Matthew di Sciascio, Corrina Wright, Sue Bell, Sam Connew, Stacey Lee Edwards, Kim Chalmers, Tennille Chalmers and Jane Faulkner

In 2014, to coincide with the introduction of more judges, the committee also made the decision to move from the old system of scoring wines out of twenty, to the system then becoming commonplace among critics and wine shows across Australia, of scoring out of one hundred points. So, where previously 15.5 points and above was bronze, 17 silver and 18.5 gold, now it's 85 bronze, 90 silver and 95 and above gold.

Not content with developing its own database and online entry system for the AAVWS, the committee also decided to build its own online judging program – WineShow Pro – which would allow judges to enter scores and tasting notes on a tablet or laptop, which would then automatically upload the data. This was a far cry – and a hugely welcome, timesaving change – from the previous system, where the judges' scores, written in pencil on paper on a clipboard, were entered manually into the system. Not only did it streamline the process, but it also increased the accountability of judges – their scores and impressions of each wine are locked in before any further discussion – as well as the value and precision of feedback that can be provided to the producers.

The Australian Wine Research Institute also developed its own online judging system during the 2010s, called ShowRunner, and although this has become the system used by many shows around the country, some – particularly those like the Geographe show and Limestone Coast show, which have strong links to the AAVWS family in Mildura – have adopted the AAVWS' WineShow Pro system instead.

In 2014, the committee also re-introduced the international judge position as a permanent fixture at the show (the last overseas judge had joined the show in 2010). And Jane Faulkner suggested they invest in bringing out Walter Speller, Dutch-born expert in Italian wines, and writer for *JancisRobinson.com*.

Jane was fast becoming an expert in Italian wines herself, travelling there regularly, visiting vineyards and cellars, and making connections; particularly in Piemonte.

'That's where I met Walter,' she says. 'At a festival called Nebbiolo Prima. We just clicked. He said, "I love how you Australians are so direct; you don't dilly dally; it's straight to the point". And then we realised we have all these other shared interests. And I said to him, you really should come over and judge. It'd be great to have your understanding.'

To coincide with the re-introduction of the position, the show also introduced another trophy in 2014, for 'International Judge's Wine to Watch'. Walter awarded it to a Langhorne Creek aglianico from Beach Road Wines, a wine he later described on *JancisRobinson.com* as 'beautiful, focused, perfumed, fluid, precise … very distinct.'

Jane says Walter 'gave the producers some cachet: you know, here's *the* Walter Speller and he says *this* about our wines. I thought that it worked brilliantly.'

The international judge's award was one of four new gongs introduced in 2014, along with the Trans-Tasman Award for Best New Zealand Wine (which went to the 2014 Waimea Estate Gruner Veltliner from Nelson), Best Fortified (Stanton and Killeen Topaque from Rutherglen), and Best Label Artwork (2013 Next Crop Graciano Tempranillo from Langhorne Creek).

The next year, 2015, saw two more new awards: Best Nero d'Avola, and Best Sparkling. Then 2016 introduced Best Aglianico (for one year only). And in 2017, no fewer than twenty different trophies were handed out at the (very) long lunch on the Saturday.

Not all these new awards lasted. Some, like the aglianico trophy, were dropped after a year or two. Some, like the Trans-Tasman award, held on for a little longer (it was discontinued in 2018). And some have continued to this day (the total trophy tally in 2022 was nineteen).

This ebb and flow of awards can, in many ways, help us chart trends and fashions in wine over the decades. And one of the most remarkable of those trends is the unstoppable rise and rise of rosé.

In 2001, at the first AAVWS, there were so few pink wines made from alternative varieties in Australia that rosé didn't even get its own class. In the early 2000s the thirst for rosé was nowhere near as unquenchable as it is today. The first rosé class appeared in 2002, but only featured six wines. Entries doubled the next year, though, and by 2005 there were enough – and style differences were becoming apparent enough – to split the class into two: drier styles (fourteen wines) and slightly sweeter styles (eight wines).

By 2012, with almost thirty wines entered in the rosé classes, it was obvious that the style had become seriously popular with Australian drinkers. So, the committee and chief judge Jane Faulkner introduced a trophy for Best

top: Walter Speller at the 2014 AAVWS

bottom: 2014 Best Label Artwork: Next Crop 2013 Graciano

Rosé, won that year by Scott Wines for their pale pink wine made from Adelaide Hills aglianico. This trophy has continued ever since. Why? Because even though rosé as a category has become about as mainstream as it's possible to be, the wines entered in the AAVWS are still made from an incredibly diverse variety of varieties: the thirty-nine pink wines judged in 2022, for example, were made from twenty-two different grapes.

Prosecco, by contrast, had a much shorter, much more dynamic, and much more homogenous trajectory through the show, from the first appearance of a handful of sparkling wines made from the grape in 2009, to getting its own class with fourteen entries in 2013, to 'graduating' in 2018 because it had become unquestionably mainstream (a decision that was much less controversial than the 'graduation' of pinot gris a decade earlier).

The story of prosecco in Australia is a classic case of 'the right wine at the right time', and a rare example of how a variety can go from obscure alternative to household name in barely more than a decade.

The Dal Zotto family in Victoria's King Valley were the first to commercially bottle a sparkling prosecco in this country, in the mid-2000s. Family patriarch, Otto Dal Zotto, was born in Valdobbiadene in the Veneto, the home of prosecco. Like many of his countrymen, Otto moved to Australia in the late 1960s and, like some other Italian migrants, planted a vineyard in the King Valley in the 1980s. Initially, he and his neighbours grew the cabernet and shiraz the local wineries wanted. Like the Pizzinis, he soon started making his own wine and planting the Italian grapes that were available at the time – mostly red varieties such as sangiovese and barbera.

'But the question was always chewing inside of me,' Otto told me in 2012. 'Why can't I make a nice sparkling wine like I remember from home?'

Amazingly, after a bit of sleuthing, in the late 1990s Otto found a small Italian grower in the Adelaide Hills

2004 Dal Zotto Prosecco

who had imported a few prosecco vines. He phoned the grower, 'talked dialect', and managed to obtain some cuttings. The slow, laborious process of propagation and planting began, and in 2004 the Dal Zottos made their first vintage.

The release coincided with a growing interest in Italian prosecco, particularly in the important US market. This global interest spilled over into Australia, and other growers and makers – particularly in the King Valley – were soon planting the grape.

Crucially, unlike rosé, which can come in a huge variety of styles from pale and dry to dark and full, the making and enjoyment of prosecco is easily, universally grasped: it's a fresh, clean, fruity-tasting fizz, often with a slight sweetness. Simple, gluggable, fun. No wonder it took off so quickly.

The prosecco explosion was given a huge boost by a marketing campaign by Campari Group – makers of Aperol – spruiking the Venetian spritz, a drink based on prosecco, mixed with bitters. In the early years of the 2010s, mixed drinks like this were becoming increasingly popular as a subset of the cocktail and craft spirits revolution then underway, both around the world and here in Australia.

A handful of new Australian gin brands emerged in the first couple of years of the decade, including West Winds in WA and Four Pillars and the Melbourne Gin Company in Victoria, kicking off a boom in craft gin. These were followed not long after by two new Australian vermouth brands, Maidenii and Regal Rogue. And in 2015, the gin and vermouth were joined by the first modern Australian amaro-style bitters, Okar, made in the Adelaide Hills by Brendan and Laura Carter, winemakers specialising in alternative varieties.

Best Label 2015: Loom Wine 2013 Tannat Durif Shiraz

'Oh, how I have been looking forward to this,' I wrote at the time. 'Ever since the artisan Australian gin craze took off a few years ago – followed by the artisan Australian vermouth craze – I've been waiting for some enterprising local booze producer to come out with a home-grown alternative to Campari. Why? Because then we'd have all three ingredients necessary for an all-Australian Negroni – and how super cool would that be? Well now my dream is real.'

What linked these new drinks was the use of indigenous Australian ingredients as botanicals, flavourings, and bittering agents. Finger lime, riberry, strawberry gum, quandong, native pepper – all these and more were appearing in our cocktails and spritzes and straight-up spirits.

Thanks to the work of high-profile chefs such as Kylie Kwong in Sydney and Ben Shewry at Attica in Melbourne, diners were becoming more accustomed to seeing these ingredients on their plates. It was perhaps only a matter of time before we'd see them in the bottle. Importantly, using native botanicals in drinks wasn't just a way of finding a new hook – a new marketing gimmick to make your product stand out in a rapidly crowding field. It also offered the potential to think very differently about bigger ideas and issues.

In the mid-2010s, for example, a team of researchers led by Professor Vladimir Jiranek of the University of Adelaide started looking into the microbiology of fermented drinks traditionally made and enjoyed by Indigenous peoples – drinks such as *way-a-linah* and *mangaitch* – travelling to the central highlands of Tasmania and the islands of the Torres Strait, taking samples of sap and nectar for analysis.

And in 2016, at the sixteenth triennial Australian Wine Industry Technical Conference in Adelaide, Kaurna man, Michael O'Brien, gave a Welcome to Country in the language of his people.

Michael Trembath

— *wine importer; AAVWS judge in 2011, 2013, 2015, 2018 and 2019 and 2021; presenter at Talk and Taste in 2013 and 2018.*

'I really enjoy judging at the AAVWS,' says wine importer Michael Trembath. 'The only reason I haven't done more is the timing of the show is not good. November is our busiest month. And it's always the first week of November, which is our busiest week.'

Michael – known to everyone as Trembles – is one of Australia's leading importers of and experts in Italian wine. He and business partner Matt Paul ship four containers a month – over 30,000 cases of wine a year – from seventy producers across Italy, from well-known brands of well-known styles (looking at you, prosecco and pinot grigio) to small batches of more quirky wines from obscure regions. No wonder he's busy in the lead-up to Christmas.

When Trembles started the business back in 1994 with then-partner Virginia Taylor, though, the market for Italian wine in Australia was very different.

'We shipped 3500 cases that year and we couldn't give the stuff away,' he says. 'Honestly, I reckon I drank more than we sold of some wines. Things have changed a lot since then.'

They certainly have. And much of that is due to the hard work of Trembles and other passionate importers like him.

His first job after completing the wine marketing course at Roseworthy in 1981 was at Moorfield's wine merchants in North Melbourne. The following year, the twenty-five-year-old was put in charge of the firm's Italian portfolio – 'because no one else wanted to do it'. The portfolio included wines from top producers like Antinori in Tuscany, but they didn't sell much beyond the few top-end Italian restaurants that needed a couple of Chiantis on their list.

'I'd only been in charge for a month or two when I got sent to Florence to the Antinori conference,' says Trembles. 'It was fabulous. Can you imagine? Hanging around the Tignanello vineyard, eating *Bistecca Fiorentina*, drinking all these wines. It was amazing.'

He was hooked. In 1992 he moved to Italy to work for Americans Neil and Maria Empson, who had been shipping wine to the US since the early 1970s. When he got back to Australia a couple of years later, he and Virginia set up their own eponymous import business, which included lots of Empson labels. And they started to educate people about Italian wine.

'Education was the key,' says Trembles. 'Because people just didn't know about Italy back then. Every time you went to talk to someone, you had to sort of start from the top. So, I developed a patter about the number of varieties and the areas and the fact that Italian wines are completely different. And they're very addictive. Once you get into the acid and the linear structure and the way the tannins are, it's hard to go back to Clare Valley shiraz.'

Trembles became a regular speaker at masterclasses and dinners and events, spreading the word about Italian wines in general and sangiovese in particular. He either worked with or got to know many of the other people trying to change Australia's wine culture at the time. Which is how he got involved as one of the judges at the sangiovese awards in 1999.

'I think no one really realised at the time what path that event in 1999 put everybody on,' he says. 'But from there, the whole thing just took off. Certainly, when you look at where we are today, with the awareness and interest in Italian wines and Italian varieties, the show has been a pretty important ingredient in that.'

As I wrote at the time, 'the AWITC is the largest regular gathering of winemakers and viticulturists, marketers and suppliers, executives, and researchers from across the Australian wine community. And this was the first time in the 48-year history of the event that it began with an Aboriginal Welcome to Country – a ceremony commonplace at other large Australian public events, whether cultural, political, sporting, or corporate. It was also – perhaps surprisingly – the first AWITC to devote substantial space in the main program to a discussion of *terroir*.'

Sue Bell, winemaker and regular AAVWS judge introduced the first *terroir* session at the conference by displaying on the screen the Australian Institute of Aboriginal and Torres Strait Islander Studies map of Indigenous Australia: a patchwork of the 250 or more distinct nations, tribes, and language groups – such as Kaurna – that existed before 1788.

'What this map shows is that different places in Australia had different practices in how they looked after the land or how they looked after themselves,' said Sue, who has Aboriginal heritage. 'If we want to harness this 40,000 plus years of human knowledge, perhaps we should think more about the concept of connection to country.'

This notion – 'connection to country' – is central to Aboriginal being, as Michael O'Brien explained: 'We talk about a physical and spiritual connection to land: that when you walk this land it becomes a part of you and you become a part of it, and so therefore we share this land with you, and you must share this land with us.'

The AWITC, and the AAVWS' own Talk and Taste sessions, weren't the only example of wine-related gabfests straying beyond the usual topics of clones, yeast nutrition and technical closures that characterised such events in the past. Suddenly, in the mid-2010s, a whole range of events popped up with people looking at philosophy and

2017 Talk and Taste: Louisa Rose, Tony Harper and Jane Faulkner

history and society – and using wine as a lens through which to view them.

Dan Sims, organiser of the popular Pinot Palooza and Game of Rhones festivals, held a series of Ted-talk-style events called Wine Day Out, which covered subjects as diverse as popular culture, the ethics of wine journalism, and diversity in wine education. Sommeliers Banjo Harris Plane and partner Meira Harel and a team of others picked up the baton a couple of years later with a series of similar events called GROW Assembly, aimed at the broader hospitality community, but featuring sometime raw conversations about the wine industry.

At Wine Day Out in Adelaide in 2016, Corrina Wright, a regular judge at the AAVWS, spoke about her experience calling out the 'boys' club' culture still prevalent in many Australian wine shows. The previous year, Corrina had encountered this culture firsthand at a wine show in Perth, when she discovered the judges' dinner was to be held at a male-only 'gentlemen's club'.

'I was pretty shocked,' said Corrina. 'I thought we'd moved on. As I've put myself out there as standing up for the rights of women and being a bit of a mentor to young women in the industry, I decided to boycott the dinner.'

Unfortunately, she said, there were other, younger women among the judging group who felt that, although they didn't agree with the choice of venue, they felt they couldn't speak out for fear of jeopardising their careers.

To help address the situation, Corrina has also become a supporter and advisor to another initiative that emerged in this time, the Fabulous Ladies Wine Society's Australian Women in Wine Awards, launched in 2015. The Society was founded a couple of years before by former psychologist and PR professional, Jane Thomson, who held several female-focussed events, wine tours, and tastings for women before establishing the awards.

'Affirmative action,' Jane Thomson told me at the time. 'I truly believe that's what's needed to see the changes we want to see in Australian wine. Some people assume we're all operating on an equal playing field. But I just don't see that at the moment.'

Except, perhaps, in Mildura every November.

During her time as chief judge, Jane Faulkner maintained the inclusive AAVWS tradition of widening the net of potential judges at the show. Not just by inviting sommeliers and writers and retailers as well as winemakers, or by aiming to ensure gender balance, but also by expanding the geographical reach.

Jane knew it was important to source more judges and speakers from outside the major south-eastern wine-producing states of South Australia, Victoria, and New South Wales, to bring a wider range of experiences and opinions into the discussion, and to promote the show to a bigger audience.

'I felt we needed more people from Western Australia,' says Jane. 'I know it's always hard from the show committee's point of view, because of budgets, and it's

2015 Pizza and Vino AAVWS dinner

more expensive to get people over from WA than just up the road. But I really felt we had to spread the love a bit.'

Jane was also chairing the Geographe Wine Show in Bunbury around this time, and made many good contacts, inviting people she met and judged with over to Mildura to take part in the AAVWS. The connections have continued ever since. Bunbury-based Meg Kopke, who was an associate at the AAVWS in 2016, for example, has established a wine retail business, MoreVino, specialising in alternative varieties. And the Geographe show has also branded itself as the 'WA Alternative Varieties Wine Show' and uses the WineShow Pro online judging system developed by the AAVWS.

Queensland was another part of the country to be welcomed into the Mildura family.

Best Label Artwork winners:

top: Delinquente Wine Co 2017 Tuff Nut

bottom: Big Easy Radio 2016 Forget Babylon

Brisbane-based wine bar owner, retailer and writer, Tony Harper, had been a regular judge at the show and big supporter of the AAVWS since 2007. He was joined by winemaker Mike Hayes from the Granite Belt, who judged at the show in 2012 and was on the committee from 2014 to 2019. During this time Mike travelled through Europe during the northern hemisphere vintage on a Churchill Fellowship grant, studying hundreds of little-known autochthonous varieties that could flourish in Australian vineyards.

'If anyone in Australia thinks that climate change is not happening, they need to visit the northern hemisphere for a reality check,' he told me soon after he got back from his trip. 'Even the older generation, growers who were once sceptical, are now changing their tune in respect to global warming. It's bloody frightening.'

In 2015, Granite Belt winery Golden Grove became the first – and as of 2023 still the only – producer outside South Australia or Victoria to win the trophy for Best Wine of Show. Admittedly, 80 percent of the grapes for that wine, a 2015 vermentino, came from the Murray Darling region, not Queensland. But at the 2022 AAVWS Golden Grove also became the first Queensland producer to win the trophy for Best White Italian Varietal (again with a current vintage vermentino) – and this time the wine was 100 percent estate-grown.

In another attempt to build networks across the country, the AAVWS introduced a fellowship program in 2014. Wine professionals – and knowledgeable enthusiasts – who are 'excited by the opportunity to explore and celebrate Australia's alternative varieties and share that newfound fervour with their networks and industry groups' can apply for an all-expenses-paid trip to Mildura during show week. They'd be staying at the Grand Hotel, touring the region, attending the dinners and tastings and awards, and visiting wineries and vineyards. The first fellow was Sydney sommelier Sarah Limacher; subsequent fellows have included writers, retailers, and educators; one of whom – James Scarcebrook – went on to start his own

Helen Healy, Daria Healy-Koljanin, Jane Faulkner, Kim and Tennille Chalmers with the Dr Rod Bonfiglioli Award at the 2018 awards long lunch

wine business, making Italian varietal wines. He has also come back to the show, joining the committee, judging, and leading the Talk and Taste session in 2021. For more about the fellows, see page 136.

In 2015, the show also introduced another new initiative, Sponsor-a-Variety, to cover the costs of facilitating the importation of a grape not currently in Australia. Winemakers and growers were invited to make the case for a variety they thought would add to the viticultural landscape: a grape that they might have tasted, or read about, or worked with overseas and thought, hey, this would grow well back home.

The first – and, so far, only – winner of the sponsorship was Anna Hooper, winemaker on the Limestone Coast. Anna's choice of grape was shavkapito, one of the hundreds of autochthonous varieties found in Georgia.

'In 2014 I spent two months in Georgia,' wrote Anna in her application. 'I travelled all over the country tasting many different varieties. I also visited the Georgian Wine Association trial vineyard where more than 500 indigenous varieties are grown in trial rows. As a finished wine, shavkapito stood out for its aromatic qualities on the nose, its liveliness, and the fact that it can produce a light to medium bodied style with character.'

2018 Glen and Judy Kelly of Artwine accepting the award for Best Wine at the 2018 long lunch

Anna also knew, from conversations with winemaker Lado Uzunashvili while in Georgia, that with its thick skins and loose bunches, the variety is expected to be disease resistant in a range of climates.

Jane Faulkner remembers Anna Hooper judging at the AAVWS in Mildura the year after she became the Sponsor-a-Variety winner.

'Anna's a really smart woman,' says Jane. 'Pint-sized pocket-rocket. She flew her plane to Mildura from the Limestone Coast to judge, which was awesome. But she got lost walking trying to find the judging venue. I mean, Mildura's a grid: it's not that hard. Needless to say, I've never flown with her since.'

At Jane's last show as chief judge, in 2018, a whole crowd of winemakers accepted awards for the first time, taking away a bunch of trophies.

Artwine became the first gruner veltliner producer to win the Dr Rod Bonfiglioli award for Best Wine of Show; Vineyard 28 from Geographe in WA took out Best Italian Red Varietal with a dolcetto; Glen James won Chief Judge's Wine to Watch with a Tasmanian-grown skin-contact friulano – and his partner, Jo Marsh of Billy

Button wines, won her first trophy, for Best Nebbiolo. McLaren Vale's Big Easy Radio won Best Label Artwork for their Forget Babylon touriga blend; and Dhiaga from Henty won Best Sparkling in their first year of entering the show.

Add these first timers to the 'repeat offenders' from South Australia (Coriole, Oliver's) and Victoria (Chalmers, Tahbilk) among others and the results in 2018 feel like pulses of alternative variety energy – of cultural change – crackling across the country.

'The tentacles that stretch out from that show really are ridiculous,' says Jane, throwing another metaphor into the mix. 'And there's a beautiful thread that connects them all. It's the Dr Rod magic. I always felt there was magic with him. And I felt that has kind of continued. I'm not spiritual. It's nothing to do with that. It's just this wonderful link that's there, that exists. You know? You just felt he was around. I remember having a little teary moment at one point. Thinking, *look, Rod, look what it's become.*

'It's the safest place for anyone to come along and have a crack with a variety without someone else going, "Ah, what the bloody hell are you doing?" I mean, I'm not saying it's all about holding hands and singing Kumbaya. But I have been at other wine shows where people are all too keen to cut others down. It's the inclusiveness that makes this show great.'

It's a lovely, positive note to end on. A rousing finish to an eventful decade in the show's evolution.

The calm before the storm.

Part Five

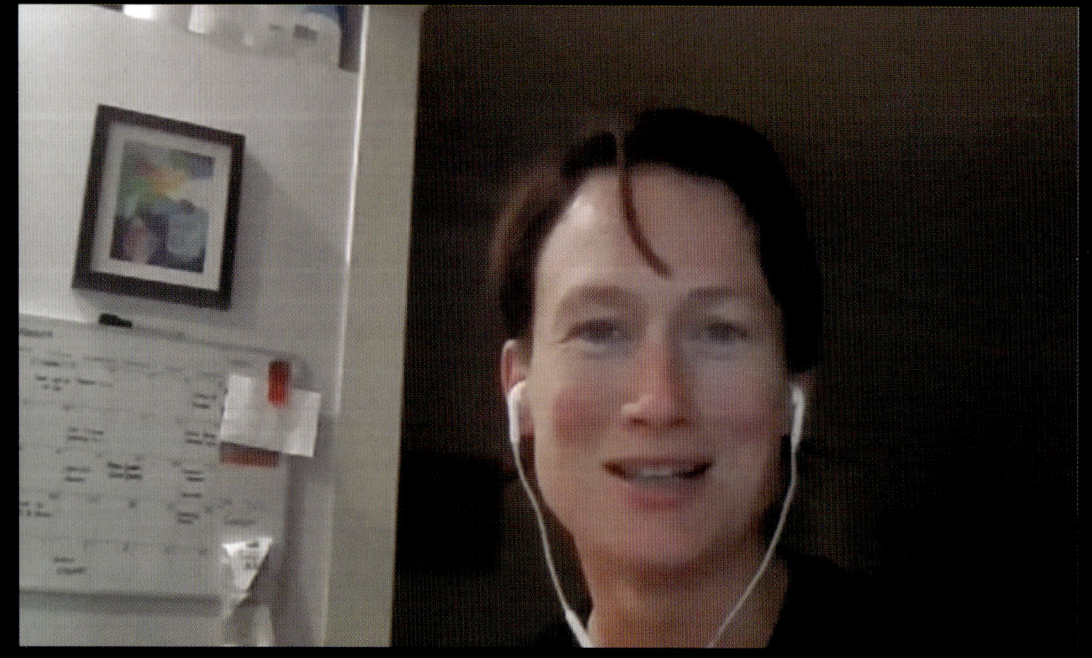

Wine in interesting times

Thursday 5, November 2020. It's the middle of judging at the twentieth Australian Alternative Varieties Wine Show. This is new chief judge Sophie Otton's second year at the helm, and she's staring at her computer screen, watching the judges' scores and comments appear as each panel works its way through another line-up of wines.

The organisers and stewards have been running this show for two decades now, so everything is going according to plan here in the footy club. With one glaring exception. Sophie Otton and her computer aren't in the same room as the judges and the stewards and the glasses and the wines. Sophie's not even in Mildura. She's beaming in on Zoom from her office at She Loves You, the small neighbourhood wine bar she owns and runs with her partner in Sydney.

The pandemic smashed any hope of this year's show being run as normal. In the middle months of 2020, as people died and more people got sick and whole cities were forced into lockdown after lockdown, it became clear that the show could not go ahead in its usual form. That nothing was normal anymore.

preceding pages: All Talk No Taste zoom seminar in 2020, clockwise from top left: Kim Chalmers, Jo Marsh, Sophie Otton and Gwyn Olsen

right: 2018 incoming chief judge Sophie Otton, centre, at Talk and Taste

So, like everyone else in the world, the AAVWS family 'pivoted'. They brought in local judges to replace the usual interstaters. They moved the Talk and Taste and the awards ceremony – and the chief judge's participation – online. And they managed, despite all the challenges of 2020, to attract a decent number of entries. The show must go on. The show did go on.

'And it all went surprisingly well,' says Sophie Otton. 'Considering that the prospect of doing it in the weeks leading up to the show had been a nightmare.'

The previous show, in 2019 – Sophie's first as chief judge – had also gone well. The handover from Jane Faulkner had been a smooth one. And it came at a time when the AAVWS was in particularly reflective, but ultimately confident mood.

In late 2018, a group of key people involved with the show had assembled in Mildura for a 'future vision' workshop. The group included then-chair of the committee, Ashley Ratcliff, co-founder Stefano de Pieri; organisers Kim and Tennille Chalmers and Helen Healy; chief steward Anita Goode; and all four chief judges, past (Tim White and me), present (Jane Faulkner) and future (Sophie).

2019 AAVWS family Bruce and Jenni Chalmers, Tim White, Helen Healy, Stefano de Pieri, Kathleen Quealy, Mark Walpole

'That was a great immersion in the culture of the show,' says Sophie. 'We had a couple of days of really taking the show apart and putting it back together, really trying to nut out what that looked like, and the relevance of the things that the show stood for, and where it was going to head to.'

The workshop facilitator had spent some time in Mildura during show week in 2018, immersed in the culture of the event. Their final report identified a couple of ways that the show could be improved, and some risks relating to the long-term viability of the show (most importantly, ensuring a smooth transition from the current, long-term management team to the next management team), but the overall impression was of a show in rude good health.

'The traditional rules of the wine show game have been largely rewritten in Mildura,' the report concluded. 'The show doesn't exist simply to benchmark wine styles and to provide medals to support winemakers' marketing activities. The AAVWS is there to pave the way for varieties new to the Australian wine landscape and to champion their cause; to provide leadership, to foster enthusiasm and support; to challenge the status quo and to do so with a sense of energy and activism; and to invite in and embrace some of the industry's characters, enlisting them to the cause. Because as [inaugural chief judge] Tim White says, quoting Anton Ego in *Ratatouille*, "The world is often unkind to new talent, new creations. The new needs friends".'

∽

Sophie Otton had extensive experience working in restaurants and retail, from the Universal Wine Bar in Adelaide in the mid-1990s to heading the team at Melbourne's City Wine Shop in the 2000s, to opening her own small bar in Sydney in the late 2010s. She had also spent many years as tasting panellist and contributor at *Gourmet Traveller WINE Magazine,* all of which made her a perfect choice as chief judge.

Sophie had a solid grounding in the wine 'classics', cemented by her time as wine director at the high-end Rockpool Bar & Grill in Sydney from 2009. But she'd also become fascinated by the rule-breakers and disruptors and rebels of the natural wine scene – particularly the Natural Selection Theory, who she described as 'a bunch of audacious young winemakers in hot pants who trooped into Rockpool, the Temple of Old Wine, one day to show me their wares'.

Sophie argues this new generation of winemakers did what the wine industry has been trying to do for years: they made wine more appealing to younger people. They made it accessible. They made it fun. They demonstrated that you didn't need a 'classical' wine education or to wear a sommelier's suit to sell wine.

'I loved the way they just didn't care what the establishment thought,' says Sophie. 'And the establishment were used to being taken notice of, to having their opinions seen as gospel. So, I found that

Anita Goode

— *winemaker; AAVWS head of stewards 2018–2022.*

Anita Goode knows exactly when she decided to get involved with the AAVWS.

'Here,' she says, reaching for her phone. She scrolls through her photos and shows me: it's a selfie of her in thick-rimmed specs next to a bloke I kind of recognise but can't quite place.

'That's me and Heston Blumenthal at Stefano's,' she says. 'Quarter to eleven at night, February 23, 2017. I'm wearing Heston's glasses. And Helen Healy had just talked me into coming to steward at the wine show.'

Anita had driven up to Mildura from her Wangolina vineyard at Mount Benson, on South Australia's Limestone Coast, to visit the Chalmers and see the varieties she'd just planted at home – malvasia, garganega, moscato giallo nosiola, prosecco, pinot blanc and greco – growing on more established vines. After her visit, she went for dinner: table for one, at Stefano's.

'Stefano had made bread soup, so I ordered a bottle of pecorino,' remembers Anita. 'The wine and the soup went really well together. I told this to the girl serving and she came back and said, "Stef wants to know who you are and how you knew he'd put that same wine into the dish. He said, once you finish your dinner, please come and sit at his table near the kitchen for a chat."'

So, Anita did, and Helen Healy was there too, and they started talking about the show, and Helen invited her to steward. And the next moment, in walk the MasterChef crew, who have been filming in Mildura with Heston Blumenthal.

'And suddenly there's this moment where I'm sitting with Heston, talking about how gut health was going to be the next biggest food trend. It was so weird. But now I know that kind of thing happens all the time at Stefano's.'

A few years before, Anita had worked as head steward at the Limestone Coast Wine Show, so she was a shoo-in for the AAVWS that November. And then, she says, at the end of the show, 'Jane [Faulkner], Kim and Helen came up and lady-mafia'd me into taking over as head steward there.'

In 2017, Anita was well into her own alternative variety journey at Wangolina.

Her family have farmed the property at Mount Benson for close to a century, and in 1999, like many other farmers during that decade, had diversified into vines to sell grapes to the region's wineries: cabernet, semillon and sauvignon blanc – 'you know, because Limestone Coast is the next Bordeaux. Apparently'. Anita studied winemaking and came back to the farm in 2001, around the same time it became clear the winery demand for grapes had dwindled and the family decided to make their own wine.

'We planted pinot gris in 2007,' says Anita. 'When it was still technically an alternative grape. But by the time we made our first wine from it in 2011, it wasn't alternative anymore.'

In 2012 Anita bought some tempranillo from the Wirrega vineyard in Mundulla, near Bordertown. And in 2015 she was offered some lagrein – vines that had been planted at the behest of Ben Glaetzer, winemaker and former AAVWS judge, in 2009.

'And then, I don't know why, but I just decided to graft some of my semillon over to something else. I mean, I *love* semillon. But no rational human being needs twenty-four tonnes of Limestone Coast semillon. Like, no one. So, I decided to keep half the block and graft half the block. And I decided that I wanted gruner veltliner.'

She phoned Larry Jacobs at Hahndorf Hill, then leading the gruner charge in South Australia, and told him she was thinking about making gruner.

'Larry got so excited. He was like, "You're gonna make the best wine out of Mount Benson! It's gonna be great!" So, I thought, okay, I'd better do it then.'

It was the best decision she ever made.

'The acceptance of our brand changed with gruner,' says Anita. 'Before, the Wangolina business had been just okay. But when the gruner came on board, we started to grow and turn an actual profit. It opened doors that had not been opened for me before. And then that led to sales of our other wines.'

Anita signed on for three years as head steward at the AAVWS, starting in 2018, but ended up doing her last year in 2022, thanks to the pandemic. And even though she has now handed over head steward responsibilities to winemaker Richie O'Donnell, she will still come back for show week, for Talk and Taste, the exhibitors' tasting, and the long lunch.

'It's addictive,' she says. 'When you're the kind of person who likes to collect grape varieties like Pokémon cards in their vineyard, you want to know everything. And you can do that if you get involved in the show.'

She'll also keep going back for the people.

'The way the judges interact at Mildura with the stewards, with the exhibitors, with the public who come to the dinners is just different: there's no segregation, there's no pomposity. It's all about sharing. And the other thing for me is how exciting the stewards at that show are. The people who come to steward in Mildura are interesting people who give a shit. They want to learn, and they want to know. And they love it.'

As a producer of alternative varieties herself, Anita says the greatest privilege of working behind the scenes at the show is gaining an insight into how the results can change people's businesses.

'A trophy may just be a trophy for some winemakers,' she says. 'But for others it's a really big deal. When you're small and you're working really hard, if you get a trophy for something it means a lot. Watching that unfold in real time is really cool.'

really thrilling. These newcomers saying, we don't want to follow anything you've done before.'

After Rockpool, Sophie moved to Billy Kwong, running a wine list dripping with natural and natural-ish, alternative styles. But in 2017, when she set up her own place – She Loves You – in Newtown, she found a balance between the two worlds, offering both more adventurous bottles alongside classics like Henschke and Cullen.

Before her first show as chief, in 2019, Sophie had also travelled across both the old and new wine worlds, visiting a natural wine fair called Zero Compromise in Georgia, and addressing the Organic Wine Conference in New Zealand. Her choices of judges reflected this breadth of vision and experience. Some were AAVWS veterans: Mark Walpole, Sue Bell, Tony Harper. And some had been judges the year before: sommelier Meira Harel, winemakers Pete Fraser from Yangarra, Belinda Thomson from Crawford River, Justin Purser, then at Best's Great Western. All had solid understanding of the long-established ways of doing things – but all were also sympathetic to the back-to-the-future disruptions of the natural wine scene.

In 2019, even though prosecco had dropped off as an eligible variety the year before, entry numbers increased, topping 800 for the first time. A sangiovese, the 2015 Bellariva from De Bortoli, took out the top trophy for Wine of Show for the first time in the event's history. Coolangatta Estate from the Shoalhaven Coast in NSW took out three awards – Best White, Best French Varietal and Best Museum Wine (a new award introduced this year) – with a nine-year-old savagnin. And Richard Leask, from McLaren Vale, won the inaugural Viticulturist Award.

The confident theme of the 2019 Talk and Taste program was 'The Future is Now'. Former chief judge Tim White conducted a tasting of wines charting the two-decade progress of the show since 1999 and Sophie chaired a panel session on the rise and rise of tempranillo. The day

top: 2019 judge Belinda Thomson at Talk and Taste

bottom: The 2015 Bellariva from De Bortoli

2019 awards long lunch

finished with an unconventional 'mini-conference of three fifteen-minute presentations' in collaboration with Wine Industry Suppliers Australia, covering digital marketing, social media, and consumer insights.

It was another successful, positive, encouraging show; an exciting debut for the new chief judge. But as everyone was busy drinking and celebrating and talking and tasting in Mildura, the east coast of Australia was burning.

Today, after three years of pandemic, and of endless rain and widespread flooding brought about by La Niña, we can all too easily forget the Black Summer of 2019/2020 and the vicious drought leading up to it.

We in the cities forget about the thick blankets of smoke that settled on Sydney and Melbourne around Christmas; the horror of hearing about fire after fire breaking out from southeast Queensland to South Australia; the images of people in Mallacoota fleeing into the sea to escape the surrounding inferno. Some of us forget, too, about the vineyards and wineries destroyed by the fires that summer in the Adelaide Hills, on Kangaroo Island, and the countless tonnes of grapes that went to waste because of smoke taint.

We remember, though, hearing about a mysterious new virus travelling around the globe in early 2020. We remember the border closures. We remember the lockdowns, the curfew, the panic. We remember because the pandemic affected all of us. And it affected all of us for month after month after month.

'We had our first planning meeting for the 2020 show in March,' says Sophie Otton. 'All of us on Zoom, which we were learning to use for the first time, trying to work out what was going to happen, because no-one knew. But the mood was overwhelmingly positive that we should hold the show in November that year. Of course, then, with the borders opening and closing, it was very hard to even think that doing the show might be a possibility as we got deeper into the reality of what we were facing. But we did it. We just did it online. Or *I* did it online.'

Because Mildura and other parts of regional Victoria were not as severely affected by restrictions and lockdowns as the capital cities, the committee were able to call in an impressive range of judges, despite the interstate travel bans. Victorian winemaker Belinda Thomson and Mark Walpole returned for a second year. Tennille Chalmers, who had been an associate in 2014 and on the management team since, and Stefano de Pieri, co-founder of the show, both stepped up to judge, as well as local Mildura winemakers Jonathan Creek, Donna Stephens and Shane Kerr – all of whom had been involved in the show for many years (Donna was an associate judge and Shane head steward at the first show, in 2001).

'We had a good strong team,' says Sophie. 'We had to recruit people who normally work behind the scenes to take part. And they judged really well. It was judging through consultation, with me sitting in my office for a

2020 White Mischief Gruner Veltliner

2020 AAVWS judges and associates: Tennille Chalmers, Jonathan Creek, Liz Richardson, Shane Kerr, Aidan Menzies, Belinda Thomson, Sierra Reed, Mark Walpole, Donna Stephens, Glen James, Stefano de Pieri and Pia Merrick

week in front of a screen, talking to them when necessary, and then making a conclusion from that. It was much more enjoyable than I expected. And it was effective.'

Because head steward Anita Goode couldn't travel from South Australia, Helen Healy was joined by long-time stewards Brendan and Kerry Steele and former head stewards, Paul Danenberg and Hugh Perez, to wrangle both the usual hundreds of bottles and dozens of people, and all the extra work that comes with COVID-safe operations. The committee also made the decision to cut the entry fees to the show in half in 2020: they were acutely aware of the huge impact the pandemic had had on everyone's financial security. As a result, 523 wines were entered by 137 producers – the lowest figures since 2012 but, given the circumstances, a remarkable result.

The awards that year were refreshingly diverse, from Hahndorf Hill winning Wine of Show and Best White with their gruner veltliner to Ricca Terra winning Best Italian White with their Bronco Buster fiano vermentino

All Talk No Taste Instagram tile from 2020

blend; and from small new label, Bondar, winning Best Red with a McLaren Vale monastrell to a huge corporate brand, Pepperjack, winning Best Italian Red with a sangiovese.

Traditionally, of course, the Friday afternoon of show week is taken up with the Talk and Taste seminar program, an interactive event that has long been a big drawcard for visitors to the AAVWS. This year it was re-branded as 'All Talk and No Taste': instead of people gathering in Mildura to sit in a room at the Grand Hotel or the Workers Club and taste wine and listen to a panel discussion, people watched and listened to guests talking about Mildura, about fiano, about sustainability, and about the impact of COVID on our wine culture – all on their computer screens.

Perhaps unexpectedly, the 2020 show also included an international judge: US-based sommelier and consultant, Cha McCoy, who beamed in for the last session of the day. She chatted with Joel and Fred Pizzini about nebbiolo, Narelle King from Tar & Roses about rosé, Alister Purbrick about the age ability of marsanne, to Mark Walpole and Kim Chalmers about aglianico, and Michael Dal Zotto about prosecco.

By November 2020, this kind of online wine event was nothing new. We were all familiar by that point with 'pivoting', to being resilient, to thinking of new ways to do things, to making the best of what was, in many ways, a disastrous situation.

At the beginning of the 2020, the wine industry had panicked – with good reason – about the sudden disappearance of some of its most lucrative income streams: restaurants, festivals, and cellar door sales. It soon became clear, though, that we're very attached to wine in Australia. Initially this manifested as a boom in retail and online sales – and online Zoom tastings – as everyone was forced to drink at home. But as lockdowns were lifted, we also flocked back to the regions, eager to spend money. Indeed, this discovery – that people are thirsty to

Jonathan Creek

— *winemaker; AAVWS steward from 2006, associate judge in 2010, judge in 2017, 2018, 2020 and 2021; speaker at Talk and Taste 2018; committee member 2017 to 2022.*

Jonathan Creek is one of the only people to have been involved with every aspect of the show, from being an exhibitor to stewarding, from associate judging to full judging, from speaking at a Talk and Taste presentation to joining the committee. Not to mention playing saxophone at Beer and Bowls.

Jono's a local. For almost twenty years, he has worked as a winemaker at Zilzie, a huge winery near Mildura that processes around 50,000 tonnes of grapes (over 3 million bottles of wine) each year. Zilzie and has been entering its wines in the show since the beginning in 2001, and has supported it through sponsorship many times over the years.

From the inception of the AAVWS, the organisers have always felt it's crucially important to draw in the local wine community, whether it be the growers and makers themselves, like Jono, or wine-passionate people from other fields, like head steward from 2009 to 2015, dentist Paul Danenberg. This approach paid off during the pandemic, of course, when the locals, and those in regional Victoria, were the only ones able to get involved.

'I started stewarding in 2006,' says Jono. 'It was fantastic for a local like me to have a national wine show on your doorstep, and it was brilliant to be involved in it. It had this culture of funkiness and fun about it, which was quite exciting as a younger member of the industry. And it featured all these varieties and styles you'd read about but not normally get a chance to taste.'

In 2009, says Jono, Paul encouraged him to put his name forward to become an associate judge. 'That was a great opportunity, too,' he says. 'I really learned to love nebbiolo through judging alongside Jane [Faulkner]. Her enthusiasm pulled you through. It was brilliant mentoring.'

Jane remembers Jono's first stint at the judging table that year.

'He said something really lovely to me at the show,' she says. 'He said: "You know, you've opened up my mind to the way we should be judging and looking at wine." It's good to think that a lot of winemakers who'd only experienced conventional shows appreciated that difference in the way we looked at wine. And that they went on to become ambassadors for that way of thinking.'

Jono has judged at several other shows – as well as the AAVWS – since then and has participated in panel tastings for *Winestate* magazine. And in 2017 he joined the AAVWS committee.

'It's a logical extension,' he says. 'You're not just participating in the show, you're actively contributing, actively learning from some of the best in the business. What I love is that this show has an emphasis on collaboration and creating an environment that's comfortable, safe, and accessible. And I certainly see links there with teaching.'

Now in his early forties, Jono has decided to ease out of winemaking by embarking on a Master of Early Childhood and Primary Education – a career he almost chose in his twenties before falling into wine and one he's now returning to. And what he's learned about modern teaching methods – creating spaces for children to explore and develop their own reasoning – has made him appreciate the AAVWS even more.

'I realised that's one of the unique aspects of this show,' he says. 'It encourages different voices.'

2021 AAVWS management team Kim Chalmers, Tennille Chalmers, Ashleah Black and Helen Healy

support their local producers – became one of the most unexpected and heartening lessons of the pandemic.

In November 2020, a couple of weeks after the AAVWS, the Australian industry was taught a much harder lesson when China announced punitive tariffs on Australian wine of 200 percent or more, effectively shutting down overnight what had become a $1.2 billion export market. And a few weeks before the show, much-loved Adelaide Hills winemaker Taras Ochota had died, at the age of forty-nine, after a couple of years battling illness.

It felt like 2020 was determined to kick the Australian wine community when they were down.

∞

In mid-2021, despite the country still being in the grip of the pandemic, the committee optimistically started planning for the twenty-first show in November, assuming – hoping – it would be able to go ahead as normal. In keeping with the anniversary theme, the first Talk and Taste sessions was set: 'Coming of Age'.

'Because it was the twenty-first anniversary,' says Sophie Otton, 'we felt that it was important to bring back

2021 chief judge on the ground Glenn James

participants and judges who had been involved before. To get the band back together to a certain extent. So, that's what we did.'

Or that's what they tried to do. But new variants of the virus emerged, new lockdowns and travel bans were enforced, regions were closed and opened and closed again. And as November approached, and Melburnians and interstaters were still prevented from travelling to Mildura, the committee was forced to limit the judges once again to locals and others from regional Victoria. It felt like 2020 all over again.

'And then, a week before the show, the Sydney restrictions were lifted,' says Sophie. 'I got a call from Helen saying, "We've got the green light! We're on!" And I said, "No, we're not. I have a small business, the wine bar, and finally I'm allowed to re-open it, and I can't leave it. You know, it's just my partner and I running it, and I've got to be there".'

So, for 2021, rather than rely on a Zoom connection with Sophie in Sydney, winemaker Glenn James also stepped in to act as chief judge on the ground in Mildura. Glenn first judged at the show in 2003 and spent a few years on the committee, as well as presenting his wines at the Talk and Taste in 2014 and judging in the first pandemic year of the show. As such, he was well placed to take on the responsibilities.

Entry numbers in the 2021 show bounced back to just under 700 – incredible, given all the challenges the wine industry was facing at the time. And a lot of long-time friends and associates of the show walked away with gongs that year, from Oliver's Taranga in McLaren Vale (their fiano was named Best White Italian Varietal, Sparkling fiano Best Fizz, and Don Oliver received the Viticulturist Award), to Kevin McCarthy (his new band MANDI – now MDI – friulano picked up Best Murray Darling and Best Label Artwork awards) and Pikes Wines (their Luccio albarino was Best White).

2021 AAVWS judges and associates: Mark Walpole, Stacey Lee Edwards, Pia Merrick, Kylie Wheeler, Tennille Chalmers, Harry Kinsman, Liz Richardson, Ray Nadeson, Justin Purser, Donna Stephens, Ralph Kyte Powell, Sierra Reed, Cindy Heley, Jonathan Creek, Glenn James, Jen Latta and Shawna Dominelli

But the wine that won the Rod Bonfiglioli award – as well as Best Red, Best Italian Red and Best Museum Wine – the 2016 Valentino sangiovese, was from a relatively new producer that had only entered the show a couple of times. And it was a wine that had a special resonance in the historical context of the AAVWS.

Santa and D'Sas is a label set up in 2013 by a couple of Victorian winemaking mates, Matthew Di Sciascio and Andrew Santarossa. In 2016, the pair purchased grapes from Greenstone in Heathcote, the vineyard that Mark Walpole had planted over a decade before. The fruit they bought came from the half-dozen different clonal sangiovese blocks – the 'really schmick new clones' Tim White wrote about back in 2003.

Mark Walpole was one of the judges at the 2021 show. He can't possibly have known that the wine he and his fellow judges gave a gold to, then an award, then another award, and then the top award, was made from vines he'd planted but no longer owned. And it must have been a bittersweet moment when he found out.

∾

Having been through the process of organising a wine show during a pandemic once, the AAVWS team were able to slip into the groove and follow the same procedural aspects again in 2021. But the prospect of holding a celebration of the show's twenty-first anniversary online was too much. So, they postponed the party and kept the Talk and Taste simple: AAVWS fellow and new committee member, James Scarcebrook in conversation with a group of the show's sponsors, discussing how the show has influenced what they do in the wine industry, and the developments they've noticed in Australia over the past twenty years.

'In 2020, the event side of show week had been much harder to manage and coordinate than the judging,' says Sophie Otton. 'When you're a part of a panel, you really need people to be engaging back and forth. And most of the time on Zoom people are just listening to you, so the committee decided to pare it back this year and hold off doing the big celebrations until next year.'

It wasn't until the first week of November 2022, then, with the worst of the pandemic beginning to recede, that the AAVWS family was reunited in Mildura and able to finally celebrate our coming of age.

As well as a sprinkling of newcomers among the judging panels – people like sommeliers Bridget Raffal from Sydney and Foni Pollitt from Perth – most of the rest of us, as had been planned for the year before, were past judges: Jane Faulkner and me, AAVWS stalwarts Sue Bell and committee president Corrina Wright, and two people who were involved in judging the first show, in 2001, winemaker Rollo Crittenden and Master of Wine Kate McIntyre.

2016 Valentino Heathcote Sangiovese

'It's kind of strange being here,' said Kate at a celebration dinner on the Thursday evening. 'I feel much more at home here than I probably should. I mean, it's been twenty-one years since I was last here judging. So obviously it must have had a big impact on me.' In fact, Kate said, it was Stefano and long-time AAVWS judge, Michael Trembath, who inspired her to do the Master of Wine program.

It felt strangely familiar to be back for me, too. I hadn't been here for show week in November since my last year as chief judge in 2011. I'd travelled to Mildura many times since then for other reasons – to visit Lake Mungo; for the future visions workshop; and just a couple of months before, in 2022, for the writers' festival – and I'd caught up with Helen and Stef and the Chalmers and others involved in the show during those visits. But this was the first time I'd taken part in the show for over a decade. And while in many ways, as Kate pointed out, it felt strangely familiar – a testament to the strong culture the show's organisers have created and maintained – it was also good to see progress. And nowhere did I see this progress more dramatically than in the quality of the top wines we tasted.

The trophy judging process at the AAVWS works like this.

Some of the trophies are arbitrary, meaning they are not decided by all the judges involved in the show. The Chief of Judges Wine to Watch, for example, is a wine that the chief judge alone feels is worthy of recognition, even though her fellow judges may not have been so enamoured – a wine that might be in the trophy taste-off but fails to pick up another award. The Stewards Choice, similarly, is awarded by the stewards, based on what they taste behind the scenes. And the Best Label Artwork is selected by the management team and the stewards.

The next tier of trophies can come from any class. The Best Organic award, for example, goes to the top certified

Drinks in the rose garden at the Grand Hotel after the awards lunch in 2022

organic wine, regardless of variety or style. Similarly, the Best Museum award can be awarded to a wine in any class, as long as it's an older vintage, and is the top scoring older vintage wine in the show.

Then there's a tier of awards based mostly on the origin of the grapes being tasted. So, for example, all the top gold medal wines in the red Italian classes – sangiovese, nebbiolo, aglianico, red Italian blends, etc – are tasted to find the Best Red Italian award; and the Iberian wines – albarino, arinto, tempranillo, mencia, et cetera – vie for the Best Iberian award.

The top wines from these last two tiers are then re-tasted to decide on the Best White, Best Red, Best Rosé, et cetera. And then from these a Best **Wine** of Show is chosen.

As you can imagine, it's a **complex** and convoluted process – or, rather, it can be if lots of gold medals are awarded on the first two days of judging across all classes. And this is precisely what happened in 2022.

Leanne Altmann

— *beverage director; AAVWS judge, 2015, 2016, 2018; speaker at Talk and Taste 2016; chief judge 2023 -*

'Leanne came up to Mildura and judged for the first time in 2015,' says Jane Faulkner, chief judge at the AAVWS from 2012 to 2018. 'And I said at the time: we have a future chief of judges here. The way she held herself, the way she was with people. She has this effortlessness about her, a friendliness, but a leadership quality, too. And now she is the chief, and that's great.'

Talking with Leanne Altmann about her job as beverage director at Trader House, the Melbourne group of food businesses that includes the always-packed Cutler & Co, Supernormal and Gimlet restaurants, I wonder how she will possibly find the time to also be chief judge at the AAVWS. 'But it's fun!' she says, smiling broadly. 'Wine is a profession *and* a hobby. So I'll get a lot out of it personally. I'll get to see what I think is the most exciting corner of the Australian wine industry up close. Don't get me wrong: we make amazing chardonnay. But if you're looking for where Australian wine is *going*, where people are challenging norms, Mildura is where you'll find those wines.'

Leanne has been impressing people since the beginning of her career. At the age of twenty-one, when she was just starting out in Adelaide, she was awarded the Daniel Pontifex Memorial Award – a travel scholarship established in the late 1990s to honour Daniel, who had died in a car accident while working at Kensington Place Restaurant in London.

'It was the most ridiculous opportunity,' she says. 'They gave you money to learn about wine and restaurants. So, I spent two months driving around France, doing stages in Paris and London.'

Returning to Adelaide, Leanne worked at restaurants like Cibo and The Manse, and the fabulous Barr-Vinum in the Barossa Valley with legendary wine marketer and raconteur, Bob McLean, before doing the Len Evans Scholarship and then starting at Andrew McConnell's Cutler & Co in Melbourne in 2009.

Leanne became interested in alternative varieties – primarily Italian, but also from other warmer regions – because of concerns about climate change.

'It resonated with me that those varieties wouldn't need water in the same way as chardonnay and shiraz,' she says. 'That came from living in the Barossa and noticing changes in flowering and veraison in the vineyards. It made sense that other varieties might work better in certain places. Even Bob McLean, after all his years working with shiraz, was adamant that mataro would be the future of the Barossa in a hotter climate.'

The next step on the road to alternative enlightenment came when Leanne developed the wine program for the opening of Supernormal.

'It wasn't like opening an Italian restaurant, and having Italian wines or Italian style wines on the list. This was an Australian restaurant with pan-Asian ingredients. There's no one reference point. I had to think about what can pair with chili and salt and umami – and all the textures of tofu. Like, what wine goes with tofu? That allowed me to have a bit more freedom with different varieties.'

She also knew that putting these lesser known, more exotic wines on by the glass was a good way to both make the list more interesting and give people a safer way of trying new styles. 'People will take a chance on a glass where they might not be willing to take a risk on a whole bottle. That's why alternative wines can be so exciting for restaurants.'

Over the last decade, Leanne has seen some fundamental shifts in Australians' awareness of certain varieties. She runs the Wine and Spirit Education Trust course for her staff, for example, and recently put on a tasting of pinot gris. All the twenty-somethings she was teaching knew what pinot gris was and had tried it heaps of times before.

'And I said, do you realise that twenty years ago, when I was starting out in hospitality, this was an alternative variety in Australia? And they were like, oh, come on. Which made me feel old.'

She thinks the next grape to go the same way as pinot gris – to become the variety that the *next* generation of hospo professionals thinks has been around forever – is fiano.

'I'm excited about how much the general consumer loves fiano,' she says. 'We are constantly being asked fiano in our venues. We put more on the list all the time. And it's being driven by normal people – not wine geeks – people who want something interesting, but not too challenging.'

There is still plenty of growth left in the alternative variety space, though. And Leanne would like the AAVWS to encourage this by broadening the diversity of the judges who get involved, and the producers who enter.

'I want there to be a currency about the show,' she says. 'I'd love to see a few more dynamic young avant garde producers entering – the ones who aren't necessarily drawn to the show system as a concept. I want them to look at the selection of judges and say, "They're the people I want to be selling my wine to", or "They're the ones who make the wines that I look up to". And seeing someone like me get involved might tempt those producers to enter, because they might see it as an entrée into selling things. I'm definitely going to reach out to the people I'd love to see there.'

top: 2022 stewards at AAVWS including long time stalwarts, Brendan and Kerry Steele third & second from right

bottom: 2022 long lunch, Bruce and Jenni Chalmers and Mark Walpole

When we judges assembled at the footy club, thirty-four glasses were lined up on the table in front of each of us. The wines ranged from a crisp, crunchy, water-white arneis to a dark, rich, fortified gros manseng, and ran the full gamut of thirty other grapes in between; from arinto to viognier, from aglianico to saperavi. We didn't know what the varieties were, or of course the identity of the producers. All we knew was that these thirty-four wines had been selected by the four panels of judges as being outstanding in the first round of judging.

Sophie instructed us to taste the wines from the line-up that were eligible for each trophy. And each judge then selected what they thought was the top wine in that taste-off by pressing a button on the relevant WineShow Pro screen on their laptop – a digital version of the old 'show of hands' method. Sophie watched these votes being cast live on her screen, and once all the votes were in, she told us which of the wines had won the award.

Except that, in at least four cases, the selection was a draw – meaning two or more wines had received equal votes from the judges. And in each of these cases – including

2021 AAVWS judge Ray Nadeson

the taste-off for wine of show – Sophie was required to cast the deciding vote.

'This was a demonstration of the calibre of wines that you judges had picked out,' said Sophie after the show. 'There was one instance where there were equal votes for three different wines. This is unprecedented. Normally in a wine show, one wine gets momentum and races through to win the top trophy. But honestly, we really had to thresh it out here.'

Not that this is a bad thing, said Sophie. In fact, quite the opposite. 'As Bridget said to me afterwards, "You know, I didn't mind which wines won because in each little taste off, the other wines were just as good".'

The wine that eventually made its way through to the top of this maze of taste-offs was the 2021 aglianico from Purple Hands in the Barossa. The grape, it seemed, was finally having its moment. Not only had an aglianico taken out Best of Show at the AAVWS for the first time, but also, the week before, a 2021 example from Hither & Yon in McLaren Vale, had walked away with the top trophy at that region's annual wine show.

It felt like such an appropriate result, too, for the show's twenty-first birthday. When I first met Dr Rod Bonfiglioli – the man remembered in the name of the AAVWS' top award – in 1999, one of the grapes he was particularly enthusiastic about was aglianico. He was certain it had a bright future in Australia. He was right.

On Saturday 5 November, the 2022 AAVWS awards long lunch took place at Willow and Ivie, a light-filled function venue outside town, surrounded by vineyards. It was a perfect Mildura day in late spring. Green and blue and bright in the sun, everyone stepping up to the occasion in bold coloured shirts and floral party dresses, enjoying the opportunity to gather again after years of being apart.

2022 steward carrying glasses at AAVWS judging

The only things missing from this typical Mildura day in November were the purple flowering jacarandas. Normally at this time of year the trees are resplendent in this region: it's one of the things visitors from cooler parts of Australia first notice and then look forward to seeing again when they arrive here. A glimpse of the impending summer, of the season unfurling across the landscape. But by November 2022, the third year of La Niña, the relentless cold and wet weather had set everything back. No jacarandas yet.

In keeping with tradition, a lot of people spoke passionately at lunch over plates of gazpacho and yabby risotto and porchetta. Bruce Chalmers told a story about Rod Bonfiglioli disappearing after a three-day, 5000-kilometre drive around Australia with the head of Rauscedo nursery back in the early days – only to be discovered snoring behind a couch when Bruce was about to sign the deal to import Rauscedo's vines.

Stefano de Pieri talked about Melbourne in the 1980s, when all the things we take for granted today – the dynamic food and wine scene, the proliferation of small bars and relaxed liquor licensing – just didn't exist. And Mark Walpole talked about the chance encounters and decisions that brought the right people together at the right time in the right place to create what became the AAVWS.

'I often sit back and wonder what the vinous landscape in Australia would now be had Alberto and Richard not met on that flight in 1996,' said Mark. 'Or if Rod had kept on working in Darwin, if Bruce had stuck to grafting chardonnay and shiraz, and if Stefano hadn't moved up here from Melbourne. I think our culture is just so much richer from being handed these twists of fate over twenty years ago.' Nothing comes from nothing.

Sophie Otton echoed Mark in her summing up of the show, saying that two decades is how long it takes for meaningful change to happen. When she started working in restaurants, she said, she had to really encourage people to be courageous, to move beyond the usual mainstream wines.

Part Four: 2019–2022

left: Kim Chalmers and Helen Healy at the 2022 awards long lunch

right: 2022 AAVWS judges and associates: James Scarcebrook, Sophie Otton, Courteney Wills, Chris Carpenter, Foni Pollitt, Max Allen, Bridget Raffal, Melissa Moore, Kate McIntyre, Nick Spencer, Sue Bell, Jane Faulkner and Richie O'Donnell

'Now,' she said, 'people are quite comfortable trying new varieties, particularly Australian new varieties, because they're looking for a different experience. It has taken twenty years, but now everyone's chomping at the bit to try something new. And look at the diversity of winemaking styles, too: winemakers have loosened up, they're not trying to make everything classic and perfect. So, the show has done a lot of good, broadening horizons and allowing people to explore without fear.'

And then, before she signed off as chief judge for the last time, Sophie addressed the Mildura locals at the heart of the Australian Alternative Varieties Wine Show – Stefano, Helen, the Chalmers, the winemakers, the judges, the stewards, the sponsors, the consumers who come to the tastings and lunches and dinners every year – with a heartfelt thank you.

'Over the last twenty-one years you have invited and welcomed over 300 judges, writers, sommeliers, winemakers, retailers, restaurateurs to Mildura from across the country,' she said. 'People from all walks of life have been associated with this show. People who otherwise may not have had a reason to be in Mildura, people who might otherwise think this is the middle of nowhere. Instead, these visitors have gone home and shared their impressions and experiences with many others. They have shared stories about the characters and personalities who make this community unique. They have portrayed Mildura not as the middle of nowhere, but as the centre of everywhere.'

We all cheered and applauded and raised our glasses of sangiovese and aglianico and albarino and gruner. And when the lunch was over, we went back to the Grand Hotel for more drinks and more talking and laughing. And, later, as the sun went down and the guitars came out, we started singing.

Afterword

What's next?

Sunrise over the Murray in flood

Thursday 3 November 2022. Just before dawn on the second day of show judging. I can't sleep; buzzing from the sensory and emotional overload of being back in Mildura and being part of the AAVWS again. So, I get up and walk down to the Murray River, over the road from the Grand Hotel and across the railway lines and the park, to watch the sun rise.

The river's the widest I've ever seen: the floodwaters that have been flowing down the Murray Darling system for months now are inundating the country as they pass. The unfathomable, unstoppable, swollen river still has a long way to rise, and months more to travel before it reaches the Murray's mouth in South Australia. Where I'm walking now will soon be underwater.

As the first glimmer of sunlight peeks through the trees on the opposite bank and a magpie calls above, I see a paddle boat moored up ahead. And for a moment, I'm sure I can hear laughter and tinkling glasses, and someone calling out to a bloke in a tinny passing by with a bottle of viognier.

It's like this all week. Ghost visions. Stepping in footprints. Not enough sleep, too much conviviality, all the talk of the past and the future. No wonder I'm delirious.

When I get back to the Grand, I pass reception and walk down the hall. The hotel still looks and feels in many ways like it did when I first came here a quarter century ago. There, on the corner, is Anna's Room, empty today but still holding the memory of that first sangiovese tasting in 1999. It's as if I can see the five of us sitting there still tasting a dozen wines before lunch.

As I walk past the dining room along the corridor, I hear echoes of voices from back then, future predictions delivered through the scent of porcini and primitivo, as Australians across the country queued in scout halls and churches to vote in the Republic Referendum.

Now, in 2022, we're heading towards another referendum, voting yes or no to enshrining an Indigenous Voice to Parliament in the Constitution. It's the first referendum since 1999, and, like the Republic, the results are not certain. I'm writing these words before the referendum is held. By the time you read this book, we may have voted. We are once again at a pivot point in Australian history.

No wonder I'm emotional.

∽

I went to a housewarming party the other day hosted by a couple of younger friends. The party was full of twenty-somethings happily drinking sparkling prosecco from Victoria's King Valley, pinot grigio from the Adelaide Hills, rosé made from sangiovese grown in South Australia's Riverland. I couldn't help but feel a tinge of pride at having played a small part in making these grapes and these wine styles entirely normal. Not alternatives anymore. Just everyday reality.

At moments like these, though, perhaps it's too easy to think like this – to think that our work with the AAVWS is done. That the transformation envisioned back in 1999 has come about. That the show and its extended family of growers and makers and sellers and communicators have indeed changed the course of Australian wine.

The reality is there's still a long way to go.

In late 2022, wine economists Kym Anderson and German Puga from the University of Adelaide published a database looking at two decades of grape variety trends across Australia's wine regions. And they revealed that where the ten most widely planted varieties in 2001 – chardonnay, shiraz, *et al* – accounted for 74 percent of the national vineyard, now, the top ten varieties account for 87 percent of the area under vine.

'True, many vignerons are exploring "alternative" or "emerging" varieties,' they wrote. 'But as yet, they make up less than 4% of the nation's vineyard area, up from 1.8% in 2007.'

In other words, although alternative varieties have more than doubled their presence in Australia in the last fifteen years (sounds impressive, right?), they still account for less than one-twentieth of the industry. What's more, the pace of change has slowed – and had been slowing even before the fires and the floods and the pandemic and the trade wars of the last few years. In fact, most of the growth in this category happened in the first decade of the show's history.

In 1999, for example, the year of the Long Italian Lunch, the *Australian Wine Industry Directory* reported seventy-five different grape varieties grown commercially in this country – with many of those being multi-purpose grapes such as sultana, for bulk wine production. Pinot gris, tempranillo and sangiovese didn't even appear on the official statistics: they were so new and so sparsely planted in Australian vineyards they were lumped together under 'other varieties'.

By 2010, the number of varieties had almost doubled and the number of producers making pinot gris, tempranillo and sangiovese (among many other new varieties) were in their hundreds. But over the following ten years, the number of commercially grown varieties rose by only twenty or thirty; some varieties are made by fewer producers now than they were then, and some are static. Nebbiolo, for example, has been sitting at around one hundred hectares and one hundred producers for at least a decade.

Perhaps it's no surprise, then (although a little disheartening) to read an article in industry journal, *Grapegrower & Winemaker* as recently as mid-2022, discussing how the 'move towards alternatives has also found its way to consumers, whose taste has begun to move ever so slightly away from … Barossa shiraz' – as though this was a recent thing – and how 'some are looking at alternatives as a potential new dawn for the sector', as if it's a new suggestion.

'It begs the question,' the article concluded. 'Is it all just a fad?'

∾

Definitely not! I would say that, of course. Yes, the alternative variety movement may be small. And it may have slowed. But it hasn't *stopped*. It's still very much alive, and it's still very dynamic. It provides depth and colour and richness to what could otherwise be a relatively homogenous Australian wine palette/palate.

What's more, it continues to offer viable and sustainable economic advantages to those who choose to diversify. Many who have taken heed of the show and planted or developed a business based on alternatives, have reaped the rewards during the recent financial difficulties.

'We've all benefited,' says Corrina Wright, current president of the AAVWS committee and champion of alternative varieties. 'We're in a situation right now in the industry where we can't sell our shiraz because there's such an oversupply – but we can sell alternative varieties a thousand times over because demand outstrips supply.'

And despite hearing stories of some warm-climate alternative varieties such as tempranillo and montepulciano suffering through the horrendous rain and flooding and disease pressure of the 2022/23 growing season, in the longer-term, in a warmer drier wine landscape, many of these varieties clearly thrive.

Take 2019, a particularly sun-baked summer in South Australia, when a lot of shiraz and cabernet was affected by the heat in the lead-up to harvest.

'But not the climate change grapes,' winemaker Steve Pannell told me at the time. 'All those Italian and Spanish and Portuguese varieties we planted a few years ago. They're fine. Montepulciano, nero d'avola, tempranillo, fiano, touriga, grenache. Still happy out there in the heat.

This will be the vintage that really shows the wisdom of having those grapes in our vineyards.'

There are many examples, too, of people continuing to push for more alternative varieties and viticultural diversity, continuing the search for The Next Big Thing.

∽

Nick Dry worked at the Yalumba nursery for eleven years before establishing his own business, Foundation Viticulture in 2019. Where the Chalmers were focused very strongly on vines from Italy, he says, Yalumba worked with French nursery ENTAV-INRA to bring in a host of varieties from the southern Rhone and across the Mediterranean – varieties like grenache blanc, carignan, cinsault, and muscardin. They also worked with individual producers to import varieties (Yalumba helped Peter Barry bring in assyrtiko from Santorini, for example).

'On top of that, we looked at the amazing old collection of vines at Best's in Great Western dating back to the

Kim Chalmers and Nick Dry at the AAVWS in 2012

nineteenth century,' says Nick. 'And we were able to access varieties like bourboulenc and picpoul noir.'

Nick has been hired to run a major – and long overdue – project, funded by Wine Australia, called the National Grapevine Collection: a coordinated attempt to assess what varieties and clones are present in the various vine collections across Australia, identify which are in demand by industry, and make them available for use.

The two biggest collections – the CSIRO's at Irymple, near Mildura, and the South Australian Vine Improvement Association's in the Barossa Valley – were closed to industry after the albarino fiasco in 2009. But following an extensive audit of the true identities of what was in the collections – hundreds and hundreds of individual vines and clones of different varieties – both have recently been conditionally re-opened.

Nick's work has been to identify exactly what varieties are in these collections and then approach industry to work out what people would be interested in planting, and how to make that happen. He's also had to bear in mind that every variety will need to be virus tested and cleaned up before being released, a process that costs $5000 per cultivar.

'We've identified about sixty varieties that are either well-known and already in demand, or are less well known have attributes that will be useful in a changing climate,' he says.

The big question, though, is what to do with the other hundreds of varieties that don't appear on anyone's wish-list. Who knows whether, lurking in those collections, there's a vine that no-one has ever heard of or yet considered planting in Australia, but, if it were, would dazzle us with its beauty and its viticultural performance.

As well as making better use of vines already in the country, some people are also continuing to look overseas for varieties that could flourish here.

Afterword

Alex Copper is a viticulturist based in the Clare Valley. Over the last few years, he has been researching drought-tolerant, heat-tolerant varieties grown in Cyprus – varieties that grow in very hot places with no irrigation. As well as studying this topic as part of a PhD – and, more recently, a Nuffield Scholarship – Alex has also imported some cuttings of the varieties, including the island's widest-grown white grape, xynisteri, and planted them in Clare. Now he's also got his sights set on Crete and Turkey, looking for more climate-change adapted grapes.

'It's not about me just making these varieties for research,' Alex told *Grapegrower & Winemaker* in 2022 (echoing the sentiments of Dr Rod Bonfiglioli a quarter century before).

'It's about the long term, giving back to the industry and getting these varieties out into different parts of Australia and seeing how they perform.

It will take a few years, but it's definitely on the cards of what we want to do for the wine industry.'

Alex is also working with another viticulturist, Paul Georgiadis, who grows and makes wine in the Barossa, and has also planted some of Alex's Cypriot vines. Paul's experience with alternative varieties dates to his days working with Penfolds, and the small block of sangiovese planted at Kalimna, along with a host of other unusual grapes, back in the 1980s. He has also worked with winemaker Steve Pannell to import a bunch of Greek grapes, including assyrtiko, agiorgitiko, xinomavro and robola (not all of which made it through the quarantine process, unfortunately). Like Alex, he is also excited about these new arrivals and their potential in a warming climate.

'I went to Cyprus to see what they're like in their homeland,' says Paul. 'We still haven't found the perfect white variety for the Barossa. I think one of these Cypriot grapes – or maybe vidiano from Crete – could be it.'

Watch this space.

~

In a corner of the family vineyard at Merbein, near Mildura, Kim and Tennille Chalmers and Bart van Olphen are also seeing whether it's possible to grow grapes in a hot climate with little to no irrigation. The grapes they've chosen for the trial are the red negroamaro, originally from Puglia, and a white variety, inzolia, originally from western Sicily. And the way they've chosen to grow the grapes – on single stakes, with no under-vine drippers – makes this unlike almost every other vineyard in this huge region.

I'm walking through the vineyard in early March, in the middle of harvest, with Bart and Kim and Tennille, and dad Bruce. The sun glares down from a cloudless sky, radiating off the bright red sand underfoot. I reach into the dark green canopy of leaves and pluck a big fat bunch of golden inzolia grapes. They're utterly delicious. My teeth chew on the thick skins and firm pulp, full of spicy, almost marmalade-like flavours. The sweet juice runs down my chin.

During the last growing season, a total of 48 millimetres of irrigation water – half a megalitre per hectare – was sprayed on the vines from overhead sprinklers to mimic rain events. And only around 200 millimetres of actual rain fell from the sky. Conventional vineyards in this part of Australia, where annual rainfall is less than 300 millimetres, usually need an extra 600 millimetres or so of irrigation; six megalitres of water per hectare; pumped from the Murray River, to produce a commercial crop. Even in Sicily and Puglia, where inzolia and negroamaro are grown without irrigation, annual rainfall is 450 and 600 millimetres respectively.

Inzolia bush vines in Merbein

The idea that you could grow these vines successfully in Merbein – where it is much more arid than southern Italy – with little-to-no supplementary water is preposterous. And yet, here they are: five-year-old bush vines thriving on 300 to 400 millimetres of water a year, throwing healthy canopies, pumping out up to eight tonnes to the hectare of fruit.

Bruce Chalmers can't believe what he's seeing – and they're his vines.

'It's stunned us,' he says as we walk through the vines. 'Just look at the lignification in those canes. Look how the trunks are coming along. And taste those grapes! It's ridiculous.'

I ask the Chalmers whether in some years they could potentially get down to zero irrigation, effectively dry-growing vines in a desert – something the viticultural textbooks and professors at wine school tell you isn't possible.

'Yes!' says Kim. 'That's the idea. We're pushing the limit.'

'We think this is a super special example for the region,' says Tennille. 'Yes, you have bush vines growing in McLaren Vale, bush vines in the Barossa. But we are *way* hotter than even those regions – which are already hot. We're proving a point that you perhaps can do that here, too.'

Bart says that, for most people in the wine industry – and for the wine trade and consumers – inland irrigated regions like the Murray Darling, where Merbein is located, are only considered to be a source of cheap, large-volume commercial wine. They're considered incapable of making wines of the quality – and with the kind of price tags – you find in 'proper', 'fine-wine', cooler-climate regions.

'When I moved here [to the Murray Darling, in 2011] other people in the industry told me, "Oh, that's the end of your winemaking career" because the region was so tarnished,' he says. 'Except for one senior winemaker, who told me, "That's rubbish. You can make quality anywhere. It's just about doing the viticulture right". And now, years later, you look at these bush vine wines and think, it's true, you can make quality anywhere.'

༄

After we've inspected the bush vines, we head back to the winery to taste this year's inzolia and negroamaro, still fermenting. And then to the nursery, where the Chalmers want to show me their latest varietal imports.

We walk into a big shed, where a dozen or so vines in pots are sitting on a table. Each one is a different variety or a different clone of the same variety. Moschofilero from Greece. Cornalin from the Val d'Aosta (no, I'd never heard of it either). And two clones – two vines in pots – of nerello mascalese from the slopes of Mount Etna.

Of all the Italian red grapes not yet available in Australia, nerello has been the most desired – the most potentially exciting. At least it feels that way. And the fact it's taken the Chalmers so long to source the material has only deepened the desire.

Nerello is an old variety that grows in sometimes incredibly stony, rubbly ground on the slopes of the still-active volcano. Like pinot noir or nebbiolo, it has an incredibly capacity for expressing subtle differences of terroir, producing wine of immense complexity and concentration – and, like nebbiolo, tannin – while still being light on its feet, almost translucent.

'For ten years we've been trying to track down a source of nerello mascalese that isn't riddled with every virus under the sun,' says Kim. 'And one that is DNA-proven to be true nerello. We went through multiple avenues, through nurseries, universities. And finally, we found Giuseppe Russo.'

Giuseppe is a client of viticultural consultant, Stefano Dini, who has been a judge and Talk and Taste presenter at the AAVWS. The Chalmers visited Giuseppe on Etna, and he agreed to provide cuttings from two nerello plants in his collection.

'Giuseppe just was really into the idea of nerello being international,' says Kim. 'Some Italians don't want anyone else to have it, but he said, "No, I want to you know how it goes in Australia". He wasn't worried. As he said, "It won't make an Etna wine. So, what's the problem?"'

It's exciting, seeing these baby vines in pots like this. To think that one day, if nerello does as well as winemakers hope, and it takes off, and is planted in lots of different places and produces a whole new wave of exciting Australian wines, it all began here, with just one or two fragile-looking plants. Just as all the nero and fiano and vermentino – and pinot grigio and prosecco – now planted in this country started out like this, propagated from one or two cuttings, mother vines planted in a pot.

Nerello mascalese growing in a pot at Chalmers nursery

Glossary

An Alternative A–Z

The grapes, explained
From aglianico to zweigelt

This is a guide to alternative grape varieties planted across Australia in 2023.

Not that long ago, non-mainstream varieties were often placed a couple of rungs down a grapevine hierarchy below 'classic' varieties such as chardonnay and cabernet (from 'noble' French regions). Grapes like viognier and tempranillo were sometimes dubbed as 'second tier' varieties, and 'lesser' varieties such as trebbiano and carignan – from the kind of warm climate regions that wine snobs looked down on – were relegated to the bottom of the pile.

This list doesn't follow that pattern because today's wine market is a much more diverse and dynamic place. Increasingly, consumers no longer see the world in terms of 'classic' regions and 'lesser' regions, or first and second tier grapes. What they care about is whether the wine is delicious. Sure, some grape varieties are inherently better than others, with the potential to produce more complex, characterful, delicious wines. But let's face it, in some regions even a so-called 'classic' grape such as chardonnay will produce decidedly 'lesser' wine – while in that same region a so-called 'lesser' variety can produce 'classic' wines.

As you go through the list, you'll see some apparent anomalies. There are a few varieties here that look to be widely enough grown and are made by enough producers to surely warrant graduation into the mainstream; to join pinot gris and prosecco as 'former alternatives'. Red varieties such as durif and petit verdot, for example, were still considered eligible for entry in the Australian Alternative Varieties Wine Show (AAVWS) in 2022. But more tonnes of both varieties are crushed each year than grenache, which is considered mainstream and is *not* eligible for the show. Similarly, chenin blanc is *not* included here as it is considered mainstream by the AAVWS, but viognier – with more hectares planted, more tonnes crushed and more producers making it – *is* still in the alternative camp.

In most cases, there is a good reason why the grape is still considered eligible to enter the show, and that reason is given in the text. But it's a topic of constant, often vigorous debate among the AAVWS committee. By the time you read this book, some of these anomalies may have been ironed out, and a couple more varieties may have crossed over into the mainstream.

Each entry on the first, more detailed list has a **picture** of the variety, tells you **where** in the world it is originally from and roughly **how long** it has been grown and made commercially in Australia. There's also some **information about the grape**, such as **what flavours** you can expect to find in the wines it makes. If the grape has a common **synonym** or synonyms (e.g., pinot gris, which can be – and often is – labelled 'pinot grigio'), those names are listed, too.

There is an indication of roughly **how many hectares** of each variety are planted across the country. This is an approximate round figure (e.g., 'around 200 hectares', or 'less than 10 hectares') because it's hard to obtain accurate information. South Australia does collect this data, for example, but it doesn't publish varieties where fewer than three growers exist in one region. Worse, there is no *national* vineyard register. And although Wine Australia records how many tonnes of most varieties are crushed each year, quite a few are reported as 'other white' and 'other red', and the survey is not compulsory, so it doesn't paint the complete picture. The non-response rate is also estimated to be around ten percent nationally – higher for smaller varieties from smaller producers (i.e., the ones likely to be the more obscure grapes). And even allowing for non-response rates, it's hard to extrapolate from tonnes back into hectares because yields vary so widely from warmer to cooler regions and from season to season.

There is also an indication of **how many producers** of each variety there are, compiled from a few sources such as the annual *Wine Industry Directory*, and records of who has entered the AAVWS. Again, with a couple of precise exceptions, these are rough figures rounded to the nearest five or ten – educated guesstimates – as it's hard, too, to keep track of exactly how many producers are making wine from each variety.

As rough as they are, these stats are included to give you an idea of how widespread each variety is and where it sits in a broader industry context. Take aglianico, for example. It might be attracting a lot of attention thanks to its success in wine shows (not just the AAVWS) in 2022. But with around twenty-five producers and less than 50 hectares planted, it has a long way to go to catch up with tempranillo's 500-ish hectares and 300 producers.

And finally, after the description of most of the grapes, there's a list of **producers** who have been awarded gold medals or trophies at the AAVWS over the last five years with wines made from that variety (or in some cases wines in which that variety is the primary grape in a blend). The **region** in brackets after each producer or brand name is the geographical indication (GI) where the grapes for that wine were grown. Where a variety has no producers listed at the end of its entry, it has not recently been – or is yet to be – awarded a gold or trophy in the show; but it is included in this main list rather than the less detailed list that follows it because of its former or potential future importance.

Red grape varieties are listed in red, **white** grape varieties in green. Where a variety is pink-skinned or purple/grey skinned (e.g., pinot gris), it has been listed with the colour of the wine most associated with that variety (so: **pinot gris**).

Aglianico

Origin: southern Italy
Grown here since: the 2000s
Area planted: less than 50 ha
Number of producers: 25

In its home in Campania and Basilicata, this long-established variety can produce complex, fragrant, age-worthy red wines with firm tannins. It has proven to be a grape well-suited to warmer sites in Australia, from the Riverina to McLaren Vale, but also does surprisingly well in cooler, higher-altitude spots like Beechworth. The grape was once thought to have come from Greece – 'aglianico' does sound a lot like 'hellenico' – but grapevine specialists dispute this theory. (image: Chalmers)

———

Chalmers (Heathcote), Fighting Gully Road (Beechworth), Izway (Barossa Valley), Prometheus (Riverland), Purple Hands/After Five Wine Co (Barossa Valley), Ricca Terra (Riverland), SC Pannell (McLaren Vale).

Albarino / Alvarinho

Origin: Portugal and Spain
Grown here since: the 2010s
Area planted: less than 25 ha
Number of producers: 20

This Iberian variety became trendy in the early 2000s thanks to its ability to make deliciously fruity, citrussy, grape-pulpy – and very seafood-friendly – whites in warm maritime regions like Galicia. As a result, quite a few Australian growers and makers sought out cuttings and planted them – and then discovered, in 2009, that the vines they'd planted were in fact the (then) decidedly un-trendy savagnin. After the shock wore off, more growers sought out cuttings of real albarino, planted them, and are now making some convincing, seafood-friendly whites. (image: PlantGrape)

———

Artwine (Adelaide Hills), Dalfarras (Nagambie Lakes), Pikes (Clare Valley), Stanton & Killeen (Rutherglen).

Arinto

Origin: Portugal
Grown here since: the 2010s
Area planted: less than 5 ha
Number of producers: 5

This newcomer to the Australian viticultural scene is traditionally grown across Portugal's regions, where it is found lending its nervy, crisp characters to seafood-whites like vinho verde. The vine's drought tolerance, late ripening and high acidity make it particularly well-suited to warmer sites in Australia, and early examples of wine made from it – dry, crisp, lean, refreshing – are promising. (image: Wine Australia)

———

Lino Ramble (McLaren Vale), Ricca Terra (Riverland).

Arneis

Origin: Piemonte, NW Italy
Grown here since: the 1990s
Area planted: less than 50 ha
Number of producers: 40

This grape can produce beautifully aromatic but dry and savoury white wines, with hints of ripe pear perfume, and an almost pear-like textural quality. It's difficult to grow, though – its name translates as 'little rascal' – which saw the vine almost disappear from Piemontese vineyards in the 1970s. Thankfully, a couple of visionary winemakers persisted, and their wines inspired a handful of Australian growers to plant it. (image: Chalmers)

Dhiaga (Mornington Peninsula), Nepenthe (Adelaide Hills), Rutherglen Estate (Rutherglen), Sam Miranda (King Valley), Symphonia (King Valley).

Assyrtiko

Origin: Santorini, Greece
Grown here since: the 2010s
Area planted: less than 20 ha
Number of producers: 1

Assyrtiko is a drought-and-heat-tolerant white grape vine traditionally grown as basket-like bushes, trained low to the stony, volcanic ground on Santorini. Despite the lack of rainfall and constant winds on the island, assyrtiko typically makes mineral-rich dry white wines notable for their high acidity and low pH but full body and robust alcohol (14 percent is not uncommon). Peter Barry of Jim Barry wines in Clare imported the first cuttings of assyrtiko in the late 2000s and is still the only (very good) producer. (image: Jim Barry Wines)

Jim Barry (Clare Valley).

Barbera

Origin: Piemonte, NW Italy
Grown here since: the 1970s
Area planted: less than 100 ha
Number of producers: 90

While that other Piemontese red grape, nebbiolo, attracts all the wine-geek attention, barbera is more widely planted in its homeland because it produces red wines that have a deeper purple colour, more generous berry fruit, softer tannin, but a lip-smacking acidity crying out for food. Along with nebbiolo and sangiovese, barbera was first made in Australia by Italian winemaker Carlo Corino in the 1970s but didn't gain a wider presence until the 1990s. (image: Chalmers)

Angullong (Orange), Billy Button (Alpine Valleys), Coulter (Adelaide Hills), First Drop (Adelaide Hills), First Ridge (Mudgee), Longview (Adelaide Hills), Michelini (Alpine Valleys), Serafino (McLaren Vale), The Other Wine Co. (Adelaide Hills).

Bastardo / Trousseau

Origin: Jura
Grown here since: the 1800s
Area planted: less than 5 ha
Number of producers: 5

This red variety is super trendy at the moment thanks to the popularity of wines from the Jura in eastern France, including the savoury, earthy reds made from this grape. It has been grown in Australia for a long time (called bastardo) as a minor variety used in port production, but a small number of producers are also using it (and calling it by its trendier name, trousseau) to make Jura-inspired reds. Also known as maturana tinta and made under this name by Saradon in the Adelaide Hills. (image: CSIRO)

Cabernet Franc

Origin: Bordeaux, France
Grown here since: the 1800s
Area planted: around 200 ha
Number of producers: 230

It feels odd to include this established Bordeaux variety in a list of 'alternative grapes' because of its long association with cabernet sauvignon and merlot as a blending component. Although it is widely grown and used by many Australian producers in precisely that way, it qualifies for 'emerging status' because only a small (although growing) number of makers bottle it as a varietal wine, or in blends where it is the dominant variety. At its best, it expresses gorgeous pure blackcurrant fruit, vibrant herbal hints and elegant, fine, snappy tannins. (image: PlantGrape)

Artwine (Clare Valley), Bleasdale (Langhorne Creek), Surveyors Hill (Canberra District), Tamburlaine (Orange).

Carignan

Origin: Spain
Grown here since: the 1800s
Area planted: around 10 ha
Number of producers: 25

Carignan has a confused history in Australia. Vines *called* carignan (or variations on that spelling – e.g., 'carignane') have been grown here since the nineteenth century but most have subsequently been identified as other varieties – bonvedro, for example, or mourvedre. Some of those older plantings may indeed be the real thing, but carignan that is *definitely* carignan (i.e., DNA tested) is a relatively recent arrival, and is showing promise, making robust, earthy reds in warm, dry regions. (image: PlantGrape)

Carmenere

Origin: Bordeaux, France
Grown here since: the 2000s
Area planted: less than 50 ha
Number of producers: 15

Common in Bordeaux vineyards before phylloxera in the nineteenth century, now a very minor variety there, but still widely grown in Chile, where it was misidentified as merlot until the 1990s. Carmenere makes wines with similar blackcurrant fruit characters you find in cabernet sauvignon, sometimes even more pronounced, but with softer tannins. Given the widespread planting and popularity of other Bordeaux varieties in Australia, we may see more appearing here. (image: PlantGrape)

_____

McGuigan (Murray Darling).

Cinsaut

Origin: southern France
Grown here since: the 1800s
Area planted: less than 10 ha
Number of producers: 30

Historically important grape in Australia, where it has been grown in warm regions such as Rutherglen and the Barossa under many different names such as **blue imperial** and used in fortified wines since the nineteenth century. A new generation of winemakers is beginning to value the fact that it thrives in hot, dry conditions and brings a perfume and freshness to a wine, especially blended with grenache and mourvedre, as well as making a deliciously crunchy, pale red wine on its own. (image: CSIRO)

_____

Corvina

Origin: Veneto, NE Italy
Grown here since: the 2000s
Area planted: less than 5 ha
Number of producers: 5

This variety – and its regional stablemate rondinella – come from the Veneto where they are used to make the red wines of Valpolicella, from lighter, cherry-scented, tart, quaffing reds to the super intense, chewy Amarone styles, made from partially-dried grapes. Grown here by only a couple of people – notably Brian Freeman, whose wines have done well in the AAVWS over the years. Has potential and it would be good to see more planted. (image: CSIRO)

_____

Dolcetto

Origin: Piemonte, NW Italy
Grown here since: the 1800s
Area planted: less than 150 ha
Number of producers: 30

The name translates literally as 'little sweet' grape, but most producers, both in its homeland of Piemonte and here in Australia produce a dry wine from it – sweetly fruited, yes (think black cherry juice) but also with nice, medium-weight fleshy characters, juicy acidity, and fine tannins. Grown in historic old vineyards such as Best's in Great Western, Victoria, since the nineteenth century, and misidentified as malbec until the 1970s. (image: Chalmers)

————

Billy Button (Great Western), Vineyard 28 (Geographe).

Durif / Petite Sirah

Origin: Montpellier, France
Grown here since: early 1900s
Area planted: less than 1500 ha
Number of producers: 90

Originally bred by botanist Dr Francois Durif in France in the mid-nineteenth century, durif was brought to Australia by viticulturist Francois de Castella in the early twentieth century. Long a feature of Rutherglen's vineyards, where it famously produced deep, dark, tannic red wines, full-bodied and grunty, that needed years in the bottle to soften, the grape has been widely planted in more recent decades to make both varietal wines and, increasingly, to provide colour and backbone in blends. Its long history and widespread acceptance arguably challenge its status as an 'alternative' variety. (image: CSIRO)

————

Atze's Corner (Barossa Valley), Billy Button (Alpine Valleys), Calabria (Riverina), Nugan (Riverina), Stanton & Killeen (Rutherglen), Tenafeate Creek (Mount Lofty Ranges).

Falanghina

Origin: southern Italy
Grown here since: the 2010s
Area planted: less than 5 ha
Number of producers: 1

Old variety from the ancient winegrowing country around Naples; produces a savoury dry white with good herbal fragrance, also useful to add complexity in a blend. Newly arrived in Australia, still rare here, and may not become as popular as fiano, but certainly has quality potential, as the recent gold medal in the AAVWS demonstrates. (image: Chalmers)

————

Chalmers (Heathcote).

Fiano

Origin: Campania, southern Italy
Grown here since: mid-2000s
Area planted: less than 300 ha
Number of producers: 100

The most commercially successful of the southern Italian white varieties adopted by Australian growers over the last two decades, fiano combines the bold fruity aromatics of, say, viognier – without being too over-the-top or cloying – with the fuller body of, say, chardonnay. At this rate, given the area planted, the number of producers (just look below at how successful it has been at the AAVWS) and broad consumer acceptance, fiano is on the cusp of becoming mainstream. (image: Chalmers)

Alex Russell / Alejandro (South Australia), Artwine (Clare Valley), Berton (Riverina), Briar Ridge (Hunter Valley), Chalmers (Heathcote), Cradle of Hills (McLaren Vale), Feathertop (King Valley), Gibson / Discovery Road (Murray Darling), Green Door (Geographe), Hesketh (Clare Valley), Hungerford Hill (Hunter Valley), Oliver's Taranga (McLaren Vale), Pikes (Clare Valley), Pinnacle Drinks / Infamous Dodger (Australia), Ox Hardy (McLaren Vale), SC Pannell (McLaren Vale), Sherrah (McLaren Vale), Sutton Grange (Bendigo), Tellurian (Heathcote), Vigna Bottin (McLaren Vale), Zerella (McLaren Vale).

Friulano

Origin: southwest France
Grown here since: the 2000s
Area planted: less than 5 ha
Number of producers: 10

You would think that a grape called friulano (or tocai friulano as it used to be known), grown in Friuli, would be an old Friulian variety. But you'd be wrong: ampelographers have shown that its origins lie in southwest France, where it's known as sauvignonasse (although it is no relation to sauvignon blanc). Either way, it produces a beautifully fragrant, savoury, richly textured whites, both in Friuli and, increasingly, in Australia, both as a varietal wine and in blends. (image: Quealy)

Billy Button (Alpine Valleys), MDI Wines (Murray Darling), Quealy (Mornington Peninsula).

Gamay

Origin: Beaujolais, France
Grown here since: the 1970s
Area planted: around 10 ha
Number of producers: 35

Very old grape originally planted in Burgundy – where, famously, it was banned in the Middle Ages – now best known as the red grape of Beaujolais, but also grown elsewhere in France, e.g., the Loire Valley, where it makes deliciously fruity, fresh reds. Has never taken off to the extent that you would expect in Australia – perhaps seen as second-fiddle to pinot noir – but is being embraced by a new, younger generation of winemakers. (image: DPIRD)

XO Wine Co. (Adelaide Hills).

Garganega

Origin: Veneto, NE Italy
Grown here since: the 2000s
Area planted: less than 5 ha
Number of producers: 5

Historically important white variety responsible for the dry and sweet (recioto) white wines of Soave in the Veneto, that combine both delicate aromatics and a textural grape-pulpy quality, as well as an ability to age in the bottle in the top examples. First made in Australia at Domain Day in the Barossa and although now grown by only a couple of producers in Australia, it has good potential to spread further. Also known as **grecanico** in Sicily and sold under this name by Politini in the King Valley. (image: Chalmers)

Gewurztraminer

Origin: Alsace, France
Grown here since: the 1800s
Area planted: around 1000 ha
Number of producers: 100

When fully ripe, gewurz – like pinot gris – is more of a pink-skinned variety than a white grape, but the wines it produces are almost always white as they are made only from the juice. A very aromatic grape, with distinctive smells of roses and lychee and spice, and a notably rich, almost oily texture, it has enjoyed huge commercial success in Australia in the past – usually in a blend, to make sweetish cheaper whites – and is still grown by some dedicated producers in cooler regions. (image: CSIRO)

Alex Russell / Son of a Bull (Tasmania), Black & Ginger (Henty), Cherubino (Pemberton), Dhiaga (Henty), Henschke (Adelaide Hills), Pike and Joyce (Adelaide Hills) Ros Ritchie (Upper Goulburn), Symphony Hill (New England Australia).

Graciano

Origin: Rioja, Spain
Grown here since: the 1990s
Area planted: less than 50 ha
Number of producers: 50

This intensely flavoured, deeply coloured red grape is best known as a minor blending partner for tempranillo and grenache in the red wines of Rioja but is also grown in other Mediterranean countries. In Australia it is often found in vineyards of producers inspired by the red wines of Spain, growing alongside – and blended with – tempranillo et al. in red and pink wines – but also finding its way into bottle as a varietal wine. (image: Chalmers)

———————

Paxton (McLaren Vale), Samuel's Gorge (McLaren Vale).

Greco

Origin: Campania, Italy
Grown here since: the 2000s
Area planted: less than 5 ha
Number of producers: 10

Of the three white grapes originally from Campania in southern Italy currently grown in Australia (the other two being fiano and falanghina), greco produces wines with the most robust, savoury character and minerality. It appears mostly in blends with other white grapes, but single varietal wines can be very successful if there's plenty of ripe fruit to match the firmness of structure. Has great potential. (image: Chalmers)

———————

Grenache Blanc (and Grenache Gris)

Origin: Spain
Grown here since: the 2000s
Area planted: less than 10 ha
Number of producers: 10

These two varieties are colour mutations of the well-known red grenache grape – blanc being white-skinned, gris being pink-skinned – and are found mostly in southern France, blended with other regional white grapes such as marsanne, viognier, bourboulenc and clairette to produce rich, textural wines. Australian winemakers inspired by these blends have planted both varieties, although there's a little more blanc than gris in the ground at this stage. (image: Nick Dry)

———————

Dune (McLaren Vale), Yangarra (McLaren Vale).

Gros Manseng (formerly Petit Manseng)

Origin: Jurancon, SW France
Grown here since: the 1990s
Area planted: less than 5 ha
Number of producers: 15

Yet another example of a misidentified variety: until the turn of the millennium, the handful of Australians growing this grape thought they had the (more highly thought-of) petit manseng in their vineyards, until ampelographic examination revealed it was in fact the more common gros manseng. Either way, as in its homeland, this full-flavoured grape makes excellent, honeyed sweet white wine, either late-harvested and bottled early, or fortified and aged. (image: PlantGrape)

Gapsted (Alpine Valleys), Symphonia (King Valley), Whistling Kite (Riverland).

Gruner Veltliner

Origin: Austria
Grown here since: the 2000s
Area planted: less than 50 ha
Number of producers: 45

The great white grape of Austria has been grown in Australia for just under two decades and has established itself as one of the top alternatives for growers in cool, higher altitude regions. Stylistically, white wines made from gruner sit somewhere between the crisp, aromatic freshness of riesling, especially when young – with a distinctive pepper-spice perfume – and the fuller body, complexity, and age-worthiness of fine chardonnay. (image: Hahndorf Hill)

Artwine (Adelaide Hills), Chain of Ponds (Adelaide Hills), Hahndorf Hill (Adelaide Hills), Linear (Tumbarumba), Longview (Adelaide Hills), Nepenthe (Adelaide Hills), Pike & Joyce (Adelaide Hills), Stage Door Wine Co. (Eden Valley), The Pawn (Adelaide Hills).

Kerner

Origin: Germany
Grown here since: the 1980s
Area planted: less than 5 ha
Number of producers: 2

Although this German grape is grown by only a couple of producers in Australia, it has been such a consistently strong performer at the AAVWS (Robinvale Wines have won no fewer than five trophies over the years for theirs) it deserves an extended mention here. Bred in the 1920s by crossing the red trollinger and white riesling varieties, it has the latter grape's perfume and, despite having lower acidity, has (at least in the case of Robinvale's biodynamically grown example) a freakish ability to age gracefully in bottle. (image: Wines of Germany)

Lagrein

Origin: Trentino, Italy
Grown here since: the 1990s
Area planted: less than 20 ha
Number of producers: 40

Thanks in part to the early success of a pioneering Australian lagrein from Cobaw Ridge (winner of Best Red at the 2000 Australian Italian Wine Awards, the precursor to the AAVWS), this variety from northern Italy has been planted by quite a few growers, who do a good job of capturing its dark cherry fruit and snappy tannins – qualities that make it a useful component of a blend, bringing verve to less energetic varieties. (image: Chalmers)

Bremerton (Langhorne Creek), Samu (Riverland), Wangolina (Limestone Coast), Wines by Geoff Hardy (Limestone Coast).

Lambrusco Maestri

Origin: Emilia, central Italy
Grown here since: the 2000s
Area planted: around 1000 ha
Number of producers: 10

Maestri comes from Emilia-Romagna, where it's one of the varieties responsible for that region's famous sparkling red wine, also known as lambrusco. The more highly-regarded lambrusco salomino variety has also been imported to Australia but maestri is the one that has taken off, partly thanks to its very deep purple colour and bold, full flavour. Indeed, the vast majority of the maestri grown here finds its way into blends as a very minor – but important – component thanks to that deep, saturated colour. (image: Chalmers)

Chalmers (Murray Darling), Countertop (Swan Hill).

Marsanne

Origin: Rhone Valley, France
Grown here since: the 1800s
Area planted: around 150 ha
Number of producers: 70

This white grape has been grown in Australia since the nineteenth century, when it was often described as 'white hermitage', a nod to its origins in the northern Rhone Valley. Produces aromatic, honeysuckle-scented white wine with some richness, especially when blended with other Rhone grapes such as roussanne and viognier, and when allowed to mature in the bottle: Tahbilk's marsannes are legendary for their ability to improve and age over decades. (image: PlantGrape)

Barwon Ridge (Geelong), Rutherglen Estate (Rutherglen), Tahbilk (Nagambie Lakes).

Malbec

Origin: France
Grown here since: the 1800s
Area planted: less than 750 ha
Number of producers: 200

Originally from southwest France but increasingly associated with Argentina – where it is widely grown and makes particularly bold red wine – malbec also has a long history in Australia. In old regions such as Langhorne Creek and the Clare Valley, malbec's intense perfume and firm structure have long lent complexity to red blends with shiraz and/or cabernet, and much of the now relatively large annual harvest of the variety is used this way. As a varietal wine, it is also particularly well-suited to the Frankland River subregion in WA's Great Southern. (image: Chalmers)

Bleasdale (Langhorne Creek), Bremerton (Langhorne Creek), Cellarmaster / Hutt River (Clare Valley), Ferngrove (Frankland River), Hither & Yon (McLaren Vale), Jim Barry / Expressions by Tom Barry (Clare Valley), Loom (McLaren Vale), Pinnacle Drinks / The Ethereal One (Fleurieu), Tamburlaine (Orange), Taylors (Limestone Coast/Clare Valley), Water Wheel (Bendigo).

Mencía / Jaen

Origin: Bierzo, NW Spain
Grown here since: the 2010s
Area planted: less than 10 ha
Number of producers: 20

Really exciting addition to the list of Iberian varieties now grown in Australia. Originally from Bierzo, in Spain's northwest, the grape produces red wines that, stylistically, have some of the spice of shiraz, the pure black fruit of cabernet franc, and the fine but grippy tannins of tempranillo. It seems to have adapted well to Australian conditions, in places as far-flung as McLaren Vale in South Australia and Frankland River in WA. (image: Oliver's Taranga)

Cherubino (Frankland River), Oliver's Taranga (McLaren Vale.)

Mondeuse

Origin: Savoie, eastern France
Grown here since: early 1900s
Area planted: less than 5 ha
Number of producers: 10

This French red is found in the Savoie region of eastern France, near the Swiss border (and in some vineyards over the border) and was brought to Australia in the early twentieth century by Victorian viticulturist Francois de Castella and has been blended with shiraz and cabernet by Brown Brothers since the 1950s. Now a handful of other producers, mostly in cooler climates, are also making aromatic, tannic red wine from it. (image: PlantGrape)

Mount Majura (Canberra District).

Montepulciano

Origin: central Italy
Grown here since: the 2000s
Area planted: around 100 ha
Number of producers: 85

Widely grown across central Italy and valued for its ability to produce good, flavoursome red wine even at high yields. Its ability to do this in relatively warm dry conditions explains why a growing number of Australian producers have planted it in their vineyards and are making deep-coloured, black-fruited, approachable red wines from it. (image: Chalmers)

Banrock Station (Riverland), Calabria (Riverina), Coriole (McLaren Vale), Chalk Hill (McLaren Vale), Delinquente (Riverland), Fourth Wave / Little Giant (Barossa Valley), Lonely Vineyard (Eden Valley), McGuigan (Murray Darling), Pinnacle Drinks / Old Fat Unicorn (South Australia), Prometheus (Riverland), SC Pannell (Langhorne Creek).

Moscato Giallo

Origin: northern Italy
Grown here since: the 2000s
Area planted: around 250 ha
Number of producers: 10

As the name suggests, the berries of this variety – one of many variations of the famously promiscuous muscat grape – are a particularly vibrant yellow (giallo in Italian). In its homeland it is often used to make sweet wine, but also contributes rich and distinctive muscat perfume to dry whites, blended judiciously with other varieties, as in Stefano de Pieri's gold medal-winning Claudia Amphora, a mash-up of malvasia istriana, moscato giallo and picolit. (image: Chalmers)

Mourvedre / Mataro / Monastrell

Origin: Spain
Grown here since: the 1800s
Area planted: less than 750 ha
Number of producers: 200

Like grenache, this old Mediterranean red grape has seen a revival of fortune over the last couple of decades, as Australian winemakers have realised the potential of the old mataro vines that have for decades been used a source of fruit for cheap blends and 'port'. Treated with love, with yields kept low, the grape can produce fabulously wild, characterful, deep, and robust red wine. As with durif and malbec, the stats show that there is quite a lot of mourvedre grown in Australia, although much of it is still going into blends. (image: CSIRO)

Bondar (McLaren Vale), Cellarmaster / Cat Among the Pigeons (Barossa Valley), Chapel Hill (McLaren Vale), Golden Grove (Granite Belt), Purple Hands (Barossa Valley), Reillys (Clare Valley), Seppeltsfield (Barossa Valley), Shingleback (McLaren Vale), Yangarra (McLaren Vale).

Muscadelle

Origin: SW France
Grown here since: the 1800s
Area planted: less than 100 ha
Number of producers: 15

Originally from Bordeaux, where it is a minor component in dry and sweet white wines, muscadelle has been grown in Australia for over 150 years to make a classic luscious, fortified wine, once known as 'tokay', now called 'topaque'. The best Rutherglen Grand and Rare topaques – dark, treacly, impossibly complex treasures – are such classic wines, and so well-established that it seems odd to consider muscadelle an 'alternative', but the fact is there are only 150 hectares and around fifteen producers – much less than many other emerging varieties listed here. (image: PlantGrape)

Morris, Stanton & Killeen (both Rutherglen).

Nebbiolo

Origin: Piemonte, NW Italy
Grown here since: the 1980s
Area planted: less than 100 ha
Number of producers: 120

The famous red grape of Piemonte, responsible for the beautiful, long-lived, tannic but elegant wines of Barolo and Barbaresco, whose name evokes the nebbia, or fog that fills the steep-sided valleys. The fact that, after more than thirty years of being grown, made and enjoyed in Australia, there are still only around 120 committed producers, shows how difficult it is to grow and make well: the variety's elusive perfume and super savoury tannins can be hard to coax into a harmonious wine. (image: Chalmers)

Arrivo (Adelaide Hills), Billy Button (Alpine Valleys), De Bortoli (Yarra Valley), Longview (Adelaide Hills), Pike & Joyce (Adelaide Hills), Protero (Adelaide Hills), Ringer Reef (Alpine Valleys), Saffron Gramophone (North East Victoria), Serafino (McLaren Vale), Symphony Hill (New England Australia), Tar & Roses (Heathcote), Vineyard 28 (Geographe).

Negroamaro

Origin: Puglia, southern Italy
Grown here since: the 2000s
Area planted: less than 10 ha
Number of producers: 10

The name means 'bitter black', which gives you an idea of the astringent, slightly chewy tannins in the grape, but, grown in an appropriately warm climate and with yields kept in check, those grainy, dusty tannins can be balanced by good round fruit and a distinctive warm, woody-spice character. (image: Chalmers)

Jacobs Creek (Barossa Valley).

Glossary   219

Nero d'Avola

Origin: Sicily
Grown here since: the 2000s
Area planted: around 100 ha
Number of producers: 70

Of all the southern Italian red grapes introduced to Australia in the last two decades this is the one that has been most successful, thanks to its eagerness in the vineyard (even in hot dry climates it grows vigorously and produces large crops) and its ability to produce dark coloured, fleshy, bold, approachable red wines. (image: Chalmers)

Calabria (Riverina), Chalmers (Murray Darling), Coriole (McLaren Vale), Dalfarras (Central Victoria), Kangarilla Road / Silent Noise (McLaren Vale), Kirrihill (McLaren Vale), Pietro (Currency Creek), Ricca Terra (Riverland), SC Pannell (McLaren Vale), Seppeltsfield (Barossa Valley), Sherrah (McLaren Vale), Wacky Grape Wine Co. / Papier Mache (Riverland), Zerella (McLaren Vale).

Pecorino

Origin: central Italy
Grown here since: the 2010s
Area planted: less than 5 ha
Number of producers: 10

Although it shares a name with a sheep's milk cheese, this pecorino is in fact a white grape from Marche in central Italy that produces wines with good fragrant freshness and crisp, even tangy acidity. It is being adopted here by a small but fast-growing number of producers who like to make and sell this style of wine; definitely one to watch. (image: Chalmers)

Petit Verdot

Origin: Bordeaux, France
Grown here since: the 1800s
Area planted: less than 1000 ha
Number of producers: 180

In its Bordeaux homeland, this is a minor grape because it's late-ripening and struggles in cooler vintages. But when it does get fully ripe, it produces wine with very deep colour, full dark fruit, and plush tannin – very useful in a blend. Here in warmer parts of Australia – where reliable ripening is less of an issue – it has been widely planted for this reason: a lot of petit verdot is harvested each year (more than grenache), but it seldom appears on the label, instead being used to embolden other varieties. Which is why it's still eligible in the AAVWS: there aren't that many varietally-labelled petit verdot wines out there. (image: PlantGrape)

Whistling Kite (Riverland).

Picpoul / Piquepoul

Origin: southern France
Grown here since: the 2010s
Area planted: less than 5 ha
Number of producers: 5

Enjoying a surge of popularity over the last decade or so, the crisp, refreshing and particularly seafood-loving dry white wines of the Picpoul de Pinet appellation, in the Languedoc, have inspired some Australian growers – notably the ever-curious Coriole in McLaren Vale – to plant the grape here, where they are making similarly successful fish-friendly whites. Some choose to label it 'picpoul' (like the appellation) and some choose 'piquepoul'. Delicious either way. (image: PlantGrape)

Pinot Blanc / Pinot Bianco

Origin: eastern France
Grown here since: the 2000s
Area planted: less than 20 ha
Number of producers: 15

Given the insatiable thirst for pinot noir, the commercial success of pinot gris/grigio, and the growing interest in pinot meunier, it's perhaps surprising that this white-skinned member of the pinot family has taken so long to catch on. But after a few years of being grown by only couple of producers, more and more examples of the grape, with its fine floral perfume and gently oily texture are appearing. (image: Chalmers)

Billy Button (Alpine Valleys), De Bortoli (Yarra Valley), Gapsted (King Valley), Sidewood (Adelaide Hills), St Huberts (Yarra Valley).

Pinot Meunier

Origin: Champagne, France
Grown here since: the 1800s
Area planted: less than 100 ha
Number of producers: 50

In France, pinot meunier is best known as the third main grape of Champagne (along with chardonnay and pinot noir), and although many Australian winemakers keen to produce top-quality fizz here have planted it for that purpose, it has also long been used here to make red wine in a style reminiscent of pinot noir, but a little earthier, that can be surprisingly long-lived: a magnum of 1970 Best's Pinot Meunier was one of the highlights of the 2007 AAVWS judges' dinner. (image: PlantGrape)

Hickinbotham (Mornington Peninsula), Moppity (Tumbarumba), Seppelt (Drumborg).

Refosco dal Peduncolo Rosso

Origin: Friuli, NE Italy
Grown here since: the 2000s
Area planted: less than 5 ha
Number of producers: 5

The 'pedunculo rosso' bit of this old Italian variety's name refers to the distinct red colouring of the stem on each bunch. Widely grown in Italy's northeast, and genetically related to teroldego, lagrein, corvina and rondinella, refosco produces medium-bodied, sometimes herbal, refreshingly tart red wine, particularly in cooler climates such as Victoria's Alpine Valleys, which has consistently performed well at the AAVWS. (image: Chalmers)

———

Billy Button (Alpine Valleys).

Roussanne

Origin: Rhone Valley, France
Grown here since: the 1980s
Area planted: less than 75 ha
Number of producers: 60

This high quality white grape, originally from the northern Rhone Valley, has benefited from a resurgence of interest in the wines of that region, and has now been planted in many vineyards in Australia, where it is often found successfully blended with the two other main Rhone whites, marsanne and viognier, to produce rich, perfumed white wines. It can also produce exceptional, long-lived varietal wine – more structural than marsanne, less heady than viognier. (image: PlantGrape)

———

Lome (Bendigo), Tahbilk (Nagambie Lakes), Yangarra (McLaren Vale).

Sagrantino

Origin: Umbria, central Italy
Grown here since: the 2000s
Area planted: less than 25 ha
Number of producers: 25

Dr Rod Bonfiglioli thought this variety had great potential in Australia, and while it has been planted by quite a few growers, the fearsome tannins in the wine have led to limited commercial success. Some (okay, the author particularly) love its uncompromising character – tasting it can be like sucking prune juice and dried blood off hot terracotta – but it's not to everyone's taste. (image: Chalmers)

———

Andrew Peace (Swan Hill).

Sangiovese

Origin: Tuscany, central Italy
Grown here since: the 1980s
Area planted: around 500 ha
Number of producers: 250

Famous grape of Chianti, Montalcino and other regions in Tuscany and central Italy, but grown all over the country. Wines are vinous, with dark cherry flavours, a twist of tannin, can age well in the cellar, becoming super savoury. Despite relatively wide planting and a high number of producers in Australia, this variety is still included in the show as there is room for it to mature in style. High-quality clones, many imported in the last two decades, are helping with this process of improvement. (image: Chalmers)

Colab & Bloom (Adelaide Hills/Fleurieu), Chrismont (King Valley), Coriole (McLaren Vale), Coulter (Adelaide Hills), Credaro (Margaret River), Dal Zotto (King Valley), De Bortoli / Bellariva (Yarra Valley), Elderton (Adelaide Hills), Fighting Gully Road (Beechworth), First Ridge (Mudgee), Galli Estate (Heathcote), Gargoyle (McLaren Vale), Hunter Gatherer (Hunter Valley), Indigo (Beechworth), Main & Cherry (McLaren Vale), Next Crop (McLaren Vale), Pepperjack (Padthaway), Pinnacle Drinks / The Ethereal One (Fleurieu), Pizzini (King Valley), Ravensworth (Hilltops), Santa & d'Sas (Heathcote), Serafino (McLaren Vale), Tar & Roses (Heathcote), Trentham Estate (Murray Darling), Yalumba (Riverland).

Saperavi

Origin: Georgia
Grown here since: the 1990s
Area planted: less than 25 ha
Number of producers: 25

The most widely planted red grape in Georgia, this dark-skinned and pink-fleshed grape is famous for producing wines with exceptionally deep, saturated purple-black colour and chewy, sometimes tart tannins. Has been embraced by a growing number of producers in Australia, especially with Georgian wine enjoying such a revival of fortune over the last decade or so. (image: DPIRD)

Alex Russell / Alejandro (Murray Darling), Billy Button (Alpine Valleys), Cirami Estate (Riverland), Gapsted (Alpine Valleys), Hugh Hamilton (McLaren Vale), La Cantina (King Valley), Patritti (Barossa), Smidge (McLaren Vale), Ten Miles East (Adelaide Hills).

Savagnin

Origin: NE France
Grown here since: the 2000s
Area planted: less than 50 ha
Number of producers: 30

This white variety was enthusiastically planted by many Australian growers in the early 2000s when they thought the cuttings they had were albarino – only to discover in 2008 that it was in fact savagnin. It makes nice, citrussy dry white wine – but excels when aged in barrel under a layer of flor yeast (like the vin jaune style of Jura), developing complex, nutty, sherry-like characters. (image: DPIRD)

———

Coolangatta Estate (Shoalhaven Coast), Crittenden Estate (Mornington Peninsula), Kangarilla Road (McLaren Vale), Soumah (Yarra Valley).

Schioppettino

Origin: Friuli, NE Italy
Grown here since: the 2000s
Area planted: less than 5 ha
Number of producers: fewer than 5

Not widely grown in Australia, and hard to pronounce (let alone spell), but comes with a great back-story (the very old variety, thought to be almost extinct in Friuli, was discovered growing in the mayor of Prepotto's garden in the early 1970s), and produces scintillating, aromatic, juicy but tannic wine. One of the varieties singled out by Dr Rod Bonfiglioli as having great potential in Australia. (image: Chalmers)

———

Bike & Barrel (Alpine Valleys).

Taminga

Origin: Australia
Grown here since: the 1960s
Area planted: less than 5 ha
Number of producers: fewer than 5

One of a handful of wine grapes bred at the CSIRO by Allan Antcliff in the 1960s and early 70s (see also cienna, tarrango and tyrian) that were subsequently planted and made into wine commercially, taminga produces very fruity, grapey whites, most successfully as a botrytis-affected sweet wine. (image: DPIRD)

———

Trentham Estate (Murray Darling).

Tannat

Origin: SW France
Grown here since: the 1980s
Area planted: less than 25 ha
Number of producers: 20

Described aptly by one Australian grower as tasting like 'dark matter lurking in a pot', tannat makes ferociously black, tannic wines, both in its homeland, where it is best known as the variety in Madiran reds, and in Australia, where it is often used as a minor component in blends, to provide structure. (image: DPIRD)

———————

Happs (Margaret River), Wines by Geoff Hardy (Adelaide Hills).

Tempranillo

Origin: north central Spain
Grown here since: the 1990s
Area planted: around 500 ha
Number of producers: 300

Just as sangiovese is strongly associated with Chianti, tempranillo is considered the grape of Rioja – even though the red wines from this famous Spanish region often contain other grapes such as garnacha (grenache) and mazuelo (carignan), and tempranillo in fact grows in many other parts of Spain, too. This association, though, perhaps explains why tempranillo took off so quickly in Australia in the 2000s to become one of the fastest-growing alternative reds – so much so that it is on the cusp of crossing over into the mainstream. (image: DPIRD)

———————

Anderson & Marsh (Alpine Valleys), Bleasdale (Langhorne Creek), Coulter (Riverland), Fox Creek (McLaren Vale), Green Door (Geographe), Hedonist (McLaren Vale), Hungerford Hill (Hilltops), La Linea (Adelaide Hills), Mayford (Alpine Valleys), McWilliams (Gundagai), Peter Lehmann (Barossa Valley), Oliver's Taranga (McLaren Vale), Serafino (McLaren Vale), SC Pannell (McLaren Vale), Tar & Roses (Heathcote), The Pawn (Adelaide Hills), XO Wine Co. (Adelaide Hills), Wangolina (Limestone Coast), Willow Bridge (Geographe).

Tinta Cao

Origin: Portugal
Grown here since: the 2000s
Area planted: less than 25 ha
Number of producers: 20

The most widely grown of the red Portuguese 'tinta' grapes (see also tinta amarela, tinta barroca and tinta negra mole), originally used in port production, more recently in dry red; seldom seen as a varietal wine, more commonly blended with the other tintas, as well as tempranillo and grenache to make Iberian-inspired wines by producers such as De Bortoli, Ricca Terra/Terra do Rio and Seppeltsfield. (image: CSIRO)

———————

Touriga Nacional

Origin: Douro, Portugal
Grown here since: the 1800s
Area planted: less than 75 ha
Number of producers: 70

The best-known and arguably the highest quality red grape of the Douro, where it has traditionally been the backbone of port production. In both Portugal and Australia (where it has been grown since the nineteenth century), touriga's spicy perfume and snappy tannins are also increasingly finding their way into red table wines, often blended with tempranillo and/or grenache, and the 'tintas'. Vineyard plantings have increased rapidly in recent years. (image: PlantGrape)

———————

Berg Herring (McLaren Vale), De Bortoli (King Valley), First Drop (McLaren Vale), Fourth Wave / Wild Folk (McLaren Vale), Gapsted (Alpine Valleys), Hither & Yon (McLaren Vale), McWilliams (Riverina), Peter Lehmann (Barossa Valley), SC Pannell (McLaren Vale), Seppeltsfield (Barossa Valley).

Verdejo

Origin: Rueda, Spain
Grown here since: the 2000s
Area planted: less than 25 ha
Number of producers: 5

From Rueda in northern Spain, this aromatic white produces full-flavoured, fruity wines, similar to sauvignon blanc. Has performed very well in Australia, in both warm and cooler climates. Surprising it's not more widely planted – although this is perhaps because it's not as trendy as that other Spanish white grape, albarino. (image: Nick Dry)

———————

Millbrook (Margaret River).

Vermentino

Viognier

Origin: northern Mediterranean
Grown here since: the 2000s
Area planted: less than 200 ha
Number of producers: 95

The origin of this grape given above is intentionally vague, as it has been grown in many places for hundreds of years – e.g., Sardinia (known as vermentino), Piemonte (favorita), Liguria (pigato), Corsica (vermentinu), and southern France (rolle). Its ubiquity shows how well adapted it is to warmer conditions – so it's no surprise to see it flourishing in similarly warm regions in Australia, where it produces vibrant, crisp, refreshing dry white wine. (image: Chalmers)

Atze's Corner (Barossa Valley), Berton (Riverland), Box Grove (Central Victoria), Carillion (Hunter Valley), Chalmers (Heathcote), Chapel Hill (McLaren Vale), Golden Grove (Granite Belt), Hastwell & Lightfoot (McLaren Vale), Kangarilla Road (McLaren Vale), McGuigan (Big Rivers), Oliver's Taranga (McLaren Vale), Pinnacle Drinks / The Ethereal One (Fleurieu), Salena (Riverland), Tempus Two (Hunter), Tim Adams (Clare Valley), Tonon (Perth Hills), Vino Intrepido (Nagambie Lakes), Yelland & Papps (Barossa Valley.)

Origin: Rhone Valley, France
Grown here since: the 1980s
Area planted: less than 750 ha
Number of producers: 240

Originally from the northern Rhone Valley and most famous for producing the rich, heady white wines of Condrieu, as well as being blended with syrah in Cote-Rotie. One of the first alternative white grapes to establish a reputation for itself in the late 1980s and early 1990s, due to its distinctive varietal aromas of apricots, jasmine, and ginger, given a major boost with the trend in the later 1990s – led by Clonakilla – of adding a splash of viognier to shiraz. (image: CSIRO)

Berton (Riverina), Artwine (Clare Valley), Castagna (Beechworth), Freeman (Hilltops), McGuigan (Hunter Valley), Millbrook (Perth Hills), Scion (Rutherglen), Whicher Ridge (Margaret River), Yalumba (Eden Valley).

Zinfandel / Primitivo

Zweigelt

Origin: Croatia
Grown here since: the 1970s
Area planted: less than 50 ha
Number of producers: 50

Tracing the identity of this grape is one of the great ampelographic detective stories. Zinfandel, once thought to be an old variety imported to California from Hungary in the mid-nineteenth century, was discovered in the 1970s to be identical to primitivo in Puglia, a variety that can trace its origins to Croatia, where its oldest varietal name is tribidrag. Makes robust, spicy, often quite alcoholic red wines. (image: Max Allen)

———

Gapsted (King Valley), Smallwater (Geographe), Terindah Estate (Geelong).

Origin: Austria
Grown here since: the 1990s
Area planted: less than 10 ha
Number of producers: fewer than 5

This Austrian grape is a crossing of blaufrankish and saint laurent, and since its inception one hundred years ago has become that country's most widely planted red variety. It has shown good promise in the few vineyards where it's grown in Australia, producing juicy, medium-bodied reds. (image: Hahndorf Hill)

———

BUT WAIT, THERE'S MORE …

The grape varieties on the following, more concise list are here for a few reasons. Almost all are less widely grown than the varieties on the previous pages – maybe one hectare here, a few rows there. Most are made by only a handful of producers, or in quite a few cases just one or two. Some varieties are listed here because they used to be more widely grown but have fallen out of fashion – almost to the point of extinction – while others are brand new arrivals in Australia, have only yielded their first or second vintage, and are still unfamiliar to growers and drinkers.

A caveat: this list is quite comprehensive but not *fully* complete. There are other varieties grown in Australia, or lurking in various vine collections, but they're not included here because they are not currently being produced commercially (as far as we know), or they haven't been entered into AAVWS for a long time – or, of course, they haven't been entered into the show yet.

Aleatico
Originally from Tuscany, now grown mostly in southern Italy; produces red wine with a floral muscat-like perfume.

Alicante Bouschet
Red-fleshed variety bred in nineteenth-century France; makes soft, full-coloured red wines, mostly blended with other grapes, but also used for deeply coloured rosé.

Aligote
This Burgundian grape produces wines similar to chardonnay but more savoury, with good acidity. Only grown by a few Australian producers at the moment but has good potential.

Alvarelhao
Northern Portuguese grape originally used as a small but important variety in port blends, but also has good potential for red wines, also blended. Only known to be grown by Yarra Yering.

Ancellotta
Red grape from Emilia-Romagna in central Italy, used there mostly in blends due to its dark colour and tannin. Blended here with primitivo by Water Wheel in Bendigo.

Ansonica / Inzolia
This grape, originally from Sicily but also grown in Tuscany, produces soft, rich, perfumed white wine. Chalmers have shown it can be grown in a hot climate with almost no irrigation.

Auxerrois / Aucerot
Very old variety from Alsace, France; historically known as aucerot in northeast Victoria, where it was once used to make sweet golden wine.

Baco Noir
Deeply coloured French hybrid, developed in the early twentieth century; useful to plump up blends, and used in that way by one Tasmanian producer, Winter Brook.

Bianco d'Allessano
Aromatic, textural white grape from Puglia, southern Italy, that shot to prominence here when it won the top trophy at the 2010 AAVWS.

Biancone
One of the many varieties once called **white grenache** in Australia, this high yielding but now quite rare white grape can trace its origins back to Corsica or Elba, where it is still grown.

Blaufrankisch
Austrian grape – also known as **limberger** in Germany and **kekfrankos** in Croatia – that makes dark, sinewy, well structured, high quality red wine.

Bogazkere
Turkish grape currently only grown in one vineyard, Tallis, in central Victoria; produces deep, full-bodied red wine in hot dry conditions. Good potential.

Bonvedro
This Iberian variety has historically been confused with carignan and mourvedre in Australia and makes similarly robust, earthy red.

Bourboulenc
Perfumed southern French variety, mostly used in blends with other white grapes, which is how Yangarra, the only producer in Australia, uses it, to gold medal-winning effect.

Brachetto
Very fragrant grape mostly used – both in its homeland of Piemonte in northwest Italy and by a couple of producers here in Australia – to make pink, sweet, moscato-like wines.

Canada Muscat
American hybrid with sweet muscat flavour, rarely grown outside Australia, where there is quite a lot planted, but the grapes are used in blends and the wines aren't labelled varietally.

Canaiolo
Old Tuscan variety, once more important than sangiovese, now a minor grape in Chianti. The one or two varietal examples made here taste rounder and less tannic than sangiovese.

Chambourcin
French hybrid, bred in the 1960s; still relatively popular in warmer, more humid Australian regions where it is suited to the conditions and makes full, rustic reds.

Chasselas
The best-known white grape of Switzerland, once grown in Victoria (originally planted by nineteenth-century Swiss winegrowers) but has now almost completely disappeared here.

Cienna
Developed by the CSIRO in the 1970s by crossing cabernet sauvignon and the Spanish grape sumoll; used mainly by one producer (Brown Brothers) to make sweet, fruity red.

Clairette
Southern French grape, used in sparkling wines and as a component of full-flavoured white blends – which is also how it is used in Australia by the few people who grow it.

Colorino
Very dark-skinned Tuscan grape traditionally used to add colour to Chianti blends; a splash is found in the Fighting Gully Road sangiovese, a consistent gold medal winner in the AAVWS.

Cortese
White grape that makes minerally dry whites in Gavi, Piemonte; performed in a similar way in the cool central Victoria vineyard where it was grown.

Counoise
Minor component in many southern French red blends, this variety, there, as here, contributes a light spiciness to the wine.

Crouchen
Old French grape, once widely grown here, especially in the Clare Valley, where it was first planted in the nineteenth-century and confused for semillon; still grown by a few producers.

Cygne Blanc
Seedling of cabernet sauvignon that produces white grapes, discovered in WA's Swan Valley – hence the name, 'white swan'.

Doradillo
Historically important Spanish white grape, once widely planted in Australia's warm irrigated regions for fortified wines and brandy, now rarely seen.

Dornfelder
Modern (1950s) German crossing, well-suited to cooler climates, makes good floral red wines with deep colour.

Fer
Very old, tannic red grape, produces firm, robust wines in southwest France. Made here by Forester Estate in Margaret River.

Fernao Pires
Portugal's most widely planted white grape, performs well in a warm climate – including the couple of vineyards it's grown in here – producing aromatic, immediately appealing wines.

Flora
Californian crossing of semillon and gewurztraminer from the 1930s; famously grown by Brown Brothers and blended with orange muscat to make a sweet wine.

Fragola / Isabella
The American variety isabella was taken to Italy in the nineteenth century, nicknamed fragola (its wines can taste of strawberry), and eventually made its way to the odd vineyard in Australia.

Furmint
Famous for being the main grape in Hungary's extremely sweet, rich, and long-lived Tokaji Aszu wines, but also makes full-flavoured, savoury dry whites (see also harslevelu).

Gouais
Ancient, historically vitally important French variety (it's the genetic parent for countless grapes including chardonnay and gamay), grown here only by Chambers in Rutherglen.

Grand Noir de la Calmette
Red-fleshed French crossing bred by Henri Bouschet (see alicante), brought to Australia with durif and other grapes in the early twentieth century, now hardly grown.

Grechetto / Pignoletto
This old Italian grape is known as grechetto in Umbria and pignoletto in Emilia-Romagna; it makes wines with a bracing acidity, useful in blends.

Grillo
Plantings of 'grillo' in the early 2000s turned out to be a rare Balkan grape called slankamanka bela; newer plantings are the true grillo and display the Sicilian variety's full golden flavours.

Harslevelu
Along with furmint, listed above, one of the main grapes of the luscious golden Hungarian Tokaji wines; now grown only by Brian Freeman in the Hilltops region of NSW.

Macabeo / Viura
White grape, widely grown in Spain (important in Rioja), also grown in southern France and – by a couple of growers – in the Riverland.

Malvasia Istriana
Of the many variations of malvasia grown across Italy, this one, originally from Croatia, is beginning to make inroads in Australia: textural, delicate, aromatic, good in blends.

Mammolo
Minor blending grape in Tuscany (and in a couple of cases in Australia); also known as sciaccarello in Corsica, where it is widely grown and produces fragrant, light-coloured wines.

Marzemino

From the genetic family of red varieties that includes lagrein, teroldego and refosco in northern Italy; makes lighter, fragrant, herbal red wine. Grown by a handful of producers.

Mavrodaphne

Old Greek variety, used to make rich sweet red wine in its homeland. Grown at Marion's Vineyard in Tasmania.

Montils

White grape from Cognac in France, grown in the Hunter Valley since the nineteenth century, now only by Mount Pleasant, historically blended into shiraz.

Muller-Thurgau

German crossing, bred in the nineteenth century, once popular in cooler parts of the world (e.g., England, New Zealand), now in decline, but found in a few Australian sites.

Muscat Hamburg

A crossing of muscat and trollinger. More of a table variety but used by a few producers in Australia as a blending grape in sweet, fortified wines, not credited on the label.

Nosiola

White grape traditionally used in sweet vin santo wines in Trentino, northern Italy, but now also used to make fragrant, textural dry whites. New arrival, good potential.

Orange Muscat

Particularly fragrant, citrussy member of the muscat family, with long tradition of being used to make fresh sweet wines in northeast Victoria (see flora, above).

Palomino

Originally from sherry country in southern Spain, and once widely grown to make Australian dry 'sherry', still championed here by a few die-hard makers of what is now called 'apera'.

Pavana

Grown and made by the Chalmers family partly as a tribute to Dr Rod Bonfiglioli, who was fond of this rare northern Italian grape and the bright crisp red wine it produces.

Pedro Ximenes

An old Spanish grape once grown widely in Australia to make sweet 'sherry' and still produced by a handful of makers in a typically rich, dark, raisined fortified style.

Petit Meslier

Rare champagne variety, known for its crisp, green-apple acidity, championed by one producer in Australia, Jo Irvine in the Adelaide Hills.

Picolit

Very old Friulian variety mostly used to make sweet wine in its homeland, but used here (albeit by very few producers) as a component of Friulian-inspired dry white blends.

Piedirosso

Old red variety from Campania, where it is widely grown around Naples and the lower slopes of Vesuvius. Makes fresh, fragrant, slightly herbal wine. New here, rarely found.

Pinotage
A crossing of pinot noir and cinsaut bred in South Africa in the 1920s and considered that country's signature red grape: rare here but at its best has good wild spicy fruit flavours.

Prieto Picudo
This grape from northern Spain produces bold, perfumed, juicy red wines and is showing glimmers of good promise in the warm Riverland region of South Australia.

Ribolla Gialla
One of the most highly regarded white grapes in Friuli, associated with the rich, textural, often skins-fermented wines made there. Recent arrival here, great potential.

Rondinella
Red grape originally from the Veneto, found in the red wines of Valpolicella; grown in Freeman vineyards in Hilltops, blended with corvina.

Rubired
High yielding American hybrid known for deep colour; widely grown in Australia but, like ruby cabernet, used to embolden blends, not bottled as a varietal wine.

Ruby Cabernet
Huge amounts of this heat-tolerant grape, an American crossing of carignan and cabernet sauvignon, are harvested in Australia, but almost all makes its way, into blends, usually uncredited.

Saint Laurent
Old Austrian variety, grown in Australia only by Hahndorf Hill in the Adelaide Hills; makes wine that tastes a little like fuller-bodied pinot noir.

Saint Macaire
Old Bordeaux variety, almost extinct there now, grown in Australia only by Calabria in the Riverina; makes cabernet-ish wine.

Sauvignon Gris
A colour mutation of sauvignon blanc: the berries are dusky pink. A couple of producers here make whites that are less aromatic and a little more textural than sav blanc.

Schonburger
Pink-skinned German crossing from the early twentieth century; produces perfumed, floral delicate white wines, suited to cool climates such as Tasmania, where it is grown on a small scale.

Souzao
Portuguese grape known for producing wines of particularly dark colour; usually blended – in both port and table wines, increasingly in Australia – with the 'tintas' (see below).

Sultana
Once hugely important to the production of cheap, bulk white wine in Australia, the use of this multi-purpose grape in wine has now dwindled to a fraction of its former size.

Sylvaner / Silvaner
Gently aromatic grape that traces its origins to Austria but is best known in France and Germany – and in a couple of cases here – for making crisp, age-worthy whites.

Tarrango
In the 1980s and 90s the most commercially successful of the CSIRO grapes (see also cienna, taminga and tyrian), recently revived by Brown Brothers; makes light, juicy chillable red wine.

Teroldego
The best examples from Trentino in Italy have good deep purple colour, intense black fruit, and snappy tannins; in Margaret River and King Valley can produce similar styled wines.

Tinta Amarela, Tinta Barroca, Tinta Negra Mole
Portuguese red grapes usually found in the same vineyards and blended with the other main 'tinta'; tinta cao, and souzao and touriga; to make modern juicy reds. Very fashionable.

Trebbiano
Widely grown around the world, this high-yielding Italian grape – known as **ugni blanc** in France – produces notoriously neutral-tasting wine. Like sultana, rarely seen in Australia now.

Trollinger / Schiava Grossa
Red grape originally from Alto Adige, also grown in Germany, makes light, perfumed wines. Grown in Australia only by Hahndorf Hill in the Adelaide Hills.

Tyrian
Another CSIRO crossing of cabernet sauvignon and the red Spanish grape sumoll; makes deeply coloured, rich wines; some medium-sized plantings but rarely seen.

Uva di Troia
The American black hybrid jacquez was once wrongly known in the Riverina as 'uva di troia'; true uva di troia, AKA **nero do troia**, an old dark, tannic Puglian grape, is a recent arrival.

Verdicchio
Old Italian grape from Marche and the Veneto, known for producing crisp dry white wines with a pleasing touch of bitterness. Grown by a couple of producers in Australia.

Verduzzo
Old Friulian variety, known for producing both fuller, textural dry whites that develop well in bottle, and rich golden sweet wines. Only made by a handful of producers here.

Vespolina
Minor red grape in Piemonte, genetically related to nebbiolo, makes fragrant tannic reds (as you'd expect, perhaps, given its genes), grown only by Ringer Reef in the Alpine Valleys.

Best Wine of Show Artwork

for winners of the Dr. Rod Bonfiglioli Best Wine of Show (2016–2022)

From 2016, the Art Vault Mildura donated an artwork for the Best Wine of Show trophy. The artists:

2016 – Geoffrey Ricardo 'Vinarium Australis' 2016, intaglio edition of 20, 29.5 x 22.5 cm

2017 – Amanda Firenze Pentney Boogie Time 2015, hand coloured linocut, unique print, 57 x 38 cm

2018 – Anita Laurence - Deakin Avenue 1 2010, linocut edition of 40, 28 x 36 cm

2019 – Rosalind Atkins 'Ampelon I' 2010, wood engraving edition of 20, 10 x 12 cm

2020 – Senye Shen, Endless Flow IV 2012, edition of 30, 42 x 44 cm

2021 – Euan Macleod 'Seated In Desert' 2016 edition of 20, etching & aquatint 40 x 50 cm

2022 – eX de Medici and Rosalind Atkins 'Lake Mungo' edition of 30, engraved and etched copper, 28.5 x 38 cm

2016: Geoffrey Ricardo

2017: Amanda Firenze Pentney

2018: Anita Lawrence

2019: Rosalind Atkins

2020: Senye Shen

2021: Euan MacLeod

2022: eX de Medici and Rosalind Atkins

Artworks

Awards / sponsors 2022–2001

2022

Venue: Willow and Ivie, 200pp, sold out within two weeks of tickets going on sale

Award	Sponsor	Winner
The Dr. Rod Bonfiglioli Best Wine of Show	Chalmers	Purple Hands Wines 2021 After Five Wine Co Aglianico
Best Red Wine	Stefano's Restaurant	Purple Hands Wines 2021 After Five Wine Co Aglianico
Best White Wine	Jamesprint	Linear Wines 2022 Gruner Veltliner
Best Red Italian Variety Wine	CHR Hansen	Purple Hands Wines 2021 After Five Wine Co Aglianico
Best White Italian Variety Wine	Duxton Vineyards	Golden Grove Estate 2022 Vermentino
Best Murray Darling Region Wine	Zilzie Wines	Gibson Wines 2022 Discovery Road Fiano
Chief of Judges (Chairman's) Wine to Watch	Orora	Quealy Winemakers Turbul 2021 Turbul Friulano
Steward's Choice	Quality Hotel Mildura Grand	Cherubino 2021 Ovale Sauvignon Gris
Best Iberian Variety	MoVida	Peter Lehmann Wines 2021 Hill and Valley Tempranillo
Best Blend	Casella Family Brands	Dune 2021 El Beyda
Tony Managan Memorial Award	Mangan Group	Whistling Kite Wines NV Classic Gros Manseng
Best Rosé	Murray Valley Winegrowers	Smallwater Estate 2022 Roze
Best Label Artwork	Tasco Petroleum	Ti Amo 2022 Fiano
Best Sparkling Wine	Longview Vineyard	*No winner awarded*
Best French Variety Wine	Yalumba Nursery	XO Wine Co 2022 Gamay
Best Museum Wine	Riedel	Tahbilk 2015 '1927 Vines' Marsanne
Best of the Rest	Mallee Foods	Linear Wines 2022 Gruner Veltliner
Viticulturist Award	Morellofert	Sam Costanzo

2021

Venue: Grand Ballroom/ Pre-recorded Online, limited audience of judges, live crosses to President, winners and Viticulturist Award judges

Award	Sponsor	Winner
The Dr. Rod Bonfiglioli Best Wine of Show	Chalmers	Valentino 2016 Sangiovese
Best Red Wine	Stefano's Restaurant	Valentino 2016 Sangiovese
Best White Wine	Jamesprint	Pikes Wines 2021 Luccio Albarino
Best Red Italian Variety Wine	CHR Hansen	Valentino 2016 Sangiovese
Best White Italian Variety Wine	Duxton Vineyards	Oliver's Taranga Vineyards 2021 Fiano
Best Murray Darling Region Wine	Zilzie Wines	Mandi 2021 Friulano
Chief of Judges (Chairman's) Wine to Watch	Orora	Kangarilla Road 2018 The Veil
Steward's Choice	Quality Hotel Mildura Grand	Dal Zotto Wines 2015 L'Immigrante Nebbiolo
Best Iberian Variety Wine	MoVida	Pike Wines 2021 Luccio Albarino
Best Blend	Casella Family Brands	Franz & Fritz 2021 White Field Blend
Tony Managan Memorial Award	Mangan Group	Paxton 2021 Graciano
Best Rosé	Amsat Oak	*No winner awarded*
Best Label Artwork	Tasco Petroleum	Mandi 2021 Friulano
Best Sparkling Wine	Longview Vineyard	Oliver's Taranga Vineyards 2018 The Hunt for Mrs Oliver Methode Traditionelle Fiano
Best French Variety Wine	Yalumba Nursery	Whicher Ridge 2019 Mademoiselle V
Best Museum Wine	Riedel	Valentino 2016 Sangiovese
Best of the Rest	Northside Wines	The Pawn Wine Company 2021 The Austrian Attack
Viticulturist Award	Morellofert	Don Oliver

2020

Venue: Grand Ballroom / Live Online, limited audience of judges, live crosses to President, winners, recorded message by Cha McCoy (USA) and Viticulturist Award judges
Notes: Best of the Rest introduced

Award	Sponsor	Winner
The Dr. Rod Bonfiglioli Best Wine of Show	Chalmers	Hahndorf Hill 2020 White Mischief Gruner Veltliner
Best Red Wine	Stefano's Restaurant	Bondar Wines 2019 Monastrell
Best White Wine	Jamesprint	Hahndorf Hill 2020 White Mischeif Gruner Veltliner
Best Red Italian Variety Wine	CHR Hansen	W Salter & Son 2020 Pepperjack Sangiovese
Best White Italian Variety Wine	Duxton Vineyards	Ricca Terra 2020 Bronco Buster
Best Murray Darling Region Wine	Zilzie Wines	Trentham Estate 2020 The Family Sangiovese Rosé
Chief of Judges (Chairman's) Wine to Watch	Wine Australia	S.C. Pannell 2019 Montepulciano
Steward's Choice	Quality Hotel Mildura Grand	Hahndorf Hill 2019 Reserve Gruner Veltliner
Best Iberian Variety Wine	MoVida	Bondar Wines 2019 Monastrell
Best Blend	Casella Family Brands	Ricca Terra 2020 Bronco Buster
Tony Managan Memorial Award	Mangan Group	Hedonist Wines 2020 Tempranillo
Best Rosé	Blue H20 Filtration	22 Degree Halo 2020 Rosé
International Judge's Wine to Watch	5 O'Clock Somewhere	La Cantina King Valley 2018 Saparavi
Best Label Artwork	Taso Petroleum	Bondar Wines 2019 Monastrell
Best Sparkling Wine	Dal Zotto	Dhiaga Wines 2020 Gewurtztraminer Dhaiga
Best French Variety Wine	Yalumba Nursery	Rutherglen Estate 2019 Shelleys Block
Best Museum Wine	Riedel	Tahbilk 2016 '1927 Vines' Marsanne
Best of the Rest (*introduced 2020*)	Northside Wines	Hahndorf Hill 2020 White Mischief Gruner Veltliner
Viticulturist Award	Morellofert	Mark Walpole

2019

Venue: Mildura Lawn Tennis Club / Lunch by Stefano
Notes: Viticulturist Award introduced / Best Museum Wine introduced / Best Nero d'Avola and Best Fortified Wine discontinued

Award	Sponsor	Winner
The Dr. Rod Bonfiglioli Best Wine of Show	Chalmers	De Bortoli Wines 2015 Bellariva Sangiovese
Best Red Wine	Stefano's restaurant	De Bortoli Wines 2015 Bellariva Sangiovese
Best White Wine	Jamesprint	Coolangatta Estate 2010 Savagnin
Best Red Italian Variety Wine	CHR Hansen	De Bortoli Wines 2015 Bellariva Sangiovese
Best White Italian Variety Wine	Duxton Vineyards	S.C. Pannell 2019 Fi Fi Fiano
Best Murray Darling Region Wine	Zilzie Wines	Stefano Docket Label 2017 Claudio Amphora
Chief of Judges (Chairman's) Wine to Watch	Wine Australia	Reillys Wines 2017 Dry Land Mataro
Steward's Choice	Quality Hotel Mildura Grand	Chaffey Bros. Wine Co. 2019 Kontrapunkt
Best Iberian Variety Wine	MoVida	Berg Herring 2018 Touriga
Best Blend	Casella Family Brands	DeBortoli Wines 2018 Vinoque Novo Tinto
Tony Managan Memorial Award	Mangan Group	Castagna NV Aqua Santa
Best Rosé	Blue H20 Filtration	Tar & Roses 2019 Tar&Roses Nebbiolo Rosé
International Judge's Wine to Watch	5 O'Clock Somewhere	Pike and Joyce Wine 2018 Innnesti Nebbiolo
Best Label Artwork	Tasco Petroleum	Hugh Hamilton Wines 2014 Oddball the Great
Best Sparkling Wine	Dal Zotto	*No winner awarded*
Best French Variety Wine	Yalumba Nursery	Coolangatta Estate 2010 Savagnin
Best Museum Wine (*introduced 2019*)	Riedel	Coolangatta Estate 2010 Savagnin
Viticulturist Award (*introduced 2019*)	Morellofert	Richard Leask

2018

Venue: Mildura Lawn Tennis Club / Lunch by Stefano
Notes: Trans Tasman Award for Best New Zealand Wine discontinued

Award	Sponsor	Winner
The Dr. Rod Bonfiglioli Best Wine of Show	Chalmers	Artwine 2018 In the Groove Gruner Veltliner
Best Red Wine	Stefano's Restaurant	Coriole 2018 Nero d'Avola
Best White Wine	Jamesprint	Artwine 2018 In the Groove Gruner Veltliner
Best Red Italian Variety Wine	CHR Hansen	Vineyard 28 2018 Dolcetto
Best White Italian Variety Wine	Duxton Vineyards	Oliver's Taranga Vineyards 2018 Oliver's Taranga Vermentino
Best Murray Darling Region Wine	Sunraysa Cellar Door & Murray Valley Winegrowers Inc.	Chalmers 2017 Appassimento
Chief of Judges (Chairman's) Wine to Watch	Wine Australia	Clay Pot Wines 2016 Taurian
Steward's Choice	Quality Hotel Mildura Grand	Bream Creek Vineyard 2017 Bream Creek Schöburger
Best Iberian Variety Wine	MoVida	Samuel's Gorge 2017 Graciano
Best Commercial Volume	Morellofert	Tahbilk 2012 Marsanne
Best Blend	Casella Family Brands	Montevecchio 2018 Mildura Rosso
Tony Managan Memorial Award	Mangan Group	Yangarra Estate Vineyard 2017 Mourvedre
Best Nebbiolo	Riedel Glassware	Billy Button 2016 'The Elusive' Nebbiolo
Best Rosé	One Idea	DeBortoli Wines 2018 Vinoque Nebbiolo Rosé
International Judge's Wine to Watch	5 O'Clock Somewhere	Artwine 2018 In the Groove Gruner Veltliner
Best Label Artwork	Tasco Petroleum	Big Easy Radio 2016 Forget Babylon
Best Nero d'Avola	Blaxland Wine Group	Coriole 2018 Nero
Best Sparkling Wine	Dal Zotto	Dhiaga Wines 2018 Gewurtztraminer Dhiaga
Best French Variety Wine	Yalumba Nursery	Bremerton Wines 2016 Special Release Malbec

2017

Venue: Trentham Estate Winery / Bus and Paddleboat
Notes: Best French Variety Wine introduced

Award	Sponsor	Winner
The Dr. Rod Bonfiglioli Best Wine of Show	Chalmers	Hither & Yon 2017 Nero d'Avola
Best Red Wine	Stefano's Restaurant	Hither & Yon 2017 Nero d'Avola
Best White Wine	Jamesprint	Crittenden Estate 2013 Cri de Couer
Best Red Italian Variety Wine	Pizzini Wines	Amadio Wines 2016 Vino Di Famiglia Rosso Superiore
Best White Italian Variety Wine	AEB Oceania	Cellarmasters 2017 Stefano Premium Range Fleurieu Vermentino
Best Murray Darling Region Wine	Sunraysia Cellar Door & Murray Valley Winegrowers Inc	Montevecchio 2017 Mildura Bianco
Chief of Judges (Chairman's) Wine to Watch	*No sponsor listed*	Yangarra Estate Vineyard 2015 Roux Beauté Rousanne
Steward's Choice	Duxton Vineyards	G. Patritti & Co. 2015 Patritti Trincadeira
Best Iberian Variety Wine	MoVida	Ricca Terra Vinters 2017 Bullets Before Cannonballs
Best Commercial Volume	Morellofert	Tahbilk 2011 Marsanne
Best Blend	Casella Framily Brands	Ricca Terra Vinters 2017 Bullets Before Cannonballs
Tony Managan Memorial Award	Mangan Group	Whistling Kite Vineyard 2017 Biodynamic Viognier
Best Nebbiolo	Riedel Glassware	Amato Vina 2015 Nebbiolo
Best Rosé	One Idea	Deliquente Wine Co 2017 Pretty Boy
Trans Tasman Award for Best New Zealand Wine	Quality Hotel Mildura Grand	Saint Clair Family Estate 2015 Saint Clair Pioneer Block 5 Bull Block Gruner Veltliner
Best Fortified Wine	*No sponsor listed*	*No winner awarded*
International Judge's Wine to Watch	Lallemand Oenology	Kimbolton Wines 2017 Montepulciano Rosé
Best Label Artwork	Tasco Petroleum	Delinquente Wine Co 2017 Tuff Nut
Best Nero d'Avola	Blaxland Wine Group	Hither & Yon 2017 Nero d'Avola
Best Sparkling Wine	Dal Zotto	*No winner awarded*
Best French Variety Wine (*introduced 2017*)	Yalumba Nursery	Crittenden Estate 2013 Cri De Coeur

2016

Venue: Mildura Lawn Tennis Club / Lunch by Stefano
Notes: Tony Managan Memorial Award renamed from Best Organic Wine / Best Aglianico this year only

Award	Sponsor	Winner
The Dr. Rod Bonfiglioli Best Wine of Show	Chalmers	Coriole 2016 Nero d'Avola
Best Red Wine	Stefano's Restaurant	Coriole 2016 Nero d'Avola
Best White Wine	Jamesprint	Saltram Winemakers Selection 2016 Fiano
Best Red Italian Variety Wine	Pizzini Wines	Coriole 2016 Nero d'Avola
Best White Italian Variety Wine	One Idea	Saltram Winemakers Selection 2016 Fiano
Best Murray Darling Region Wine	Sunraysia Cellar Door & Murray Valley Winegrowers Inc	Montevecchio 2016 Rosso Mildura *and* Trentham Estate Wines 2016 Trentham Estate la Famiglia Sangiovese Rosé
Chief of Judges (Chairman's) Wine to Watch	Yalumba Nursery	Jim Barry Wines 2016 Assyrtiko
Steward's Choice	Duxton Vinneyards	Graham Stevens Wines 2015 Fleurieu Tempranillo
Best Iberian Variety Wine	MoVida	St Hallett Wines 2015 Touriga Nacional
Best Commercial Volume	Morellofert	Tahbilk 2016 Marsanne
Best Blend	Morellofert	Montevecchio 2016 Rosso Mildura
Tony Managan Memorial Award (*renamed from Best Organic Wine in 2016*)	Mangan Group	919 Wines NV Pale Dry Apera
Best Rosé	Quality Hotel Milduara Grand	The Yalumba Wine Company 2016 Yalumba Y Series Sangiovese Rosé
Trans Tasman Award for Best New Zealand Wine	Riversun Nursery	Saint Clair Family Estate 2015 Saint Clair Marlborough Premium Gruner Veltliner
Best Fortified Wine	CHR Hansen	Pfeiffer Wines NV Seriously Fine
International Judge's Wine to Watch	Food & Wine Travel	Fighting Gully Road 2014 Aglianico
Best Label Artwork	Tasco Inland	Ten Miles East 2015 Savperavi
Best Nero d'Avola	Blaxland Wine Group	Coriole 2016 Nero d'Avola
Best Sparkling Wine	Dal Zotto	*No winner awarded*
Best Aglianico (*only 2016*)	Riedel Glassware	David Premium Vineyards 2015 Rogue Series 'Moon Child' Aglianico

2015

Venue: Mildura Lawn Tennis Club / Lunch by Stefano
Notes: Best Spanish Variety Wine renamed to Best Iberian Variety Wine / Best Sparkling and Best Nero d'Avola introduced

Award	Sponsor	Winner
The Dr. Rod Bonfiglioli Best Wine of Show	Chalmers	Golden Grove Estate 2015 Vermentino
Best Red Wine	Stefano's Restaurant & Mildura Brewery	Hither & Yon 2015 Nero d'Avola
Best White Wine	Jamesprint	Golden Gorve Estate 2015 Vermentino
Best Red Italian Variety Wine	*Not listed*	Hither & Yon 2015 Nero d'Avola
Best White Italian Variety Wine	One Idea	Golden Grove Estate 2015 Vermentino
Best Murray Darling Region Wine	Sunraysia Cellar Door	Golden Grove Esate 2015 Vermentino
Chief of Judges (Chairman's) Wine to Watch	Yalumba Nursery	Aronui Wines 2014 Single Vineyard Albarino *and* Simão & Co. Wines 2015 Ugni Blanc
Steward's Choice	Macquarie Agriculture	Loom Wine 2014 Loom SV Sangiovese
Best Iberian Variety Wine (*renamed from Best Spanish Variety Wine in 2015*)	MoVida	Taylors Wines 2015 Taylors Tempranillo
Best Commercial Volume	Morellofert	Tahbilk 2010 Marsanne
Best Blend	Casella Wines	SAMU Wines 2015 Nero d'Avola Merlot
Best Organic Wine	Mangan Group	Gemtree Wines 2015 Luna de Fresa
Best Nebbiolo	Riedel Glassware	Grove Estate Wines 2013 Sommita Nebbiolo
Best Rosé	Quality Hotel Mildura Grand	Gemtree Wines 2015 Luna de Fresa
Trans Tasman Award for Best New Zealand Wine	Riversun Nursery	Arouni Wines 2014 Single Vineyard Albarino
Best Fortified Wine	CHR Hansen	Stanton and Kileen Wines NV Grand Topaque
International Judge's Wine to Watch	Select Events	Beach Road Wines 2014 Greco
Best Label Artwork	Tasco inland	Loom Wine 2013 Tannat Durif Shiraz
Best Nero d'Avola (*introduced 2015*)	Blaxland Wine Group	Hither & Yon 2015 Nero d'Avola
Best Sparkling Wine (*introduced 2015*)	AEB Oceania	Dalfarras Wines 2015 Daflarras Prosecco

2014

Venue: Paddleboat Mundoo / Frank Camorra & Stefano
Notes: Best Label Artwork / International Judge's Wine to Watch / Best Fortified Wine / Trans Tasman Award for Best New Zealand introduced

Award	Sponsor	Winner
The Dr. Rod Bonfiglioli Best Wine of Show	Chalmers	S.C. Pannell Wines 2013 S.C. Pannell Tempranillo Touriga
Best Red Wine	Mildura Brewery	S.C. Pannell Wines 2013 Tempranillo Touriga
Best White Wine	Jamesprint	Oliver's Taranga Vineyards 2014 Fiano
Best Red Italian Variety Wine	Orlando Wines	Hither & Yon 2014 Nero d'Avola
Best White Italian Variety Wine	One Idea	Oliver's Taranga Vineyards 2014 Fiano
Best Murray Darling Region Wine	Sunraysia Cellar Door	Calabria Family Wines 2013 Calabria Private Bin Vermentino
Chief of Judges (Chairman's) Wine to Watch	Yalumba Nursery	Davis Premium Vineyards 2013 Rogue Series Hunter Valley Vermentino
Steward's Choice	Macquarie Agriculture	Beach Road Wines 2013 Fiano
Best Spanish Variety Wine	MoVida	S.C. Pannell Wines 2013 Tempranillo Touriga
Best Commercial Volume	Morellofert	Yalumba Wine Company 2013 Yalumba Y Series Tempranillo
Best Blend	Casella Wines	S.C Pannell Wines 2013 S.C. Pannell Tempranillo Touriga
Best Organic Wine	Mangan Group	Whistling Kite Vineyard 2013 Biodynamic Montepulciano
Best Nebbiolo	Riedel Glassware	T'Gallant Winemakers 2012 Odysseus
Best Rosé	Tasco Inland	Nova Vita Wines 2014 Firebird
Trans Tasman Award for Best New Zealand Wine (*introduced 2014*)	Riversun Nursery	Waimea Estates 2014 Waimea Gruner Veltliner
Best Fortified Wine (*introduced 2014*)	Best Bottlers	Stanton & Killeen NV Rare Topaque
International Judge's Wine to Watch (*introduced 2014*)	Danenberg Dental Surgery	Beach Road Wines 2012 Aglianico
Best Label Artwork (*introduced 2014*)	Healy and Daughter	Next Crop Wines 2013 Graciano Tempranillo

2013

Venue: Trentham Estate Winery / Lunch by Dag Demarkov / Bus & Boat
Notes: Best Spanish Variety Wine (White and Red) introduced this year only

Award	Sponsor	Winner
The Dr. Rod Bonfiglioli Best Wine of Show	Chalmers	S.C. Pannell Wines 2012 Tempranillo Touriga
Best Red Wine	Quality Hotel Mildura Grand	S.C. Pannell Wines 2012 Tempranillo Touriga
Best White Wine	Jamesprint	Ceravolo Premium Wines 2013 Ceravolo Cortese d'Ashton
Best Red Italian Variety Wine	Orlando Wines	Whistling Kite Vineyard 2012 Biodynamic Montepulciano
Best White Italian Variety Wine	Mildura Brewery	Ceravolo Premium Wines 2013 Ceravolo Cortese d'Ashton
Best Murray Darling Region Wine	Sunraysia Cellar Door	Trentham Estate Wines 2013 Verdejo
Chief of Judges (Chairman's) Wine to Watch	Yalumba Nursery	K1 by Geoff Hardy 2012 Gruner Veltliner
Steward's Choice	Macquarie Agriculture	Mayford Wines 2012 Tempranillo
Best Spanish Variety Wine (White) *(introduced 2013 only)*	MoVida	Trentham Estate Wines 2013 Verdejo
Best Spanish Variety Wine (Red) *(introduced 2013 only)*	Riedel Glassware	S.C. Pannnell Wines 2012 Tempranillo Touriga
Best Commercial Volume	Mangan Group	Tahbik 2011 Marsanne
Best Blend	Casella Wines	S.C. Pannell Wines 2012 Tempranillo Touriga
Best Organic Wine	Morellofert	Whistling Kite Vineyard 2012 Biodynamic Montepulciano
Best Nebbiolo	Riedel Glassware *(transfered to Spanish red)*	*No winner awarded*
Best Rosé	Tasco Inland	Glen Roy Winemakers 2013 Bellwether Nero d'Avola Rosé

2012

Venue: Old Mildura Homestead / Lunch by Stefano
Notes: Best Rosé introduced

Award	Sponsor	Winner
The Dr. Rod Bonfiglioli Best Wine of Show	Chalmers	S.C. Pannell Wines 2008 Nebbiolo
Best Red Wine	Quality Hotel Mildura Grand	S.C. Pannell Wines 2008 Nebbiolo
Best White Wine	Jamesprint	Saltram Wine Estate 2012 Fiano
Best Red Italian Variety Wine	Orlando Wines	Cirami Estate 2012 Lagrein
Best White Italian Variety Wine	One Idea	Saltram Winemakers 2012 Fiano
Best Murray Darling Region Wine	Mildura Wines	Trentham Estate Wines 2008 Noble Taminga
Chief of Judges (Chairman's) Wine to Watch	Yalumba Nursery	Chalmers Wines Australia 2012 Lambrusco
Steward's Choice	Casella Wines	Mount Majura Vineyard 2010 Graciano
Best Spanish Variety Wine	The New Spanish Bar & Grill	Rosemount Estate Project 2011 GMG
Best Commercial Volume	Riedel Glassware	Tahbilk 2011 Marsanne
Best Blend	Macquarie Agriculture	Rosemount Estates 2011 Rosemount Nursery Project GMG
Best Organic Wine	Mangan Group	BJ&VA Bassham 2012 Bassham Lagrein
Best Nebbiolo	Danenberg Dental Surgery	S.C. Pannell Wines 2008 Nebbiolo
Best Rosé (*introduced 2012*)	Select Events	Scott Winemaking 2012 La Provo Aglianico Rosata

2011

Venue: Seasons Restaurant / Stefano with Seasons. Wine tutoring by judges
Notes: Best White Italian Variety Wine renamed from Best Italian Variety / Best Red Italian Variety Wine

Award	Sponsor	Winner
The Dr. Rod Bonfiglioli Best Wine of Show	Chalmers	Protero Wines 2006 Nebbiolo
Best Red Wine	Quality Hotel Mildura Grand	Protero Wines 2006 Nebbiolo
Best White Wine	Jamesprint	Scott Winemaking 2011 Scott Fiano
Best Red Italian Variety Wine (introduced 2011)	Orlando Wines	Protero Wines 2006 Nebbiolo
Best White Italian Variety Wine (renamed from Best Italian Variety)	Orlando Wines	Scott Winemaking 2011 Scott Fiano
Best Murray Darling Region Wine	Mildura Wines	Robinvale Organic & Biodynamic Wines 2008 Kerner
Chief of Judges (Chairman's) Wine to Watch	Yalumba Nursery	Clan del Sud 2010 Green Man Malvasia
Steward's Choice	Casella Wines	Greenstone Vineyards 2010 Colorino
Best Spanish Variety Wine	The New Spanish Bar & Grill	Juniper Estate 2010 Juniper Crossing Tempranillo
Best Commercial Volume	Macquarie Agriculture	The Yalumba Wine Company 2011 Yalumba Y Series Viognier
Best Blend	Riedel Glassware	Mount Majura Vineyard 2010 TSG
Best Organic Wine	HHO Events	Robinvale Organic & Biodynamic Wines 2008 Kerner

2010

Venue: Grand Hotel / Lunch by Stefano / Wine tutoring by judges

Award	Sponsor	Winner
The Dr. Rod Bonfiglioli Best Wine of Show	Chalmers	Salena Estate Wines 2010 Ink Series Bianco d'Allessano
Best Red Wine	Qualiity Hotel Mildura Grand	Westend Estate 2008 Calabria Aglianico
Best White Wine	Jamesprint	Salena Estate Wines 2010 Ink Series Biacno d'Allessano
Best Italian Variety	Binjara Vine Nursery & Riedel Glassware	Salena Estate Wines 2010 Ink Series Bianco d'Allessano
Best Murray Darling Region Wine	Mildura Wines	Cellarmaster 2010 Stefano de Pieri Tre Viti
Chief of Judges (Chairman's) Wine to Watch	Yalumba Nursery	T'Gallant Winemakers 2007 Claudius *and* MicheliniWines 2008 Teroldego
Steward's Choice	Casella Wines	The Pawn Wine Company 2008 En Passant Tempranillo
Best Spanish Variety Wine	The New Spanish Bar & Grill	Mazza Wines 2008 Tempranillo
Best Commercial Volume	Macquarie Agricultural	Casella Wines 2010 Yellow Tail Malbec
Best Blend	Advanced Scripting	Cellarmaster 2010 Stefano de Pieri Tre Viti
Best Organic Wine	Mangan Group	*No winner awarded*

2009

Venue: Grand Hotel / Lunch by Stefano / Wine tutoring by judges
Notes: The Dr. Rod Bonfiglioli Best Wine of Show renamed from Best Wine of Show

Award	Sponsor	Winner
The Dr. Rod Bonfiglioli Best Wine of Show	Chalmers	S.C. Pannell Wines 2007 Nebbiolo
Best Red Wine	Quality Hotel Mildura Grand	S.C. Pannell Wines 2007 Nebbiolo
Best White Wine	Jamesprint	Beach Road Wines 2009 Fiano
Best Italian Variety	Binjara Vine Nursery & Riedel Glassware	S.C. Pannell Wines 2007 Nebbiolo
Best Murray Darling Region Wine	Mildura wines	*No winner awarded*
Chief of Judges (Chairman's) Wine to Watch	T'Gallant	d'Arenberg 2007 The Censosilicaphobic Cat *and* Beach Road Wines 2007 Greco di Tufo
Steward's Choice	Cellarmasters Wines	Mount Majura Vineyard 2008 Tempranillo
Best Spanish Variety Wine	The New Spanish bar & Grill	Brown Brothers Milawa Vineyard 2008 Graciano
Best Commercial Volume	Macquarie Agricultural	Brown Brothers Milawa Vineyard 2008 Pinot Grigio
Best Blend	Advanced Scripting	*No winner awarded*
Best Organic Wine	Mangan Group	Robinvale Biodynamic & Organic Wines 2008 Kerner

2008

Venue: Trentham Estate Winery / Lunch by Dag Demarkow / Bus and Paddleboat
Notes: Best Spanish Variety Wine introduced

Award	Sponsor	Winner
Best Wine of Show	Mildura Grand Hotel	Mayford Wines 2006 Tempranillo
Best Red Wine	Quality Hotel Mildura Grand	Mayford Wines 2006 Tempranillo
Best White Wine	Jamesprint	Tahbilk 2004 Marsanne
Best Italian Variety	Chalmers	David Hook Wines 2006 Barbera *and* Dal Zotto Wines 2008 Arneis
Best Murray Darling Region Wine	Mildura Wines	Trentham Estate La Familgia 2008 Pinot Grigio
Chief of Judges (Chairman's) Wine to Watch	Advanced Viticulture & Management	Quealy Winemakers 2008 Nome Tocai Friulano
Steward's Choice	Cellarmasters Wines	Coriole 2008 Fiano
Best Spanish Variety Wine (*introduced 2008*)	The New Spanish Bar & Grill	Mayford 2006 Tempranillo
Best Commercial Volume	Macquarie Agricultural	Tahbilk 2004 Marsanne
Best Blend	Stefano de Pieri	Wrattonbully Vineyards 2006 Marsanne Viognier
Best Organic Wine	*No sponsor listed*	Robinvale Organic & Biodynamic Wines 2008 Kerner

2007

Venue: Avoca Paddleboat / Lunch by Peter Webley of Stefanos / Wine tutoring by judges
Notes: Steward's Choice introduced / Journalism Award discontinued

Award	Sponsor	Winner
Best Wine of Show	Riedel Glassware	Pizzini Wines 2002 Nebbiolo Pizzini
Best Red Wine	Riedel Glassware	Pizzini Wines 2002 Nebbiolo Pizzini
Best White Wine	Jamesprint	Tahbilk 2003 Marsanne
Best Italian Variety	Chalmers	Pizzini Wines 2002 Nebbiolo PIzzini
Best Murray Darling Region Wine	Mildura Wines	Robinvale Wines 2002 Kerner
Chief of Judges (Chairman's) Wine to Watch	Winetitles	Brown Brothers Milawa Vineyard 2007 Vermentino *and* Freeman Vineyards 2003 Rondinella Corvina
Steward's Choice *(introduced 2007)*	Cellarmasters Wines	Robinvale Wines 2002 Kerner

2006

Venue: Avoca Paddleboat / Lunch by Stefano / Wine tutoring by judges
Notes: Chief Judge's (Chairman's) Wine to Watch introduced / Best Wine in an Alternative Closure discontinued

Award	Sponsor	Winner
Best Wine of Show	Mildura Grand Hotel	Arrivo 2004 Nebbiolo
Best Red Wine	Heinrich Cooperage	Arrivo 2004 Nebbiolo
Best White Wine	Jamesprint	Yalumba Eden Valley 2005 Viognier
Best Italian Variety	Chalmers	Arrivo 2004 Nebbiolo
Journalism Award	Australian & New Zealand Grapegrower & Winemaker Magazine	Louise Radman, *Spanish Siren*, *The Adelaide Magazine* September 2006
Best Murray Darling Region Wine	Murray Valley Winegrowers Inc. and Telstra	Trentham Estate 2005 Lambrusco Maestri
Chief of Judges (Chairman's) Wine to Watch *(introduced 2006)*	évOAK	*No winner awarded*

2005

Venue: Avoca Paddleboat / Lunch by Stefano / Wine tutoring by judges
Notes: Best Murray Darling Region Wine introduced / Journalism Award introduced

Award	Sponsor	Winner
Best Wine of Show	Jamesprint	Yalumba Eden Valley 2004 Viognier
Best Red Wine	Mildura Grand Hotel	Yalumba 2004 Hand Picked Tempranillo Grenache Viognier
Best White Wine	Jamesprint	Yalumba Eden Valley 2004 Viognier
Best Italian Variety	Chalmers Nurseries	T'Gallant Winemakers 2005 Pinot Grigio
Best Wine in an Alternative Closure	Riedel Glass	Yalumba Eden Valley 2004 Viognier
Journalism Award (*introduced 2005*)	Australian & New Zealand Grapegrower & Winemaker Magazine	Max Allen, *In the Know, Australian Gourmet Traveller,* November 2005 Issue
Best Murray Darling Region Wine (*introduced 2005*)	Murray Valley Winegrowers Inc.	Trentham Estate 2005 'The Family' Moscato *and* Murray Darling Collection 2005 'Murray Cod' Vermentino

2004

Venue: Avoca Paddleboat / Lunch by Stefano / Wine tutoring by judges

Award	Sponsor	Winner
Best Wine of Show	Mildura Rural City Council	Pizzini Wines 1998 Nebbiolo
Best Red Wine	Mildura Grand Hotel	Pizzini Wines 1998 Nebbiolo
Best White Wine	Jamesprint	Beringer Blass Wine Estate T'Gallant Tribute 2004 Pinot Gris
Best Italian Variety	Chalmers Nurseries	Pizzini Wines 1998 Nebbiolo
Best Wine in an Alternative Closure	*No sponsor listed*	Beringer Blass Wine State T'Gallant Tribute 2004 Pinot Gris

2003

Venue: Avoca Paddleboat / Lunch by Stefano / Wine tutoring by judges
Notes: Best Wine in an Alternative Closure renamed from Best Wine in Stelvin Closure

Award	Sponsor	Winner
Best Wine of Show	Sunarysia Area Consultative Committee	Yalumba Eden Valley 2002 Viognier *and* Tahbilk 1997 Marsanne
Best Red Wine	Mildura Grand Hotel	Scaffidi Gulf Breeze 2002 Nebbiolo
Best White Wine	Jamesprint	Yalumba Eden Valley 2002 Viognier *and* Tahbilk 1997 Marsanne
Best Italian Variety	Chalmers Nurseries	CA Henschke & Co. 2002 Innes Pinot Gris
Best Wine in an Alternative Closure *(renamed from Best Wine in a Stelvin Closure)*	Regional Development Victoria	C Henschke & Co. 2002 Innes Pinot Gris

2002

Venue: Grand Hotel / Lunch by Stefano / Wine tutoring by Phil Reedman
Notes: Best Wine in Stelvin Closure introduced

Award	Sponsor	Winner
Best Wine of Show	Sunraysia Area Consultative Committee	Yalumba Eden Valley 2001 Viognier
Best Red Wine	Mildura Grand Hotel	Scaffadi Estate Talunga 2001 Sangiovese
Best White Wine	Jamesprint	Yalumba Eden Valley 2001 Viognier
Best Italian Variety	Chalmers Nurseries	Redbank Sunday Morning 2002 Pinot Gris
Best Wine in a Stelvin Closure *(introduced 2002)*	Department of Innovation and Regional Development	Gibbston Valley Wines 2002 Pinot Gris

2001

Venue: Grand Hotel / Awards lunch featuring wines of Primo Estate with Joe Grilli

Award	Sponsor	Winner
Best Wine of Show	National World Travel	Redbank Sunday Morning 2001 Pinot Gris
Best Red Wine	Mildura Grand Hotel	Mc Guigan Wines 2000 Verdot
Best White Wine	Jamesprint	Redbank Sunday Morning 2001 Pinot Gris
Best Italian Variety	Chalmers Nurseries	Redbank Sunday Morning 2001 Pinot Gris

Published by Melbourne Books
Level 9, 100 Collins Street,
Melbourne, VIC 3000
Australia
www.melbournebooks.com.au
info@melbournebooks.com.au

Copyright © Max Allen 2023
Title: Alternative Reality: How Australian wine changed course
Author: Max Allen
ISBN: 9781922779069

A catalogue record for this book is available from the National Library of Australia

All rights reserved. No part of this publication may be reproduced, stored in a retrieval system, or transmitted in any form or any means electronic, mechanical, photocopying, recording or otherwise without the prior permission of the publisher.

Every attempt has been made to locate the copyright holders for material quoted and images printed in this book. Any person or organisation that may have been overlooked or misattributed may contact the publisher for correction in any future printing.

Publisher: David Tenenbaum
Cover design: Marianna Berek-Lewis
Book design: Ellen Cheng

Australian Alternative Varieties Wine Show

The Author

Max Allen is an award-winning journalist and author, and a lecturer in wine studies at the University of Melbourne. Max has been writing about booze for thirty years: he is the wine and drinks columnist for the *Australian Financial Review*, long-time contributor to *Gourmet Traveller Magazine*, Australian correspondent for *JancisRobinson.com* and a regular presenter at masterclasses and festivals around the world. Max has authored or co-authored over a dozen books, including *The History of Australian Wine*, *The Future Makers*, *Red and White*, and *Intoxicating: Ten Drinks That Shaped Australi*a.

Max Allen and fellow former chief judge Jane Faulkner at the show in 2022

Acknowledgements

Thanks to Helen Healy and the whole team at the Australian Alternative Varieties Wine Show, all the amazing stewards and delivery drivers and restaurant staff and hot-desk operators and sponsors who make the show possible every year. Thanks to the hundreds of judges and talkers and tasters who have travelled to Mildura over more than two decades and become part of the AAVWS family. Thanks to Sandy Hathaway at Wine Australia and Kym Anderson and German Puga for invaluable help compiling the A-Z (and Sandy for proofreading it!). Thanks to everyone who has provided images. And thanks to Stefano de Pieri, Bruce and Jenni Chalmers, and the late Rod Bonfiglioli for dreaming the whole thing up in the first place and then making it a reality.

Some of the material in this book originally appeared in different form in various publications, including the *Australian Financial Review*, *Gourmet Traveller*, *Gourmet Traveller WINE*, *JancisRobinson.com* and *The Weekend Australian*.

Image credits

All photographs are courtesy of the AAVWS archives and include the work of Graham Downie & Diana Byrne (Apricot Films), Darren Seiler, Harry Rekas, Keiran Mangan, Adam Hobbs (Admedia), Sophie Louise, Ben Gross and Roberto Pettinau, except: Max Allen: pages 1, 76, 179, 188, 200; Chalmers: endpapers, 48, 196; Chalmers / Adam Hobbs (Admedia): 199, 203; Coordinated Imagery Program, DELWP, Vic.: opposite page 1; Anita Goode: 164 and 256; Hill Smith Family Estates: 65; Adrian Lander: 10; Richard Lyons: 56; Kristoffer Paulsen: 180; Quealy and McCarthy family: 36; David Ridge: 112 (bottom centre); James Scarcebrook: 136; Grant Scicluna: 136.

The cartoons on pages 12, 44, 78, 118 and 160 are by Matt Skinner, AAVWS judge in 2007.

Bottle shots and label images supplied by the producers.

Grape variety images on pages 202-228 courtesy of Max Allen; Chalmers / Adam Hobbs, Admedia; © Copyright CSIRO Australia; Hahndorf Hill / Larry Jacobs; Jim Barry Wines / Don Brice; Nick Dry, Foundation Viticulture; Oliver's Taranga; PlantGrape, Institut Agro Montpellier, INRAe, IFV; Quealy Wines / Adrian Lander; Western Australia Department of Primary Industries and Regional Development (DPIRD); Wine Australia; Wines of Germany.